The
Romantics
and Us

The Romantics and Us

❧

Essays on
Literature and Culture

❧

Edited by Gene W. Ruoff

R

Rutgers University Press

New Brunswick and London

Acknowledgments appear on page 331

Library of Congress Cataloging-in-Publication Data
The Romantics and us : essays on literature and
culture / edited by Gene W. Ruoff.
  p. cm.
  Bibliography: p.
  ISBN 0-8135-1498-3 (cloth)—ISBN 0-8135-1499-1 (pbk.)
  1. English literature—19th century—History and criticism.
2. Romanticism—England—Influence. 3. American literature—20th
century—History and criticism. 4. United States—Civilization—
20th century. I. Ruoff, Gene W.
PR457.R647 1990
820.9'145—dc20   89-36069
                                                            CIP

British Cataloging-in-Publication information available

Contents

Culture

Acknowledgments

This book brings together the presentations given at a public conference and lecture series, "The Romantics and Us," in Chicago in the spring of 1988. My thanks go first of all to my collaborators in this venture, whose good talk and good writing have made it a pleasure. Because the conference and lectures were held in conjunction with the appearance of the exhibition, "William Wordsworth and the Age of English Romanticism," I also thank my fellow members of its executive committee, M. H. Abrams, Michael C. Jaye, Kenneth R. Johnston, Stephen Parrish, Robert Woof, Jonathan Wordsworth, and Jamil Zainaldin, for their tireless work in providing such a memorable occasion.

The staffs of the Chicago Historical Society, host to the exhibition and lecture series, and of the Chicago Circle Center of The University of Illinois at Chicago, host to the conference, did much to make the events a pleasure for audiences and speakers alike.

The conference, lecture series, and book have all been generously supported by a grant from the National Endowment for the Humanities, Division on General Programs. In this case, the spirit of NEH has been exemplified by the cheerful support and firm guidance of Wilsonia Cherry, who worked from the beginning to help me in shaping the project.

My project assistant, Linda Vavra, handled with aplomb all the complicated logistics of the conference and lecture series, making me the envy of my fellow scholars, and her keen eye has served well in the editorial preparation of the volume.

My editor at Rutgers University Press, Leslie Mitchner, has once more been a delight to work with. Stuart Mitchner, my copyeditor, has won unanimous praise from the contributors for his thoroughness, helpfulness, and tact. It is good to publish books with friends.

The

Romantics

and Us

Introduction

The title of this volume hovers between the abstract and the personal. The term *romantic* names nothing, either in the singular or the plural, because it had little contemporary authority. Our best cultural maps of early nineteenth-century British literary thought, Samuel Taylor Coleridge's *Biographia Literaria* (1817) and William Hazlitt's *The Spirit of the Age* (1825), use the word only in passing, and then to denote something romance-like, a mode of exotica somewhere between the supernatural and the quotidian. As cultural shorthand—the only quality my subsequent uses will allow—the word now assembles for us a group of writers in Britain who flourished roughly between the outbreak of the French Revolution and the passage of the Reform Bill of 1832. So far were they from constituting a movement that they actually considered their esthetic, cultural, and political differences at least as important as their similarities, and most of them would be uncomfortable to find themselves inextricably linked in our anthologies and set courses.

What we have come to call *romantic* is neither more nor less than a belated codification of literary practices which have been induced—fluidly, unsystematically, and selectively—from a highly diverse body of writings. Unlike some terms for more recent artistic movements—modernism, imagism, vorticism, futurism, and surrealism, which possess legitimate historical warrants—romanticism seems to have as much potency to obscure as to clarify individual artistic phenomena.

But words which do not name still may have a remarkable power to provoke and evoke, and it is this force which has been used to gather the essays presented here. Twelve American critics, half of whom are also distinguished poets, were invited on the occasion of the Chicago appearance of the exhibition, "William Wordsworth and the Age of English Romanticism," to address the topic "The

Romantics and Us." Delivered first as public lectures, their essays were revised for inclusion in this volume. The *us* of the title was patently seductive, an attempt to draw forth responses more immediate and personal than rehearsals of the classic moderns' quarrels with their sense of the romantic. The hope was that the title would function as a Rorschach blot, compelling at once description and self-description.

The desire for a more individually engaged assessment of the relations between the cultures of romanticism and this century has been realized. This is a volume in which we learn that Alicia Ostriker was a Garrison Keillor "shy person" as an undergraduate; that John Matthias had to learn to write about Suffolk before he could write about South Bend; that James Chandler and Bruce Springsteen were nursed upon the selfsame hill in Asbury Park, New Jersey; and that Diane Wakoski is not now and has never been a biker. (That last one hurts.) I will take such revelations as an adequate excuse for a personal tone in this introduction. The fact that I will be talking about academic experiences should not put off the general readers for whom this book is intended. Although romantic and modern literature were created by writers outside the academy, almost all current readers' ideas of the tensions between modernism and romanticism have been shaped by their experiences in college classrooms, which have frequently marked their first sustained encounters with a William Blake or a William Wordsworth, a William Butler Yeats or a Wallace Stevens. Our responses to these writers, then, are almost all schooled responses, and the ways in which that schooling has mutated are part of our common experience.

If the idea of exploring affinities between romantic writers and the writers of this century raises few eyebrows, that is due in considerable measure to the recent efforts of some of the contributors to this volume. In such books as *Transformations of Romanticism in Yeats, Eliot, and Stevens* (1976) and *Romantic and Modern: Revaluations of Literary Tradition* (1977), George Bornstein has done more than any other literary historian to demonstrate the negotiations between romanticism and high modernism. In different ways Robert Pinsky's *The Situation of Poetry: Contemporary Poetry and Its Traditions* (1977) and Charles Altieri's *Self and Sensibility in Contemporary American Poetry* (1984) have helped to clarify the traditional moorings of recent poetry, including its romantic attachments. Indeed, whatever Altieri writes about, Wordsworth is seldom far beneath the surface. John Hollander's finely detailed and wide-ranging treatments of poetic tropes and techniques, especially *The Figure of Echo: A Mode of Allusion in Milton and After* (1981), have drawn copiously from both romantic and later texts. The critical work of Louis Simpson has ranged from *Three on the Tower: The Lives and Work of Ezra Pound, T. S. Eliot, and William Carlos Williams* (1975), to *A Revolution in Taste: Studies in Dylan Thomas, Allen Ginsberg, Sylvia Plath, and Robert Lowell* (1978), to *The Character of the Poet* (1986). It has always been marked by greater interest in poets and poems than in categories, movements, and exclusionary polemics. We can safely claim to have a subject, because we have a literature on it. As the dates of these books might suggest, it was not always so.

When I entered graduate school at Wisconsin in the early sixties, I saw myself as a card-carrying modernist. I was in love with Dylan Thomas, and to this day cannot fully trust anyone who has not been (or still is). My idea of a great research library would have been one in which the Grove and New Directions paperbacks were all shelved together. Madison may not have epitomized the intellectual world of this age, but even its idiosyncrasies and excesses seemed to point in the direction of the characteristic. It was not an auspicious place to be a modernist, but then what was? My first embarrassment was discovering that Thomas was not a modern poet. Yeats, Eliot, and Stevens were, but Thomas was something else—a something with which no one was quite comfortable. I carried my torch for a few more years, but the only place I ever found to write about him was in my first graduate seminar—in romanticism, of all things—taught by Karl Kroeber, for whom I did a comparative study of childhood in some poems by Wordsworth and Thomas. Kroeber was kind, but people looked at me oddly.

The state and status of Wisconsin modernism reflected to an almost parodic degree the divisions in the American academy of letters. The reign of literary history was absolute in the fields that mattered. In British writing the eighteenth century had fairly recently been established as a field worthy of serious study, but English literature was still generally thought to have happened between Chaucer and Milton. American literature ran out of steam around Mark Twain. The great maps of these areas were already drawn, and what remained to be done was niche scholarship: useful, solid studies of underregarded but historically significant subjects—say, Thomas Shadwell. It was not that faculty representing traditional periods were out of touch with contemporary writing or current critical trends, because the best of them were remarkably widely read, and the works of this century were decently represented in freshman and sophomore courses. They just felt, as Kroeber has recently remarked to me, that anyone who has to be *taught* the contemporary must be hopeless. The literary historians, who did biographical criticism, straightforward genre study, and some history of ideas, comprised about ninety percent of the faculty. But in an odd way they felt themselves embattled.

The modernist faculty seemed to be constituted reflexively against the dominant force. In their teaching, if not entirely in their scholarship, their concern was for the intrinsic study of literature. None claimed to be a New Critic, but history ended at their classroom door, or at least it began there. Modernism was magisterially autonomous, a formation with its own history which was not to be elucidated by appeals to earlier eras. Like Jay Gatsby, it had sprung from its own Platonic self-conception. If modernism had origins at all, they were sordid and distinctly Gatz-like, unspoken, perhaps unspeakable.

Wisconsin's modernists were a sturdy band. They had to be: never more than three or four strong at the senior level, they were directing a staggering proportion of the department's doctoral dissertations. The late John J. Enck, to whom I became closest, did greats—Henry James, James Joyce, Wallace Stevens—and remains for me the quintessential modernist. Trained in the literature of the renaissance, his first book was on Ben Jonson, but his true love was the high modern. To study James with him was to sit at the feet of the Master in the graduate equivalent of a catechism class. The novels were our bible, and the New York edition prefaces our summa theologica. The creed was actually chanted. Woe unto him who confused art with life or could feel, however fleetingly, some possible advantages to the scenic, rather than dramatic, method. Woe doubly unto her who might imagine that *Washington Square* owed something to Jane Austen, whom James had consigned to fictive naiveté—a teller but no maker—or who felt that *The Bostonians* sounded suspiciously like a novel of ideas. Fine minds could not be so easily violated.

Enck's major achievement as a scholar, *Wallace Stevens: Images and Judgments* (1964), came only two years before his distressingly early death. Its final words, summing up Stevens's poetic, are equally descriptive of Enck's critical virtues: "native and cosmopolitan, vigorous and aloof, uncompromising and witty, primordial and elegant, idiomatic and stylized." Even writing in homage, though, I am struck by how much has been omitted: call it the price of modernism. Enck's treatment of a few anthology-pieces should give some sense of the dimensions of the problem. "Anecdote of the Jar" is one of Stevens's best-known poems:

> I placed a jar in Tennessee,
> And round it was, upon a hill.
> It made the slovenly wilderness
> Surround that hill.
>
> The wilderness rose up to it,
> And sprawled around, no longer wild.
> The jar was round upon the ground
> And tall and of a port in air.
>
> It took dominion everywhere.
> The jar was gray and bare.
> It did not give of bird or bush,
> Like nothing else in Tennessee.[1]

Enck lucidly explores the poem's dialectic between nature and culture. But at the point where his commentary expands from the verbal to the conceptual, he turns to a later Stevens essay, "John Crowe Ransom: Tennesseean," in an attempt to capture what for Stevens might have been the effect of the Tennesseeness of the jar's environment. His swerve has a dual force, moving in the direction of the modern—Ransom—and the intrinsic—Stevens's sensibility and private mythology. Another swerve might have been more illuminating: to the most famous pot in the language, Keats's Grecian urn. For surely it is there that the dialectic between nature and art is played out most fully, and that is the vantage point from which to register the power Stevens attributes to the artifact, even when it is stripped of its classical heritage and depicted story. A similar

problem afflicts Enck's reading of "Sunday Morning." For an analogue to the glorious passage,

> Death is the mother of beauty, mystical,
> Within whose burning bosom we devise
> Our earthly mothers waiting, sleeplessly,

he turns anachronistically to Paul Valéry's "Le Cimetière marin,"
which appeared in *La Nouvelle Revue Française* five years after "Sunday Morning" was published in *Harmonium*. Enck's recourse to the
modern and to the continental is telling, especially when so many
subsequent critics have spotted "Ode on Melancholy" peeking between Stevens's lines.

One sometimes wonders how much earlier poetry the modernist
critics of past generations knew. So far as Enck is concerned, he was
a reader of enormous range and depth, and I seldom found anything
he did not know. His work on Stevens is an example of that deliberate unremembering which enabled the making of modernism. Only
three earlier poets in English are taken seriously enough to be
quoted and find their way into his notes, and all are prelapsarians,
who wrote before the watershed Eliot termed the dissociation of
sensibility: Spenser, Donne, and Marvell. The entire nineteenth
century is represented by two continental adoptive moderns, Baudelaire and Nietzsche. High modernism threatens always to erase
Anglo-American writing of the nineteenth century, and the erasure
has a dual purpose: to evade questions of influence which would im-
peril modernism's autonomy, and to differentiate the intrinsic mode
of modernist commentary, which tends to venerate the deep self
and the deep text, from the extrinsic, historical mode of commentary on earlier writings.

If much modernist criticism of decades past now seems either
fiercely isolationist or smugly mandarin, the causes lie in the politics of the academy. To establish a place in the university curriculum
for the serious study of recent and living writers took as enormous
an act of the will as our own time has witnessed in the advents of
feminist and multicultural scholarship. The success of the modernist effort is beyond dispute, and its effectiveness is registered nowhere more fully than in its influence on romantic criticism during
the past three decades. During the time of the formation of high

modernism, romantic scholarship was largely a pale imitation of the prevailing modes of historical commentary on earlier periods. It had enumerated a set of features characteristic of the writings of the period, giving us our hoary (if almost forgotten) tags: love of nature, love of the common man, interest in childhood, interest in primitive cultures, veneration of the classical past, elevation of feeling over reason, and so forth.

The newer romanticism, epitomized in the career of M. H. Abrams, did not set itself so much against the limitations of that earlier historicism as against the disdain of the modernists.[2] *The Mirror and the Lamp* (1953) is perhaps too early to reflect fully Abrams's program, but it does indirectly challenge the autonomy of modern literary formalism by displaying its roots in romanticism's expressive poetics. An essay like "Coleridge, Baudelaire, and Modern Poetics" (1966; reprinted in *The Correspondent Breeze* [1984]) explores both the intellectual continuities and socio-political divide between romanticism and modernism. *Natural Supernaturalism* (1971) boldly rewrites two centuries of literary practice to establish the romantic as the seedbed of the modern. In retrospect, the great vitality of romantic criticism over the past three decades may be a result of its marginal status well into the 1950s: as a relatively non-canonical field of study, romanticism could develop with little constraint from the older historicism, while the anti-romantic bias of modernism kept it free from the narrow dogmatism of that field, to which it nevertheless owes its greatest intellectual debts.

The current situation in romantic studies, which is marked by a widely dispersed unmaking of the newer romantic settlement of Abrams and such distinguished inheritors as Harold Bloom, Geoffrey Hartman, and Thomas McFarland, also reflects the ongoing tension between romantic and recent writing. Although it is magnificently camouflaged by the authoritative intellectual range of these critics, their newer romanticism has been characterized by a remorseless exclusion of romantic literary practices which are not assimilable to the tenets of modernism. Even if we limit ourselves to canonical writers, we can see clearly that the cost of this accommodation with modernism has included, along with its reductive emphasis on internalization in the writings of Blake, Coleridge, Wordsworth, Shelley, and Keats, the sacrifice of Byron, Austen, and Scott.

The symbiosis between the romantic and the modern I have sketched has colored literary practice, literary criticism, and literary history. It is so culturally pervasive that even a freshman student, who may have read few romantic or modern texts, can come to the classroom knowing why he prefers the latter. If such a dynamic, tangled relationship suggests that fresh examinations of the topic are in order, it should also suggest that these are unlikely to be unitary in character. Although a volume bringing together poets and critics, modernists and romanticists, could never have had unity as a major concern, it did envision a blend of voices. The actual structuring of the book, though, entailed the crude taxonomy reflected in its table of contents, a classification of the essays which divides them along lines which might have been roughly predictable, but according to principles which I, at least, found unexpected.

The first three essays appear under "Testimony": they are attempts by Diane Wakoski, John Matthias, and Alicia Ostriker to respond directly to the summons of the volume by addressing the impact of their romantic forebears on their own art. All three essays are intensely personal, and none is interested at all in questions of periods or movements. They usefully remind us that poets respond to poets and poems, not to cultural abstractions, and that they respond in unusual ways. Who, for example, would have suspected that poets so different as Diane Wakoski and John Matthias would both present homages to Wordsworth? Neither of their Wordsworths is currently fashionable, and they are strikingly different. Wakoski was captivated early both by a Wordsworth with intimate secrets, which he simultaneously kept and divulged, and by the populist Wordsworth of the Preface to *Lyrical Ballads,* who taught her to honor her own language. Matthias's Wordsworth arrived later in his life, not as a rebel or revolutionary, but as the writer of "Home at Grasmere," a mentor who could instruct in the arts of domestication. Matthias's essay is itself a kind of *Prelude,* a spiritual pilgrimage in which the academic experience of the stateside Vietnam generation plays the unsettling role of Wordsworth's sojourn in France and its bitter aftermath in England. Ostriker, the only poet in the volume who has devoted continuing scholarly attention to a single major romantic writer, relates her extended love affair with William Blake, in which he has played a variety of parts, from hero to antagonist to ally, in both her critical writing and her poetry.

The section entitled "Continuity" contains five essays, all of which argue directly or indirectly for relations along a continuum between romantic and more recent writing. Louis Simpson's essay on Wordsworth and Proust heads the section for two reasons: the French novelist is the earliest of the moderns discussed extensively in the section, which proceeds upon roughly chronological lines, and Simpson's is the most militantly traditional—in this context the most romantic—essay in the volume. He is interested in those moments of experience in Wordsworth and Proust which seem simultaneously to be most personal—revelations of the deepest reaches of the individual mind—and most transpersonal—revelations of some ultimate power outside the self. Simpson says he is "suspicious of influences"; George Bornstein is not, but he demonstrates that poetic influence operates in devious ways, which can often be mistaken for rejection. He writes of the efforts of two great early moderns, William Butler Yeats and Wallace Stevens, to decenter the national hegemony of English verse, not by stripping their poetry of its romantic allegiances, but by remaking its romanticism in distinctive Irish and American idioms. Bornstein's differentiation of the nationally rooted romanticism of Yeats and Stevens from the "modernized cosmopolitanism" of poets like Ezra Pound and T. S. Eliot is especially valuable.

John Hollander and Robert Pinsky avoid the polemical questions implicit in connecting romantic with later writing by concentrating on mutations in specific forms and figures. Hollander's topic is ekphrastic verse, poems "addressed to silent works of art, questioning them; describing them as they could never describe—but merely present—themselves; speaking for them; making them speak out or speak up." Hollander provides detailed examples of the tendency of romantic and later poems to incorporate the gazer into the description of the artwork, but his concern is throughout for the individual rather than the characteristic. The same may be said of Robert Pinsky's essay, tracing mutations of the figure of city sky, which modulates between the "pastoral calm" of Wordsworth and the "revolutionary ardor and urban claustrophobia" of Blake. Pinsky presents his essay as a "poetry reading," tracing in his selected poems lines of affinity which reach from Wordsworth and Blake through Baudelaire and Gerard Manley Hopkins to Hart Crane and Elizabeth Bishop. Pinsky's impeccably crafted readings present themselves as artless, and like Hollander's, the effect of his essay is to sink difference in the pursuit of the community of art.

Charles Altieri closes the section with an essay exploring the paradox that while Wordsworth "exerts very little direct influence on contemporary American poetry," he may be the best "exemplar for the basic models of lyrical intensity and even of ideal lyric emotional economies that pervade contemporary poetry." Altieri reviews a recent dispute in criticism of contemporary poetry over the value of Wordsworthian poetic principles, almost all of which have been derived from the Wordsworth of the preface to *Lyrical Ballads,* before going on to suggest another Wordsworthian model, based on his practice in the extended lyrics (exemplified by "Nutting") as more appropriate. The viability of this model is then pursued through examinations of poems by William Stafford, Ann Lauterbach, and Robert Hass.

Depite their diversity in subjects and angles of approach, the essays in "Continuity," all by writers who are generally perceived as modernists, share central values. They agree not only that romantic poetry is relevant to the poetry of this century, but that this relevance is virtuous. Properly understood, the romantic achievement underwrites some of the highest achievements of our own age. The essays in the final section, "Culture," all written by critics whose interests lie primarily in romanticism, are no less certain of the pertinence of romantic art to our age, but they are manifestly unsettled about the virtue of that continuity. They are altogether darker readers of both romantic and modern culture.

Karl Kroeber begins the section with an essay that questions a fundamental credo of modernist art criticism, that only with the arrival of abstract, subjectless art in this century "did painting fully realize its true nature and become self-sufficient." Kroeber speculates that a major effect of emptying painting of subject has been to empty it of story, to "de-narrativize" it. When told from a modernist perspective, the rise of landscape in the nineteenth century to rival and eclipse history painting has seemed a step toward the subjectless ideal of painting for its own sake. Kroeber counters this interpretation of cultural movement with reconsiderations of J. M. W. Turner's *Ulysses Deriding Polyphemus* and John Constable's *The Hay Wain* and *Salisbury Cathedral from the Water Meadows,* calling attention to the story-values of these works. For Kroeber, storyless art is ethically

enfeebled, and while romantic artists were clearly narrative revi-
sionists, they should not be understood as proto-abstractionists.
Implicitly, of course, Kroeber's thesis jars against the high valuation
of romantic and modern lyricism characteristic of the essays in
"Continuity."

James Chandler's essay finds no absence of story in modern culture, for he is discussing Hollywood epic cinema. Chandler's concern
is to establish the impact of Sir Walter Scott, whose contemporaries
would have considered him the central writer of their times, on the
art of America's greatest film-maker, D. W. Griffith. Chandler's patient examination of the ways in which Griffith goes beyond the
vulgar Scottism of his literal source, Thomas L. Dixon's *The Clansman,* to recreate in *Birth of a Nation* an epic filmic equivalent of
Scott's mode of epic historical romance, is wholly persuasive. If we
were not aware that the parallel is new to film studies, we would feel
that we have always known it. The troubling undercurrent of
Chandler's essay stems from our recognition of how naturally the
power of Scott's romantic achievement has lent itself to Griffith's
advocacy of one white nation, under God, indivisible, with liberty
and justice for itself.

In a more directly polemical vein, Anne K. Mellor isolates two
aspects of romantic ideology, its "celebration of the creative process
and of passionate feeling," to measure against the responses of two
great women writers of the day, Jane Austen and Mary Shelley. According to Mellow, the egoistic claims of the masculine romantic
ideology were answered contemporaneously by women writers
who saw, in Mary Shelley's case daily and at first hand, its destructive potential. The romanticism of our own day, then, is marked by
its failure to attend to that counter-voice, which Mellow offers as a
second and unexplored romanticism.

My own essay, "Romantic Lyric and the Problem of Belief," was
not part of the conference or lecture series. It is both an extension of
the argument of this introduction and a reflexive response to themes
running through several of the essays in the collection.

If, as remarked above, Louis Simpson's is the most traditionally
romantic essay in this volume, Clifford Siskin's concluding contribution is the most radical. Siskin is concerned with the way in
which changes in literary genre configure new kinds of human behaviors, exemplified here by the apparent coincidence of the rise of

romanticism and the idea of the professional. For Siskin, the 1830s does not mark the end of a romantic era, but rather the point at which the "constructs and strategies" of its "texts became 'normal' within and for the very culture that had produced them." Romantic art, he argues, "has prescribed—written before—both the 'real' world it supposedly reflects and the very means by which we understand that world." Siskin's claim for the ongoing influence of romanticism is the largest in the volume, but he argues that both romanticism and professionalism are at this moment in a state of profound conceptual crisis.

One should not assume from the contents of this collection that romantic hagiography is alive and well only in the writings of contemporary poets and modernist scholars, and that all romanticists are vexed and self-vexing. A different cast of players could surely have produced a different drama. But that is a drama for someone else to produce.

Gene W. Ruoff

Notes

1. Citations of the poetry of Wallace Stevens are from *Collected Poems* (New York: Knopf, 1954).
2. This statement risks oversimplifying a complex intellectual situation. For an intriguing analysis of M. H. Abrams's work from a different perspective, as a mediation between New Criticism and Harvard historicism, see Jonathan Arac, *Critical Genealogies: Historical Situations for Postmodern Literary Studies* (New York: Columbia University Press, 1987), esp. 77–80.

Testimony

Whitman? No, Wordsworth
The Song of Myself

❧

Diane Wakoski

JUSTICE IS REASON ENOUGH

He, who once was my brother, is dead by his own hand.
Even now, years later, I see his thin form lying on the sand

where the sheltered sea washes against those cliffs
he chose to die from. Mother took me back there every day for
over a year and asked me, in her whining way, why it had to
    happen

over and over again—until I wanted
never to hear of David any more. How
could I tell her of his dream about the gull beating its wings
effortlessly together until they drew blood?

Would it explain anything, and how can I tell
anyone here about the great form and its beating wings. How it
swoops down and covers me, and the dark tension leaves

me with blood on my mouth and thighs. But it was that dream,
you must know, that brought my tight sullen little

brother to my room that night and pushed his whole taut body
right over mine until I yielded, and together we yielded to the
  dark tension.
Over a thousand passing years, I will never forget
him, who was my brother, who is dead. Mother asked me why
every day for a year; and I told her justice. Justice is
reason enough for anything ugly. It balances the beauty in the
  world.[1]

I wrote that poem when I was an undergraduate at Berkeley in
1958, and even though I wrote my first poem when I was seven
years old (about a rose bush) and continued to write poetry, especially love sonnets modelled on Shakespeare and Petrarch, throughout my high school life, it wasn't until I wrote this poem that
anyone began to pay any serious attention to my poetry, or that I
began to discover what poetry could be, for me.

   I still think that what poetry is all about is secrets.

   Beautiful, secret things, wrapped with many layers and put into a
specially-made box, and that all those layers of wrappings are the
figures of speech, the gorgeous language, the rhythms; and at the
poetry reading, the stories and charming talk of the poet which engage our attention—which is then focused on our finally opening
the box and looking at whatever's in there: the grail, your mother's
alcoholism, Christ's robe, the picture of your mother with a man
who wasn't your father, your husband's drug addiction, the first
time you were sexually aroused, the only time you killed a living
thing. Something secret, something taboo, something only you,
the poet, can reveal to the world. Poems *need* these big secrets,
whether they are Freudian, biographical, evolutionary, or social, historical, political. A poem has to reveal a secret, or it simply isn't a
good poem.

   A poem is an act of disguise, but the disguise, like a good murder
mystery, must offer clues to its revelation, and the reader must feel
that he can discover what's really in the box, or he won't care for the
poem or bother to try to make the discovery. The reader doesn't
want that secret flaunted or made obvious, either; he wants to unwrap, carefully, ingeniously, each beautiful layer; and then, most of
all, he wants that secret to mean something to his own life, his own
questions about birth, or death, or love, the big things.

Like every young poet, I started by imitating the superficial aspects of the poets and poems I read. By the time I was an undergraduate at Berkeley, I had all the Freudian secrets of my childhood that everyone else had, but I had no idea how to reveal them; or even perhaps that they *were* secrets, or could be beautifully wrapped treasures in boxes anyone else might want to unwrap. I don't think I realized how different my 1940s life had been from other children's—growing up without a father, in a woman's haunted world, with the image of my storybook father, the chief petty officer in the Navy, occasionally appearing magically in my life. Sex even in its usual Freudian terms was absent from the world I lived in, sterilized and neuter.

I trust my mind. I have always trusted my mind, and not done badly with that trust. When I was a sophomore in high school in 1953, our wonderful English teacher, Dale Rulison, introduced us to the poetry of Robinson Jeffers. She played the recording of Dame Judith Anderson reciting Jeffers's "*Medea*," and it was my first contact with the dramatic use of classical legends and stories.

I have always trusted what my mind did that year, though never really understood it. Indelibly, as if I were an infant biologically imprinting something that I was supposed to be, I discovered that I thought I was Medea and that her life was mine. Now, I was just a little brain with glasses who even in the early sexual-ripening-stage of Southern California beach parties and necking in cars hadn't yet found boyfriends or dates or, of course, sex. And there was none in the all-female home I came from. So, why I identified so thoroughly with the powerful woman, the sorceress, Medea, who had been betrayed by her lover, Jason, and after saving him and bearing children by him was then abandoned for another bride, a politically expedient one, I do not know. I suppose it was part of my missing-father drama, but in fact, it doesn't matter. What does, is that it happened in my mind, and from that moment on, I began to have some idea about what poetry could be/what I would have to do to make poetry out of my life. Jeffers's poem, "Cassandra," a beautiful haunting lyric also imprinted itself on me, and we all know that I have chosen deliberately the role of the maverick in my life and certainly my poetry career, believing that I am always speaking the truth which most people cannot bear to hear or, at least, to believe, and which they must ignore.

However, what is important to this occasion, the celebration of our antecedents among the nineteenth century British romantic poets, is that my life began to blossom with the taboo, as sex entered it, and my responses were nice traditional, 1950s responses: shame, guilt, secret-keeping. My problem was that I still hadn't learned the art of disguise in poetry, even though now I know that Shakespeare was probably keeping secrets too: who was the "dark lady" of the sonnets? I still didn't know that Dante had never even met, to say nothing of, touched Beatrice, or that we still can't be sure who she was, historically. I have written an essay which I hope some of you will trouble to read called "Creating A Personal Mythology," which is about my processes of coming to this revelation of what poets do: make myth out of their personal lives, their autobiographies. I wanted so much to reveal my pain, my feelings, but was so fearful of telling the secrets themselves. I wanted truth, not the guilty facts, and trusted that this was what poetry was for; but how, how to accomplish it?

When I was a sophomore at Berkeley in 1957, I studied the romantic poets and fell in love with Keats and Wordsworth. But what I remember best about that class is the day when our professor told us that Wordsworth had had an affair with a woman when he went to France, Annette Vallon, and been the father of an illegitimate child. Where, where, could I find him writing about this in his poems? I devoured them, looking for this fact, this truth. I wasn't much of a scholar then, as I am not one now. Easily bored with details, I wanted to read fast, read everything, read on and on through his poetry, which I did. I found lots of child-mother imagery in his poems, but I never found the pain, the longing, the rejection and sense of loss I was looking for. What I did find was acceptance. Over and over, I found an almost stoic, at times beatific acceptance that beauty *was* everywhere.

What I also began to do, as I read his poems, was to search each one, to see if layer after layer of language was wrapped around what must, to me, be the secret at the heart of each poem, his affair and his illegitimate child. Looking for Wordsworth's guilty secret, which I was sure that he could not have been able to talk about and therefore must have had to find some way to write about, became my task.

Either I was a poor reader—certainly I was a hasty one—or there *is* no evidence that this event dwelt long and painfully in Wordsworth's mind. Had I been a feminist, then or now, I would probably have decided that a man could not suffer these things as a woman must, and written him off as superficial; but instead, the search for this secret made me a lifelong reader of Wordsworth's poems, a lover of that meditative voice and the lovely sense of balance he achieves in looking for the beauty in the world. I still look for references to Annette Vallon and beguile myself that when he is talking about Nature or even about Dorothy or his wife that it is really only another wrapping of the secret. Wordsworth does not, as Baudelaire did, look for beauty in evil; and in fact, unlike most other romantics, he did not seem to be fascinated with evil or pain or the realities that I felt life was made up from.

I have always regretted not having a classical education, and additionally I have regretted not having an education which insisted on the memorization of poetry. But, one poem which I was asked to memorize was Wordsworth's "Daffodils," when I was in the eighth grade, and I suppose that event had its imprinting effect on me as well. As a child growing up in Southern California I had no idea of what spring flowers could mean coming after the bleak winter landscape. To me, the key word in that poem was "lonely":

> I wandered lonely as a cloud
> That floats on high o'er vales and hills,
> When all at once I saw a crowd,
> A host, of golden daffodils;
> Beside the lake, beneath the trees,
> Fluttering and dancing in the breeze.[2]

And more important, I heard in the lovely last stanza all the echoes of Shakespeare's love sonnets, which I was already poring over as a thirteen-year-old, and trying to imitate:

> For oft, when on my couch I lie
> In vacant or in pensive mood,
> They flash upon that inward eye
> Which is the bliss of solitude;
> And then my heart with pleasure fills,
> And dances with the daffodils.

I knew when I was thirteen, from Shakespeare and from this one poem by Wordsworth, that I had permission to do what I loved best to do—to sit and think about the world, and to write my meditations about it. What I didn't know was *how* to do this. I still didn't understand that these men had big secrets they couldn't tell, and what poetry does is wrap, in one beautiful layer after another, those secrets, whether they are chocolate, or sex, or rubies, so that the unwrapping is as much a pleasure as finding and receiving the secret, the gift beneath the wrappings.

Let me change the subject to Walt Whitman, for a moment. My eighth grade learning about Wordsworth was more fortunate than my eighth grade learning about Whitman. Of course, there were no grammar school hints in 1950 that Whitman might have had his secrets too. At least I did not have to memorize it, but

O Captain! My Captain! our fearful trip is done,
The ship has weather'd every rack, the prize we sought is won.
The port is near, the bells I hear, the people all exulting
While follow eyes the steady keep, the vessel grim and daring.[3]

—that did not even strike me as poetry. I knew I didn't want to write anything like that. I think I thought it was because it was about Lincoln and politics, but of course I know that I might have responded differently had we read, instead

When lilacs last in the dooryard bloom'd,
And the great star early droop'd in the western sky in the night,
I mourn'd, and yet shall mourn with ever-returning spring.

Ever-returning spring, trinity sure to me you bring,
Lilac blooming perennial and drooping star in the west,
And thought of him I love.

If nothing else, that last line, "And thought of him I love," would have had me off and running through Whitman's poems looking for his lost love and its secrets.

What if I had read, instead, that haunting section of "Song of Myself" where Whitman portrays a lonely woman inside her house, looking out her window at naked young men swimming, and longs for their touch, to be bathing with them? What if I had read:

Twenty-eight young men bathe by the shore,
Twenty-eight young men and all so friendly;
Twenty-eight years of womanly life and all so lonesome.
. . . .
The beards of the young men glisten'd with wet, it ran from their
    long hair,
Little streams pass'd all over their bodies.
An unseen hand also pass'd over their bodies,
It descended tremblingly from their temples and ribs.
. . . .
They do not think whom they souse with spray.

It hasn't been until recent years, when we've all discovered what a Whitman tradition is, that I have more carefully and joyfully read Whitman's poetry; and I think that while all the aspects of the Whitman tradition which we poets of the eighties embody in our poems are there—the democratic vision, the use of common language, the gravitation towards taboo attitudes about sex and religion and politics, and most important, the claiming of the heroic role for ourselves and our personal quests as heroic ones—for me a more real source of these same attributes comes from Wordsworth, or the way I read and perceived Wordsworth when I was young.

As I began my wild race through Wordsworth's poetry, I found what is to me today the most important piece of writing that he did, his Preface to the *Lyrical Ballads*. Almost everyone who studies poetry is familiar with a small passage from the Preface, which is often used to define poetry; "I have said that poetry is the spontaneous overflow of powerful feelings; it takes it origins from emotion recollected in tranquility" (460). And some students are also familiar with another passage from the Preface:

What is a Poet? To whom does he address himself? And what language is to be expected from him?—He is a man speaking to men: a man it is true, endowed with more lively sensibility, more enthusiasm and tenderness, who has a greater knowledge of human nature, and a more comprehensive soul, than are supposed to be common among mankind; a man pleased with his own passions and volitions, and who rejoices more than other men in the spirit of life that is in him; delighting to contemplate similar volitions and passions as manifested in the goings-on of the Universe, and habitually impelled to create them where he does not find them. To these qualities he has added a disposition to be affected more than other men by absent things as if they were present; an ability of conjuring up in himself passions, which are indeed far from being the same as those produced by real events. (453)

If I had been looking as avidly for secrets in Whitman, I could have discovered much of this same message there, but I wasn't, thanks to "O Captain! My Captain!" I was looking for guilty secrets in Wordsworth, and without realizing it, stumbling over a guilty secret of my own: I was from the lower classes. I had no educated relatives, and I didn't want to speak like a commoner; I wanted to disguise the fact that I WAS a commoner. I wanted to be a fairy tale princess, taken from her Cinderella peasant life, or from the rude hut in the woods, to the Prince's palace where my natural aristocracy and beauty would shine through and past all the false royalty. I wanted, not to speak from my common origins, but to be listened to, as I was sure no one from common origins ever was. In the Aristotelian tradition, commoners don't have speaking parts.

What I learned the first time I read those versions of Wordsworth's "Preface" to the *Lyrical Ballads* was that people now were supposed to listen to the common voice. Here was an educated poet, saying that the language of poetry had become false and untrue because it had lost its roots in common speech. He said,

The earliest poets of all nations generally wrote from passion excited by real events.

Hah! Me. My real and guilty secrets. And, he said,

they wrote naturally, and as men: feeling powerfully as they did, their language was daring, and figurative. In succeeding times, Poets, and Men ambitious of the fame of Poets, perceiving the influence of such language, and desirous of producing the same effect without being animated by the same passion, set themselves to a mechanical adoption of these figures of speech, and made use of them, sometimes with propriety, but much more frequently applied them to feelings and thoughts with which they had no natural connection whatsoever. A language was thus insensibly produced, differing materially from the real language of men in *any situation*. (465)

Oh, my! This was what I had been struggling with. I had learned the sonnet forms, acquired a rhyming dictionary, faithfully practiced the (to me, crude) metrics, and produced over a hundred sonnets which seemed, I supposed, good for a high school student but in fact were awful poetry. And I knew that. Here I was at Berkeley, with my sonnets being sneered at by the other editors of the literary magazine, and trying to figure out what made good poetry. I certainly had the passion, but the language was not part of that passion. I continued to be assaulted with the problem of not being able to tell my secrets, and thus the passion did not seem to be anchored in either real experience or the language that Wordsworth called "of any situation."

As I have narrated in my essay on "Creating a Personal Mythology," it was actually a poem by William Butler Yeats which was a turning point for me. "Leda and the Swan." I am not sure why that neo-classical poem did it; but suddenly snapped in me was permission to invent my life. A fictive self which would be more believable—no, more acceptable—than my lower middle class Southern California prim and prissy self, with her secrets, secrets probably not all that interesting if revealed.

Isn't that what Freud is all about? Translating our normal sexual dramas into the classics? So, I invented the story of my twin brother, of our incestuous relationship, of his teenage suicide. I didn't have to invent the hateful mother, but I invented a version of her which seemed more believable, and I didn't invent the sexual guilt, but I invented a different, more interesting reason for it. I reinvented my secret, so that I could wrap it and then unwrap it, lovingly, and reveal it in the poem with which I began this talk.

It really wasn't until I wrote a collection called *The Motorcycle Betrayal Poems* and another one called *Dancing on the Grave of a Son of a Bitch,* that the fictive self which had started as the Diane who loved her twin brother David too much grew into the personal mythology most people know my poetry by, the questing Diane who looks for love, sex, and romance as if it were the Grail, the woman who still knows her life was shaped when her father abandoned her, the young handsome fairy-tale father she will always long for and pursue, just as elusive as the cup from which Christ drank at the last supper.

The next milestone for my poetic quest, after "Justice Is Reason Enough," is a poem called "The Father of My Country." It is my best known poem, included in the *Norton Anthology* and other popular sources. It is a poem about the beautiful memories, and the erotic and sexual memories I have from childhood and how they shaped me into the kind of lonely, questing woman I am. It probably represents the Freudian way in which I put the Oedipal myths together with my personal myth, the story of Medea's betrayal. The poem accepts the pain, the anger, and the beauty as simultaneous in what I think of as a kind of Wordsworthian meditation.

THE FATHER OF MY COUNTRY

All fathers in Western civilization must have
a military origin. The
ruler,
governor,
yes,
he is
was the
general at one time or other.
And George Washington
won the hearts
of his country—the rough military man
with awkward
sincere
drawing-room manners.

My father;
have you ever heard me speak of him? I seldom
do. But I had a father,
and he had military origins—or my origins from
him
are military,
militant. That is, I remember him only in uniform. But of the
    navy,

30 years a chief petty officer,
Always away from home.

It is rough/hard for me to
speak now.
I'm not used to talking
about him.
Not used to
naming his objects/
objects
that never surrounded me.

A woodpecker with fresh bloody crest
knocks
at my mouth. Father, for the first
time I say
your name. Name rolled in thick Polish parchment scrolls,
name of Roman candle drippings when I sit at my table
alone, each night,
name of naval uniforms and name of
telegrams, name of
coming home from your aircraft carrier,
name of shiny shoes,
name of Hawaiian dolls, name
of mess spoons, name of greasy machinery, and name of
stencilled names.
Is it your blood I carry in a test tube,
my arm,
to let fall, crack, and spill on the sidewalk
in front of the men
I know,
I love,
I know, and
want? So you left my house when I was under two,
being replaced by other machinery, and
I didn't believe you left me.

This scene: the trunk yielding treasures of
a green fountain pen, heart-shaped mirror,
amber beads, old letters with brown ink, and

the gopher snake stretched across the palm tree
in the front yard with woody trunk like monkey skins,
and a sunset through the skinny persimmon trees. You
came walking, not even a telegram or post card from
Tahiti. Love, love, through my heart like ink in
the thickest nubbed pen, black and flowing into words.
You came to me, and I at least six. Six doilies
of lace, six battleship cannon, six old beerbottles,
six thick steaks, six love letters, six clocks running
backwards, six watermelons, and six baby teeth, a six
cornered hat on six men's heads, six lovers at once
or one lover at sixes and sevens; how I confuse
all this with my
dream
walking the tightrope bridge
with gold knots
over
the mouth of an anemone/tissue spiral lips
and holding on so that the ropes burned
as if my wrists had been tied

If George Washington
had not
been the Father
of my Country,
it is doubtful that I would ever have
found
a father. Father in my mouth, on my lips, in my
tongue, out of all my womanly fire,
Father I have left in my steel filing cabinet as a name on my birth
certificate, Father, I have left in the teeth pulled out at
dentists' offices and thrown into their garbage cans,

Father living in my wide cheekbones and short feet,

Father living in my Polish tantrums and my American speech,
    Father, not a
holy name, not a name I cherish but the name I bear, the name
that makes me one of a kind in any phone book because
you changed it, and nobody

but us
has it,
Father who makes me dream in the dead of night of the falling
    cherry
blossoms, Father who makes me know all men will leave me
if I love them,
Father who made me a maverick,
a writer
a namer,
name/father, sun/father, moon/father, bloody mars/father,

other children said, "My father is a doctor,"
or
"My father gave me this camera,"
or
"My father took me to
the movies,"
or
"My father and I went swimming,"
but
my father is coming in a letter
once a month
for a while,
and my father
sometimes came in a telegram
but mostly
my father came to me
in sleep, my father because I dreamed in one night that I dug
    through
the ash heap in back of the pepper tree and found a diamond
    shaped like
a dog and my father called the dog and it came leaping over to him
    and
he walked away out of the yard down the road with the dog
    jumping
and yipping at his heels,

my father was not in the telephone book
in my city;
my father was not sleeping with my mother

at home;
my father did not care if I studied the
piano;
my father did not care what
I did;
and I thought my father was handsome and I loved him and I
    wondered
why
he left me alone so much,
so many years
in fact, but
my father
made me what I am
a lonely woman
without a purpose, just as I was
a lonely child
without any father. I walked with words, words, and names,
names. Father was not
one of my words.
Father was not
one of my names. But now I say, George, you have become my
                                                        father,
 in his 20th century naval uniform. George Washington, I need your
love; George, I want to call you Father, Father, my Father,
Father of my country,
that is
    me. And I say the name to chant it. To sing it. To lace it around me
    like weaving cloth. Like a happy child on that shining afternoon in
the palmtree sunset with her mother's trunk yielding treasures,
I cry and
cry,
Father,
Father,
Father,
have you really come home?[4]

   One of the matters which Wordsworth struggles with in the Preface is how you can put together the passion at the heart of poetry
which draws people to it and the language which turns that passion
into literature and makes it endure. One sentence of Wordsworth's

has stuck in my mind all these years: "But the first Poets, as I have said, spake a language which, though unusual, was still the language of men" (466). Ignore the "spake." It was easy for me to ignore in the fifties. What called my attention was the sense that the language of poetry had to be simultaneously "unusual" and "common." I had worked to get the commonness out of my poetry, but realized now that what Wordsworth called "prose" was the commonness he meant. Perhaps reading that essay caused another snapping in my mind which allowed me to write "Justice Is Reason Enough"? Mulling in my mind Wordsworth's ideas about how the poet needs a common language, but his also defending the natural poetic nature of metrics (this was a struggle that all of us, as also the moderns had struggled, were going through—how to make a free verse, free from traditional prosody—that was easy, we hadn't studied Latin or Greek—but still using some kind of rhythmic structures.) Mulling over Wordsworth's convoluted but interesting arguments about how poetry could be like prose with metrics. Of course, I could have learned this from reading Whitman's poetry! His prose prosody is still what all of us employ. But I didn't yet think Whitman was interesting, had any secrets; and so I wasn't much interested in his verse. I knew Wordsworth had a secret and that gave me a kinship I latched onto and have never let go of. His Preface has been my manifesto for the past thirty years.

> Poets do not write for Poets alone, but for men. Unless therefore we are advocates for that admiration which subsists upon ignorance, and that pleasure which arises from hearing what we do not understand, the Poet must descend from this supposed height; and, in order to excite rational sympathy, he must express himself as other men express themselves. To this it may be added, that while he is only selecting from the real language of men, or, which amounts to the same thing, composing accurately in the spirit of such selection, he is treading upon safe ground, and we know what we are to expect from him. (457)

One of the reasons I have been so angry with Marjorie Perloff for years (besides the fact that I am not a feminist and she dismissed me in her now infamous review, "The Corn Porn Lyric," as being "just another feminist") is that she wrote to the effect that if Wakoski would stop hanging around truck stops and spend more time studying poetry, she might write better verse. The fact is that the studied part of my poetry, the truck-stop and motorcycle betrayal part of my poetry, is what I learned from Wordsworth and reaffirmed in Whitman—the common parts of my life and language which I had to reclaim after learning to write sonnets and sestinas and old-fashioned verse which avoided the secrets, the forbidden and the taboo, including my own lower class origins. How could a critic, especially one as brilliant and perceptive as Perloff, not see that?

To Wordsworth's credit, if that is where credit is due, my most successful collection has been *The Motorcycle Betrayal Poems,* and readers have bought my personal mythology so thoroughly that they still come up to me after poetry readings and ask me where my motorcycle is or try to engage in technical conversations about bikes. Of course, if they have really read my poems, they know that I have never ridden motorcycles, only lived with and been betrayed by a man who raced and repaired them.

Secrets, secrets. Our failures are our greatest secrets, though no one cares about them until they are aged, like good wine, stored in our cellars, covered with dust, and kept away from the light for some years. Secrets wrapped in layers of our clever or interesting or mythic or beautiful telling.

Taking the final prerogative of a poet asked to speak about her connections with these great poets of the past, I will conclude this presentation with a poem of my own, taken from *The Motorcycle Betrayal Poems,* published in 1972. Before I read this poem which is called "The Pink Dress," let me say that the title derived from creating a variation on a title by William Carlos Williams, "The Pink Church," and my sense that for women, love *is* the main religion and the main politics. A woman's sense of identity comes from how successful she is as a lover, and as a beloved: it is a myth that is bigger than our autobiographies and dominates us all, whether we are bankers or astronomers or housewives or poets. The secrets in all of my poems are the truth of how I have succeeded, or more usually, failed at love, sex, and romance, my trinity, my grail.

THE PINK DRESS

I could not wear that pink dress tonight.
The velvet one

lace tinting the cuffs with all
the coffee
of longing. My bare shoulder
slipping whiter
than foam
out of the night to remind me
of my own vulnerability.

I could not wear that pink dress tonight
because it is a dress
that slips memories like
the hands
of obscene strangers
all over my body.
And in my fatigue I could not fight away the images
and their mean touching.

I couldn't wear that pink dress,
the velvet one you had made for me,
all year, you know.

I thought I would tonight because
once again
you have let me enter your house
and look at myself
some mornings
in your mirrors.

But
I could not wear that pink dress tonight
because it reminded me
of everything
that hurts.
It reminded me of a whole year
during which
I wandered,
a gypsy,
and could not come into your house.
It reminded me of the picture of a blond girl
you took with you to Vermont

and shared your woods with.
The pretty face you left over your bed to stare
at me
and remind me
each night
that you preferred her face to mine,
and which you left there to stare at me
even when you saw how it
broke me,
my calm,
like a stick smashing across my own
plain, lonesome face,
and a face which you only
took down
from your wall
after I had mutilated it
and pushed pins in it to get those smug
smiling eyes off my cold
winter
body.

I couldn't wear that pink dress tonight
because it reminded me
of the girl who made it,
whom you slept with
last year while I was sitting in hotel rooms
wondering why I had to live
with a face
so stony no man could love it.

I could not wear that pink dress
because it reminded me
of how I camp on your doorstep now,
still a gypsy,
still a colorful imaginative beggar
in my pink dress,
building a fire in the landowner's
woods, and my own fierceness
that deserts me

when a man
no, when you
show a little care and concern
for my presence.

I could not wear that pink dress tonight.
It betrayed all that was strong in me.
The leather boots I wear to stomp through the world
and remind everyone
of the silver and gold and diamonds
from fairy tales
glittering in their lives.
And of the heavy responsibility
we all must bear
just being so joyfully alive
just letting the blood take its own course
in intact vessels
in veins.
That pink dress betrayed my one favorite image
   —the motorcyclist riding along the highway
   independent
   alone
   exhilarated with movement
   a blackbird
   more beautiful than any white ones.

But I went off
not wearing the pink dress,
thinking how much I love you
and how if a woman loves a man who does not love her,
it is, as some good poet said,
a pain in the ass.
For both of them.

I went off thinking about all the girls
you preferred to me.
Leaving behind that dress,
remembering one of the colors
of pain.

Remembering that my needs
affront you,
my face is not beautiful to you;
you would not share your woods with me.

And the irony
of my images.
That you are the motorcycle rider,
Not I.
I am perhaps,
at best,
the pink dress
thrown against the back
of the chair.
The dress I could not wear
tonight.[5]

Finally, let me point out, as a critic should, those lines in the middle of the poem,

And of the heavy responsibility
we must all bear
just being so joyfully alive
just letting the blood take its own course
in intact vessels
in veins.

I took seriously that lesson from Wordsworth's Preface, that "the end of Poetry is to produce excitement in co-existence with an over-balance of pleasure," (459) and his admonition that "we have no sympathy but what is propagated by pleasure: I would not be mis-understood: but wherever we sympathize with pain, it will be found that the sympathy is produced and carried on by subtle combina-tions with pleasure" (455).

My original goal in writing poetry was to make people interested in the pain I had experienced, the pain which was caused by my search for pleasure. Wordsworth taught me about the balancing, the co-existence of the two which had to exist to make good poetry. I could never have learned this lesson from my transcendental father,

Walt Whitman, even if I had earlier discovered that he too had secrets. Whitman's "Song of Myself," is undiluted celebration, with no acknowledgment of pain. Secrets are coupled with pain, for me. Wordsworth's lonely songs of himself are what taught me to apprehend and accept the commonness of both beauty and pain. More important, their co-existence in poetry.

Notes

1. Diane Wakoski, *Trilogy* (New York: Doubleday, 1974), 11.
2. William Wordsworth, *Selected Poems and Prefaces,* ed. Jack Stillinger (Boston: Houghton Mifflin, 1965). All subsequent Wordsworth quotations are from this edition and are cited in the text.
3. Walt Whitman, *The Complete Poems* (New York: Penguin, 1984). Subsequent Whitman quotations are from this edition.
4. Wakoski, *Inside the Blood Factory* (New York: Doubleday, 1968), 16–20.
5. Wakoski, *The Motorcycle Betrayal Poems* (New York: Simon and Schuster, 1972), 157–160.

Places and Poems

A Self-Reading and a Reading of the Self in the Romantic Context from Wordsworth to Parkman

❧

John Matthias

My title is awkward and long, but it is intended to suggest as accurately as possible what I intend to talk about this afternoon. I was invited to discuss my own work in the context of romanticism, and, although that initially seemed perhaps a rash and certainly an immodest thing to do—egotistical, but not sublime—the temptation to accept, proceed, and see what happened simply in the end overcame good sense. For what does my work have to do with romanticism? I have never admitted it had anything to do with it. Furthermore, I must confess that I have only read the romantics systematically once, and that the one time was under the stern eye of Yvor Winters at Stanford University in the middle sixties. Yvor Winters—the great *anti*-romantic of twentieth century criticism. I can still hear him growling in his mockery, adding a line to the Immortality Ode:

> The Rainbow comes and goes,
> And lovely is the Rose,
> The baby's playing with his toes.

And I can hear him pause in a lecture on Whitman to tell us that a student seemed to have written "Good descriptive elements!" in the margin of the text he was considering. "Ladies and gentlemen," he said, "these are *bad* descriptive elements."

Well, that was graduate school, and one reason for my being here at all is that I went to England to write poetry in 1966 rather than finishing graduate school. But although I never again systematically read the romantics in an academic and responsible way, I *have* read certain romantic texts for more pressing personal reasons since which will be seen to have something to do with the self-reading threatened in my title and the issue of place which provides, I hope, a legitimate connection between my own work and that of Wordsworth, Francis Parkman, and, incidentally, some of the artists whose paintings surround us today in the Historical Society.

However, as I have said, I am by no means an expert on romanticism and I am therefore anxious to defer to some critics who are experts in order to provide a context for my remarks. All other things being equal, I want to cite the work of people making a direct contribution to this conference, whether in person or through their essays appearing in Kenneth R. Johnston and Gene W. Ruoff's *The Age of William Wordsworth* or in the catalogue for "William Wordsworth and the Age of English Romanticism."

I was interested to find Morris Dickstein writing in the Johnston-Ruoff volume that "perhaps the crisis of feeling described by so many writers in the nineteenth century is something we no longer experience in any significant way," but going on to argue that nonetheless "a crisis of feeling is a consistent, unrecognized symptom of contemporary criticism itself. As our critical vocabularies have flourished on the analytic side, they have atrophied on the affective side. We have no accepted language in which to examine what really moves us in a writer."[1] Dickstein is remembering and commending the language of Matthew Arnold and John Stuart Mill. Arnold, he reminds us, "paid tribute to Wordsworth's 'healing power' that revived the wounded capacity for feeling in his contemporaries," while Mill, as everyone knows, turned to Wordsworth "for medicine for [his] state of Mind" having become, as a result of his rigorous analytical and utilitarian training, a kind of stock or stone in which, he felt, all feeling might be dead.[2] Wordsworth himself, of course, had feared much the same thing. Writing in book 10 of the

1805 *Prelude,* he speaks of the period when his own early habit of analysis in the categories of Godwinian rationalism, together with his agonized support of the Revolution, brought him to the state of mind which the famous lines describe:

> Thus I fared,
> Dragging all passions, notions, shapes of faith,
> Like culprits to the bar, suspiciously
> Calling the mind to establish in plain day
> Her titles and her honours, now believing,
> Now disbelieving, endlessly perplexed
> With impulse, motive, right and wrong, the ground
> Of moral obligation—what the rule,
> And what the sanction—till, demanding proof,
> And seeking it in every thing, I lost
> All feeling of conviction, and, in fine,
> Sick, wearied out with contrarieties,
> Yielded up moral questions in despair. . . .
>
> (889–900)

Wordsworth, like Mill, had sought to be a reformer of the world, and, like Mill, had cultivated a "habit of analysis" which had "a tendency to wear away the feelings" and "strengthen the associations between causes and effects [and] means and ends."[3] Although I do not have a vocabulary at my disposal adequate to reanimate for contemporary discourse the affective side of a critical language which, as Dickstein correctly notes, has atrophied—certainly not anything better than Arnold's language or Mill's—I need to record the fact that at a particular point in the 1960s I went as intentionally to Wordsworth as one might reach for the right medicine in the medicine chest, and I went to him remembering what he had done for Mill and how his own distorted and traumatized emotional life was reoriented and restored to proper health through memory and the disciplined play of an imagination interacting with nature in a particular place.

It is a bit shy-making to acknowledge that one needed and actively sought the Wordsworthian therapy for a state of mind that seems in retrospect almost a parody of the one he describes, but so in fact I did. I was not, I suppose, untypical of my generation in the

1960s by becoming sufficiently caught up in the machinery of protest and the language of neo-Marxist analysis to feel in the end both
confused and inauthentic, "dragging passions, notions, shapes of
faith / Like culprits to the bar," and subjecting everything, including the pleasures I took in a new marriage, in the birth of my first
child, in solitude, and in the arts to a rigorous inquisition with respect to means and ends considered in the context of political activism. I remember telling a friend in late 1968 that I felt oddly off
balance, that I was trying to regain that balance by reading Wordsworth. I also remember his response: "In a year like this one's been,"
he said, "I'm prepared to believe anything."[4] The sixties, like the
1790s and the first decades of the twentieth century, briefly held out
millennial expectations leading one to find, with Wordsworth, that
it was bliss to be alive and very heaven to be young. But if Robes-
pierre and Stalin led the dialectics of two revolutions to gag on their
own contradictions, sixties activism simply exhausted the emotional
energy of its partisans without producing much more than the temporary radicalization and political self-consciousness of an outraged
fraction of the middle class. "A dull, dishonest decade," as W. H.
Auden called the 1930s? Well, it certainly wasn't dull.

It's not that I exactly abandoned "present objects, and the busy
dance / Of things that pass away" for "a temperate show / Of objects that endure" by turning to Wordsworth at this time, and eventually he led me neither to a Natural Supernaturalism, nor a Via
Naturalitar Negativa, nor a Burkian Second Nature, nor an Established Church,[5] but simply to a place—and not *his* place either, but
a place of my own. Or, to be absolutely accurate, he led me to *realize* that I had been led to a place of my own. Perhaps I misread him;
or at any rate misread him at crucial points (the Spots of Time, the
Prospectus, crossing the Alps, Mount Snowdon), for, as many critics have made clear to me, Wordsworth is not always the sort of
poet of place I thought he was.[6] In any case, two years before turning in my post-activist consternation first tentatively to standard
anthology pieces and then in earnest to "Home at Grasmere" and
The Prelude for whatever therapy they could provide, I had begun
to spend my summers at my wife's home in the tiny village of
Hacheston, in Suffolk. Arriving one year by ship—a Russian ship
named for the romantic poet Lermontov, in fact—I bade my farewell to the sixties radical in a parodic idiom that was Byronic rather

than Wordsworthian. Although written in the middle seventies, it casts off a persona from the late sixties which had begun to vanish from my actual life the more I travelled to Suffolk and the longer I lived there. It also casts off anything that might have been left of my superficially assimilated Marxism except for its epistemology (which I still found useful in spite of the parenthetical joke), leaving me "with children and a wife" and "middle class for life."

> Said Marx (correctly)
> men will make their history, all right,
> but not exactly
> as they think or choose.
> (Even he had everything to lose
> with that excuse.)[7]

It was my wife, of course, who introduced me to Hacheston, the Aldeburgh coast, Orford, Framlingham, the rivers Stour and Alde and Orwell and Deben, and other places the names of which are utterly resonant for me now but which at first meant nothing. I had spent most of 1966 and '67 in London, only rarely venturing into the countryside and writing my first published poems under the influence of an eclectic range of American modern and postmodern poets. My sense of "the country" was as generic as my sense of trees and flowers and crops—which is to say totally generic. And I didn't, indeed, "make history," my private history, exactly (or anything like) I might have thought or initially chosen. In the end, I chose what I had been given, but at the beginning I didn't even see that I had been given something. Utterly urban to the age of twenty-five, I had grown up in an uninteresting city—Columbus, Ohio—which had given me only a negative sense of place, a sense only of a place I wanted to be away from. California was melodramatically impressive, but clearly wasn't mine—and I remember too that I arrived there just in time for the success of Philip Roth's first book, *Goodbye, Columbus,* which an ex-student of Roth's liked to taunt me with, then singing out for good measure: "Oh me Oh My Oh/Why did I ever leave Ohio?"

It took several years of summer visits—roughly from 1967 to 1970—for Suffolk to begin to do its work on me, and it took Wordsworth in *The Prelude,* "Home at Grasmere," "Poems on the

Naming of Places," and related works of the period 1798–1814 to make me consciously aware of what I had begun unconsciously to feel—namely, that whatever I was and whatever I was going to write that might have any merit was bound up, for the present at least, with a place I had come to love, and that I was going to have to learn, somehow, to write *from* that place as well as about it. It doesn't matter that Wordsworth's place was the Lake District and that mine turned out to be Suffolk—for surely Karl Kroeber is right when he says of Wordsworth and Constable that "their art makes us feel not that we would enjoy Cumberland or East Anglia but that we are at home on the earth."[8] Predictably, once I found that I could feel "at home on the earth" in Suffolk, I also found that I could write with a good deal of sympathy about Ohio. But only in Suffolk! And it's fair to say that Constable *had* made me feel that I would enjoy East Anglia.

I love the way Kroeber in *Romantic Landscape Vision* talks about Wordsworth taking possession of his place in "Home at Grasmere" like a predator or a pre-agricultural Indian in contrast to Constable, whose relationship to place in a painting like *The Leaping Horse* is compared to farming, which is, as Kroeber says, "a shaping of the natural world." "A farmer who does not understand nature," Kroeber notes, "will plant crops in poor soil, pasture sheep in the wrong field, generally will not get the most out of the land, animals, and plants. But to make nature work to his advantage, the farmer must be aggressive, must rearrange natural patterns. Constable, analogously, is true to nature in order to reshape it."[9] Kroeber finds the various versions of *The Leaping Horse* showing Constable "maneuvering the phenomena which are his subject to realize some mental scheme, not a chance falling out of events. Yet he is not arbitrary. His originality lies in rejecting conventional artistic schemes (the sublime, the picturesque, and so on) while refusing merely to copy natural appearances. His psychic patterns and nature's physical patterns, 'in here' and 'out there,' must be made to *fit*."[10] This description reminds me very much of what a contemporary farmer-poet, Wendell Berry, has said of his own work in a book called *Standing By Words*. Berry begins a long essay on "Poetry and Place" by asking if the connections he once saw and wrote about between his work on the Kentucky hill farm where he lives and his work as a poet has anything to it. What he wrote was that "the place has become the form of my work, its discipline, in the same way the sonnet has been the form and discipline of the work of other poets: if it doesn't fit it's not true."[11] At the end of his essay, Berry concludes that, in its essentials, his initial observation was sound. The farm is not, of course, a literary form, "but it is *like* a literary form, and it cannot properly be ignored or its influence safely excluded by any literary form that is made within it. Like any other form, it requires us to do some things, and forbids us to do others. Some acts are fitting and becoming, and some acts are not. If we fail to do what is required and if we do what is forbidden, we exclude ourselves from the mercy of Nature; we destroy our place, or we are exiled from it."[12]

But Wordsworth's personal and poetic relationship to Grasmere Vale is not like that of the figurative painter-farmer or the literal farmer-poet. Kroeber stresses the fact that in "Home at Grasmere" (and one can add as well books 1 and 13 of *The Prelude*), Wordsworth and his sister "are newcomers to the vale" and that Grasmere is a place they *choose* to live in which provides "a territory in which to roam." What Wordsworth does in Grasmere is "to fit himself to nature, and fit nature to himself, not in the fashion of a farmer, a pastoral poet, or a modern exurbanite, but, strange as it sounds, in the fashion of a predator such as a wolf."[13] This is a wonderful analogy, I think, and, though Kroeber does not press it, he says he "knows no better way to define the poet's preferred relationship to nature, because it excludes conventional attitudes toward possession and property in its emphasis upon territorial familiarity."[14] Dropping the lycanthropic comparison, Kroeber ultimately settles on an analogy between Wordsworth's attitude to place and "that found in preagricultural societies, whose concepts of 'land possession' are to us almost incomprehensible . . ." but who seem "to feel that they belong to their territory as fully as it belongs to them."[15] Perhaps Bruce Chatwin's recent book about the "songlines" of the Australian aborigines provides an extension of this analogy which is usefully far-fetched. One might see Wordsworth on a kind of aboriginal walkabout singing, as Chatwin writes of the aborigine following the labyrinth of invisible pathways which constitute the songlines, "the name of everything that crosses [his] path and so singing the world into existence." Chatwin tells us that there is "hardly a rock or a creek or a stand of eucalyptus that isn't an 'event' on one or other of the songlines. In other words, the whole of Australia can be read as a musical score." [16] So, in its domestic and circumscribed terms, can the world of Grasmere Vale in Wordsworth's poetry.

If farming provides an analogy for the form of a Constable painting and a poem by Wendell Berry, clearly Wordsworth's relationship to the prospect before him in Grasmere is analogous to the prospect before him in his writing. In all three cases, the work at hand is like the artist's chosen relationship to his place. The self in Wordsworth, having been spiritually dis-placed during the period of his revolutionary sympathies, takes up residence in a place which is like a poem and a poem which is like a place. Kroeber reminds us that he treats the mind, too, as a territory, as a "haunt" and a "region" in the conclusion to "Home at Grasmere" which became the "Prospectus" for *The Recluse,* and that he defines the self as an entity "created through deliberate fitting of one's individuality to the external world and of the external world to one's mind." [17] In the enclosed and self-contained world of his place, he is, Kroeber feels, suggesting a third analogy to accompany those of the predator and the preagricultural Indian, like a child "in the microcosmic environment of a garden, a farm, or a country place." [18] Furthermore, because he appears to do no work, his life seems indolent. Raisley Calvert's legacy has freed him for his poetry. He is in a position, as Whitman said, to "loaf and invite the soul."

I wonder how many people know, let alone enjoy, "Home at Grasmere." It causes critics like Goeffrey Hartman a good deal of embarrassment, [19] and it gives us Wordsworth at his most Whitmanic, writing ecstatically, allowing the words to tumble over themselves all but out of control. This is not a poetry of emotion recollected in tranquility: it reads in places like an attempt to write a poetry of lovemaking while actually enjoying sex. It is important for an understanding of the kind of influence I am trying to acknowledge to point out that this poem is not the sort of thing I approved of intellectually or held as a conscious model or recommended to anyone else—which is why, in fact, I was reading it, as it were, in secret. It seemed, and it still seems, something very strange; and it is something I read seriously only once.

The opening of *The Prelude* is similar, but more restrained and more controlled. It too is concerned with the business of getting started with the right poem in the right place. The place, again, sponsors the poem. Wordsworth contemplates "Long months and undisturbed delight / . . . in prospect" in his "known Vale." This time he "spares to tell of what ensued, the life / In common things"—having done just that in "Home at Grasmere"—but instead grapples with a range of possible subjects, suffers indeed a kind of temporary writer's block brought on by the very freedom and the range of possibilities he contemplates, and then, remembering the Derwent, surrenders to memory, evokes the earliest "spots of time," and at last realizes that the poem that he must write will tell "the story of [his] life." Thousands of lines later, the poem returns to its beginning and the poet returns to Grasmere, the place, as it were, containing the present memories of the poet's far-flung past as the binding of the book contains the pages of its telling. And in books 12–14, where Grasmere is re-introduced and the spots of time return, the writing, under the influence of Dorothy's ministrations, begins, now and then, to echo that of "Home at Grasmere."

But it's now past time to say that my own initial relationship to place in Suffolk and then later in East Anglia more generally, a relationship brought to full consciousness in part by a reading of Wordsworth's relationship to *his* place, was neither like that of a farmer nor that of a predator or an Indian; it was, oddly and literally, that of a spouse. When I married my wife I also married East Anglia, Suffolk, the Adelburgh and Orford coasts, the river Deben, the town of Woodbridge and the village of Hacheston. My initial response to English village life was pretty condescending. This was the place where farmers got on with whatever it was that farmers did and where my wife's parents lived in retirement in a rambling house which had been pieced together by joining three Elizabethan cottages made of local mud and horse hair. But the house itself became in a couple of years as numinous for me as Howards End is for Margaret Schlegel, and my mother-in-law, a repository of all the local legends and a fine amateur historian, proved to be, especially after the death of her husband, as mysterious a presence as Mrs. Ramsey herself and as nurturing an influence on my family as all the Wordsworth women put together. Accepting, as one does and must in a marriage with children, a life which made me a father and a son-in-law as well as my wife's lover and friend, I slowly opened myself to the full geological, topographical, natural, historical, and social context of the region where I came, able during these summers to loaf and invite the soul, to write.

In a paragraph which is more general than Wendell Berry's describing the manner in which a poem can be like a farm or Karl Kroeber's on the way a poem can resemble the territory of a predator, Jeremy Hooker writes in an afterword to his new book of poems that, consciously returning to his own original home in the south of England, he was "thinking of a poem that is like a place."

> Entering a place that is new to us, or seeing a familiar place anew, we move from part to part, simultaneously perceiving individual persons and things and discovering their relationships, so that, with time, place reveals itself as particular identities belonging to a network, which continually extends with our perception, and beyond it. And by this process we find ourselves not as observers only, but as inhabitants, citizens, neighbours, and locate ourselves in a space dense with meanings.[20]

If this is essentially what Wordsworth did, first with such abandon in Grasmere and in "Home at Grasmere," and then more soberly throughout the vale and in the poems it later sponsored, it is also what I sought to do in Suffolk, both in the place itself and in those poems I wrote which tried to take the measure of the place and find my proper station in it. But my initial explorations were necessarily tentative, as "Epilogue from a New Home," my first sustained poem written there, makes clear.

> There's a plague pit
>   just to the edge of the village.
> Above it, now mostly covered with grass,
>   a runway for B-17s: (American
> Pilots back from industrial targets). Tribes
>   gathered under my window;
> They'd sack an imperial town: I'll wave
>   to my wife at the end of the Roman road.
> At night I said
>   (the odd smell of the house recalling home)

"My father sits up in his grave.
    I'm too unstrung to love you now. Look:
Children play in the garden with bones."

Enclosed within a boundary of stones
    they died in isolation. All of us have
Colds; we visit the parish church and read: "Names.
    The numbers of persons who died of bubonic plague."
Grey-stone cottages across the road,
    a stream at the end of the church-yard,
Giant harvesters working the mechanized farms. . . .

Yesterday I walked to see the black,
    malignant huts that held the bombs.
After the war, nobody tore them down. Some
    are full of hay. Mechanics counted, standing
There, the number of planes that returned. I don't
    understand the work men did in the fields, or do.
I don't know the names of the crops. I don't
    know the uses of gears.
A church has grown on every hill like a tree.

Green on green: texture, shade, & shadows:
    opening out, folding in, surrounding.
Before the planes, someone counted ships: counted
    once that ancient one across the Deben
Where, from Woodbrige, you can almost see the site
    where his retainers set about to bury it,
A cenotaph, a King's.

Cynouai says: "I don't like my name. I won't have
    a name and I'll just be a girl."
Laura, three and deferential, understands. I open
    a bottle of wine.[21]

These lines from 1972 register something of the post-Vietnam state
of consciousness parodied in the poem written on board the Lermontov and quoted earlier. But here, as the elements constituting
the place begin coming together—the Roman road, the ruined air

base, the farm, the cottages, the Sutton Hoo ship burial, Woodbridge, the Deben, the church with its memorials to those who died
of plague (perception of which is conditioned partly by the shock of
my father's recent death and partly by the first full realization that I
was now myself a father)—the healing process, I think, can be seen
to begin. But it's important to stress that from the beginning the
place for me was inseparable from what I was reading about it, and
the following stanzas are distinctly bookish. This husband and father aimed also to be a historian of sorts, and the poems do not
draw much, as Wordsworth does, on oral sources and traditional
lore, but on books.

> A whir of looms where wool was wealth:
>   (*nidings voerk, nidings voerk*) the baths long
> Drained, the polyglot army long before withdrawn.
>   If the Trinovantian coins & the legionary oaths,
> If the pentatonic lyre in the Royal Ship
>   prefigure here a merchant—*upon his head*
> *A Flaundrish bever hat*—,
>   is that more odd
>   than that my children's rhyme recalls
> The plague, the unattended fields & the dissipation
>   of the feudal claims, or that the final
> Metamorphosis of Anna's luck should find its
>   imagery—like Christ's—in bas-reliefs
> Depicting animals domesticated by domesticating
>   Saxon heirs?

> We picnic by these graves, these strata of
>   the dead: Celtic, Roman, Viking, English—
> All of them killers, all of them dead, they'd moralize
>   on one another's end. Christian to pagan, power
> To power, and I am also implicated here: the woodwose
>   in the spandrels of a door lifts up his club,
> A voice begins to speak of Fifteen Signs.[22]

These last three stanzas sound to me a bit more confident and
rooted than the initial stanzas do. Fearing, perhaps, the dangers of
the picturesque, what Wordsworth in *The Prelude* calls a "strong

infection of [his] age—giving way / To a comparison of scene with
scene, / Bent overmuch on superficial things, / . . . with meager
novelties / Of colour and proportion," I turned early on to books
and documents and histories to discipline my seeing. Now this is,
strictly speaking, anti-Wordsworthian. James Chandler has shown
clearly Wordsworth's aversion to documentary history together with
his feeling that it posed a threat to his oral and traditionary material—"a plague on your industrious antiquarianism," he wrote
to Scott who had offered to send him some documents about the
Norton Uprising for "The White Doe of Rylstone"[23]—and Karl
Kroeber argues that the form and subject of *The Prelude* are largely
explained by Wordsworth's "effort to escape the limiting condition
of history" and work only with "what has been transformed by tradition or imaginative enthusiasm into legend."[24] For myself, however, any fitting of the mind to the external world very soon required
learning from the books in my mother-in-law's library, the documentary contents of which seemed as much a part of the soil as the
flints I turned up with the toe of my shoe. I met with few Michaels
or Pedlars or leech gatherers in Suffolk, but 1969 was the year that
Ronald Blyth—that Wordsworth with a tape recorder—published
Akenfield, and shortly after that I carried on my walks the books on
Suffolk and The Iknield Way by those Wordsworthian wanderers
Julian Tennyson and Edward Thomas.[25] And there were also specialized and scholarly books—whole bibliographies of such—which
I read with pleasure for materials they provided for the structures I
began to build. The poem from which I have been quoting ends:
"I'm but half oriented here. I'm digging down." The facts I learned
from books were what I dug with.

> *The child is father of the man*
> but not the child the poet meant.
> The child of flesh and blood
> and not the ghost of former selves
> is father of the man. . . .[26]

So begins the conclusion of a poem for my daughter written late
in the series of East Anglian poems from the first decade of summer
visits there. In the end, much of what I wrote was a result of watching my children play in their grandmother's garden. It has always

surprised me that Wordsworth, who wrote so much about himself as a child, wrote so little about his children. If my own route to the responsibilities of being an adult was through my children, it was also through my children that I found the route to childhood. And one thing that I wanted to learn on my way to childhood and back again had something to do with the meaning of play. In "Double Derivation . . . ," a poem glossed by another addressed to Robert Jacoby, my older cousin, I drew on Johan Huizinga:[27]

> In proper costume, Homo Ludens wears
> Imagination on his sleeve,

and went on to speak of "a field in Suffolk / So like the one we used to play in, in Ohio, / When we were boys." Feeling increasingly rooted in East Anglia, I had begun—East Anglia had made it possible for me—to remember Ohio without condescending to what was an authentic richness in my own early experience. And so I ask my cousin if *he* remembers

> all those games
> we used to play: the costumes,
> All the sticks & staves, the whole complicated
> paraphernalia accumulated to suggest
> Authentic weaponry and precise historical dates,
> not to mention exact geographical places . . .

all of which constituted

> a world of imagination,
> Lovely and legitimate, uncovering, summer after
> summer, a place that we no longer go,
> A field we do not enter now, a world one tries
> to speak of, one way or another,
> In a poem. . . .

But remembering Robert and remembering the games through which we tried to fit our minds to the external world and the external world to our minds, I remembered also another cousin, James. This one valued *work* instead of play. With his "bicycles / and paper routes and baseballs" he was a "miniature / Adult" who "looked askance at our elaborate rituals. He laughed outright, / Derisively. No mere chronicler, he was reality itself." The *news* was, as I go on to tell my cousin,

> that he, not you and I, made
> Without our knowledge, without our wigs and
> epaulets, with bricks he had a right
> To throw, binding rules for our splendid games.[28]

In an article I'm truly grateful for, Jeremy Hooker has said about this aspect of the poem that "the poet at his creative play makes poems that are themselves worlds, but makes them out of the stuff of reality, which exists independently of him, makes its own claims, questions the poet, and calls him to witness all that is not himself."[29] That was certainly the intention of the lines, but there is still an unresolved (and probably unresolvable) tension between a world of play and a world of work, the world of a child and the world of an adult, the world of a daughter or son and the world of a parent, the world of Suffolk summers (nurturing memories of childhood) and the world of midwestern American winters (forcing attention to the obligations of the present moment). Karl Kroeber, you will remember, finally likened Wordsworth's relation to his valley to the manner in which "a child fits himself to, and makes fit his demands, the microcosmic environment of a garden, a farm, or a country place." This is very like the microcosmic environment of the game according to the rules of which a child plays and of the poem according to the conventions of which the poet writes. But how does it relate to a world of work and adult responsibilities and the contemporary fact that the place we find where, for a while, we can loaf and invite the soul, is almost certainly going to be some kind of temporary haven which, one way or another, is separated from the place in which we earn our living—the Wendell Berrys are certainly very rare—and which, once found, is all too likely to be lost?

Jeremy Hooker is, I think, the best British critic of literature seen in relationship to place. In his 1985 collection of essays, *The Poetry of Place,* he argues that "poetry of place after Wordsworth cannot be understood outside a context of loss"[30] and develops a paradigmatic history of post-Wordsworthian poetry by reading representative poems by Arnold, Clare, Hardy, Edward Thomas, and the tragic

Ivor Gurney. Already with Matthew Arnold, Hooker finds Wordsworth's security in a shared humanity vanishing from poetry and
his sense of an order embracing all mankind, along with a corresponding confidence in the spiritual and cultural centrality of poetic
utterance, diminishing to an elegiac investiture of particular places
"with the poet's spirit . . . [and] the localization of the poetic within
an England whose dominant culture has no use for it. A resulting
narrowing of focus, in poems as well as ideas of poetry, has trans-
ferred its voice from an order embracing man and nature to the
hills." [31] When Arnold writes "I know these slopes; who knows
them if not I," Hooker hears an expression of cultural isolation, of a
culturally marginal role, more than he does an expression of a characteristic temperament. The effects of such isolation in Clare and
Hardy make of place, Hooker feels, "a refuge or escape from an unmanageable or unlovable society or nation," [32] while in Thomas and
Gurney (and in Thomas's prose master, Richard Jeffries), he finds a
melancholy fulfillment of these tendencies in work where the worship of nature becomes concentrated in a particular place to such
an extent that, should the place be taken away, nothing will be left
at all. [33]

If the poet in his place had been able to *work* and invite the soul
rather than loaf and invite the soul (or, once utterly displaced, des-
perately remember), would Hooker's history look any different?
Only Clare and Hardy, among comparatively recent poets, had a
real and active, if ambiguous and strained, relationship with their
communities. That I respond somewhat defensively to the work of
poets shown by Hooker to be cut off by their trade and their self-
consciousness from the organic life of the place they love probably
only means that my own experience of place is much like theirs. I
arrived in Suffolk, after all, unconsciously *seeking* "a refuge or escape from an unmanageable or unlovable society or nation." And
I didn't live there like a native of the place—whether a farmer, a
craftsman, a doctor, or a teacher—but as a relative and friend of natives and a writer who, though he might experience and describe
the place in fresh and unfamiliar ways, would never be fully integrated with its life unless he stayed there and worked there. I was
more than a tourist, but less than a citizen of the place. And mightn't
a poet consult more deeply the Genius of the Place in his poetry if
he were constrained to consult it in every aspect of his daily life? [34]

By the time I came to write a review of Hooker's book, I was troubled and perplexed. It was 1984 and I had been commuting between the place I wrote in Suffolk and the place I worked at the University of Notre Dame for more than fifteen years. Moreover, the summer before I wrote the review I had sat at my desk within two hundred yards of the St. Joseph River in South Bend, Indiana, and written the most sustained and ambitious cycle of poems I had yet produced about East Anglia dealing in part with those three rivers in Suffolk which I loved so much, the Alde, the Deben and the Stour. "Why not," I asked, "a poem about the St. Joseph?" The review began by trying to sort that question out.

I think the reason is that while the St. Joseph is rich with associations that might stimulate another poet—La Salle came down this river, the Potawatomi lived nearby, the continental divide split it from the Kankakee and created a famous portage, Francis Parkman wrote about it, etc.—for me it is associated entirely with the kind of daily grind that prevents poetry from being written (or river banks from being explored). It is the river I cross in my car to go to work. Last summer was the first summer in years that I did not spend in East Anglia, that part of England where for more than a decade I have felt both welcome and free—free in the sense that Donald Hall has in mind when he speaks about emotions deriving from "a place associated not with school or with conventional endeavor or with competition or with busyness," but a place "where we have loafed and invited the soul." I know and love the Suffolk rivers—have loafed and invited the soul on their banks—but have no feeling at all about the St. Joseph, even though I have lived beside it for most of the past fifteen years. On the banks of the St. Joseph I sought, I think, to summon back emotions I have felt on the banks of the Alde, the Deben, and the Stour. The writing, I suppose, expresses a kind of nostalgia, a compensation for loss. Loss of what? Well, of the place. A year ago we lost the house in Suffolk and it isn't clear when or if we'll be returning to East Anglia.[35]

It's interesting that in the poem I wrote, a poem exploring not only the rivers and river routes connecting locality with locality and time with time, but also the ancient paths or tracks dating back to the neolithic period known as ley lines, the chief human presences should have been Constable and Edward Thomas. I had no idea when I wrote the poem that the Constable painting I was dealing with was one of those worked up in London from the oil sketches made in East Bergholt between 1810–1811 which recalled not the place in the Stour Valley where Constable any longer lived and worked, but the place he had lost by moving to London after his marriage and could only possess again through the emotional charge of his expressionistic later manner. As for Edward Thomas, his book on the Icknield Way, the chief ley line explored in the poem, was his *last* on the English countryside. I imagine him before his death in 1917.

> Home, returned on leave, exhausted,
> bored by prose he's published only months before
> and talking with a friend who asks:
> *and what'll you be fighting for over there?*
>
> he picks a pinch of earth up off the path
> they're walking and says: *This*
> *For this,* he says,
> *This this this*
> *For*
>
> > > > *this*[36]

As of course Edward Thomas *did* say before leaving to die in the war. During the Napoleonic wars, Constable painted and Wordsworth wrote poetry for much the same reason.

If my own place had been lost except in memory—one attempt to visit it found the house itself converted into a "Bed & Breakfast"—what was there to do? Making a virtue of necessity, and concerned about some of the questions I have just raised, I decided to stay in Indiana for a while and read a little history.[37] I thought I could *try* to feel "at home on the earth" even in South Bend. Moreover, as an act of will, though still believing firmly with David Jones that the poet must "work within the limits of his love," I began to write a long poem which I intend to conclude by reading a section from called "Facts from an Apocryphal Midwest." I could only hope that an act of will might, in the curious processes of composition, become an act of love. At any rate, I began to grapple with some midwestern American geography, geology, prehistory, and history that parallel in many ways those I was working with in the long East Anglian poem I had finished two years before. The chief trails this time—American ley lines, as it were—began as prehistoric paths down which Lake Superior copper was carried from the early days of the Mound Builders until the collapse of their particular economy and way of life. These trails, and especially the St. Joseph-Kankakee portage, were later used by the Potawatomi, the Miami, and other local Algonquian tribes, as well as by the Iroquois on their raids into the area, and by the French explorers, traders, and missionaries. Again, as in the East Anglian poem, three rivers figure in the topographical configuration that emerges: the St. Joseph (which the French called the River of Miamis), the Kankakee (also called the Seignelay), and the Illinois. The dominant historical figure in the poem is Réné-Robert Cavelier, Sieur de la Salle. Ironically, once I had begun my research and composition, I found myself stimulated by exactly those things which I said in the review of Jeremy Hooker's book might stimulate "another poet"—LaSalle's voyage through the great lakes and journey along the local rivers and trails, Algonquian (mostly Potawatomi) history and mythology, the geological and geographical transformations which occurred during the last glacial recession, and most of all the prose of Francis Parkman in the volume of *France and England in North America* called *La Salle and the Discovery of the Great West*. The entire poem is, in a way, a homage to Parkman.[38]

Never having walked a foot along the banks of the St. Joseph river, I now followed Parkman as Parkman—who must have trudged virtually through my back yard on his visit to the area in 1867—followed La Salle who followed his Indian guide along the portage trail to the Kankakee marsh. With respect to the self, the solution seemed to be this: that I, who had little feeling for the place I would evoke and engage, should embody myself in a figure who had great feeling for it, who in turn embodies himself in the figure who initially explored that place, contended against it, and had perforce to fit his mind to the external world to survive and the external world to his mind to prevail.

Now what about Parkman and Wordsworth? Aside from some fascinating biographical similarities—both courted in their early lives the "ministry of fear," both were cared for by their sisters, both expanded their domestic entourage to include yet other nurturing women, both grieved deeply for lost brothers who were sailors, and both were plagued by neurasthenic ailments brought on by writing (in Parkman's case, the victory of creative will over illness is nothing short of inspiring)—Wordsworth and Parkman are Romantic opposites.[39] We know that Wordsworth saw "little worthy or sublime / In what the Historian's pen so much delights / to blazon," but we should also know that this particular historian, according to his biographer, "could not abide Wordsworth and his followers." "He loved nature," Charles Farnham tells us, "but not as a lover who sits down quietly for intimate communion."[40] He had a love, Farnham says, "of the real" and a nature which did not include "a poet's capacity for revery and contemplation." Moreover, he "deplored the modern tendency to discover objects of sympathy in vagabonds" and the like—vagrants, pedlars, shepherds, or leech gatherers—and was instead drawn to the heroic, even, indeed, the chivalric.[41] As capable as Wordsworth of sublime effects—of infusing a panoramic landscape with a light as remarkable as Turner's[42]— his sublime was anything but egotistical; he possessed, in fact, a high degree of Negative Capability and "seized with certainty the salient traits of men and women, courtiers and savages, priests and politicians, seigneurs and peasants, nuns and *coureurs de bois.*"[43] But if there is a Turner in him, there is no Constable, for he "cared not for highly humanized landscapes" and "the charms of rural England are not mentioned in his diaries."[44] Given the dual focus of his histories—the protagonists seen at first close-up and then dwarfed by the panoramic landscapes that envelop them—we need for visual analogues both paintings like West's *The Death of General Wolf* and Turner's *Hannibal Crossing the Alps.* In fact we need a whole academy of painters that would include, along with West and Turner, such different artists as Joshua Reynolds, Thomas Cole, George Caleb Bingham, and, when we enter the Jesuit mind, El Greco.[45]

But I must soon read from the poem or I fear we'll never get there. Everyone who reads or reads about Francis Parkman understands the manner in which La Salle embodies both active characteristics of Parkman's personality and also, in La Salle's life of action, distorted versions of characteristics which would have found expression had not illness made an invalid of the author of *The Oregon Trail* and the journals which he kept of his early exploration of the Magalloway. There is something of Parkman in many of his major characters, but La Salle is an alter ego, a dark Byronic brother, a tragically flawed Coriolanus. He is one of the great characters in

American literature, and one of the most troubling. Groping for comparisons, critics have mentioned Melville, Milton, and even Homer, as well as Scott, Byron, Cooper, and Shakespeare.[46] In a fascinating analysis of the psychology of composition, Howard Doughty quotes a letter to Martin Brimmer: "I conceived literary ambitions, and, at the same time, began to despise the literary life." And Doughty comments: "However inflexible he was on one level in pursuit of his chosen task, one senses a resistance to the 'calling' of authorship—to his role of artist and creator—which some sub-conscious mechanism of the psyche like illness was required to overcome. . . . At any rate there is something almost uncanny in the way his complex of maladies shaped his life to the best deploy-ment of his powers."[47] This, then, is the man I follow who in turn follows La Salle across Lake Michigan, up the St. Joseph River, across the portage to the Kankakee, and to the Illinois within a few dozen miles of where we are this afternoon. My own language bleeds into Parkman's which in turn bleeds into La Salle's. The poem, the sixth section of *Facts From an Apocryphal Midwest,* is called "The Boat Maker's Tale."

>He'd sent the Griffin on back to Niagara
>loaded with the furs he thought
>would pay his debts. . . .
>>Colbert walked in shadows

>at Versailles, the river to be named for him
>named otherwise by Onangizes, called
>himself, like Colbert's king, the shimmering sun.

>Frontenac, Onnontio to Green Bay's Ouilamette
>and all the rest of Gigos clan,
>dreamed a map of colonies and little forts

>stretching from above St. Joseph on the lake
>down the river of Miamis
>to the marshy waters of that languid

>tributary to be named one day for Seignelay
>whose own necrology of ships
>made him Minister among the idle admirals

in the shipyards and the ports of France.
Stretching farther still . . .
Stretching well beyond that river to the one

that only Joliet and Père Marquette
among the French had ever seen & named & spoken of
saying that *no land at all no*

country would be better suited to produce
whatever fruits or wheat or corn
than that along this river that the wild cattle

never flee that one finds some 400 in a herd
that elk & deer are almost every
where and turkeys promenade on every side. . . .

From the day a man first settled here
that man
could start to plow . . .
> But Cavelier, La Salle,

had sent the Griffin on back to Niagara.
He'd build a second ship
to sail down the rivers he would find. . . .

For he himself had said in Paris, sounding
just like Père Marquette, *it's all*
so beautiful and fertile, free from forests

full of meadows brooks and rivers all
abounding there in fish & game
where flocks and herds can even be left out

all winter long. All winter long!
And it was nearly winter now in Michillimackinak.
The King had said to him *We have received*

with favor a petition in your name and do
permit your exploration
by these presents signed with our own hand

but now he was in debt. Migeon, Charon—
they'd seized the beaver pelts
and even skins of skunks—Giton, Pelonquin!

Names of enemies. But there was Henri Tonty here;
there was, indeed, Count Frontenac.
These he'd name against the plotting creditors.

The Ship will fly above the crows, he'd said,
his patron governor's heraldic mast-
head besting Jesuits in a Niagaran dream of power.

He had his Récollets to do whatever of God's work
there was. Hennepin, who strapped
an altar on his back and cured the fainting

Father Gabriel with a confection of hyacinths!
And Gabriel himself; and Zénobe.
They'd sung *Te Deum* well enough upon the launching.

He'd have them sing a good deal more than that—
Exaudiat, Ludovicus Magnus!—
once they'd reached the Colbert's mouth, the sea.

The ship *had* nearly flown across the lakes.
In spite of an ungodly pilot
and in spite of god knows dreadful storms

she'd been the equal of the Erie and the Huron.
How she'd sailed out beyond Niagara!
Her canvas billowed & she fired her five small guns

to the astonishment of Iroquois along the banks.
Then a freshening northwest wind.
Down the lake and to Detroit's narrow straights

she sailed until she met a current there strong
as the bore before the lower Seine—
and twelve men leapt ashore to pull her over, through.

They marvelled at the prairies to the east & west
and stopped to hunt, and hung their
guyropes full of fowl and drying bearskins.

From wild grapes the priests prepared communion wine.
Then they were in Huron where the gale
attacked them and they brought down mainyards, tacked

with trysail, then lay long to the till.
The pilot blasphemed damnably while all the rest
cried out to Anthony of Padua

who calmed the winds and brought the ship to port
at Michillimackinak beside
the mission of St. Ignace, Père Marquette's fresh grave.

That was in the early autumn when the Ottawa
and Huron fishing fleets
were strung across the lakes from Saint Marie du Sault

to Keweenwa, from Mackinac to Onangizes' islands
in Green Bay. He'd worn his scarlet coat
with its gold lace and flown the banner of the king

while all his men fired muskets & he stepped ashore.
That was autumn, when the sun
still burned their necks & missionaries harvested.

But it was nearly winter now and he would be he said
in Illinois country when the rivers froze.
Heavy clouds blew in from Canada on northern winds.

The ship had sailed away. And so they
set forth on the lake in four canoes: fourteen men
who bore with them a forge & carpenters' &

sawyers' tools to build the Griffin's twin
beside a fort they'd also build on high ground near
the navigable lower Illinois.

They cried out to each other in the dark.
For it was dark before they were across the lake.
It stormed again as when the Griffin

rocked and shook on Huron, waves against the fragile
birchbark, rain in their red eyes.
Anvil and bellows, iron for nails and bolts,

pit-saws, arms, and merchandise for gifts
and trade when they had reached the Illinois town below
the portage weighed them down.

Gunsmith, blacksmith, joiner, mason, master-
builder Moyse Hillère—
they paddled for the further shore with Cavelier

and three priests and the guide. Half of them
were cousins to *coureurs de bois*
and would desert. Two of them were felons.

All of them washed up together with the breaking
waves beside
the mouth of the Miamis

                    and gorged on grapes, and wild haws, &
on the carcass of a deer that had been killed by wolves.

Here they stayed for twenty days, and built a tiny fort, and spiked
the hill they built it on. They took nine soundings of the river's
mouth, marking out the passage that a ship might take with buoys
and bearskin flags. The first brief snow blew in across the lake well
before December and ice began to form along the river's edge. Occasionally, La Salle's Mohegan guide could find a deer to kill, or
bear, and brought them meat; but food was scarce and all of them
began to urge La Salle to press on to the portage and to Illinois or
Miami camps where they might find, in covered pits, a gleaming
hoard of winter's corn. When Tonty finally came with men who
had been sent ahead from Fort Niagara but had scattered in the
woods, the party numbered thirty-four. Four were left behind with
messages and maps for those who would arrive to reinforce them

when the Griffin sailed back past Michillimackinak and down Lake
Michigan & anchored here. If the Griffin wasn't lost. If the furs to
pay off creditors had not been stolen by the pilot and his men. If all
of them had not sailed straight to join the outlaw trader Dan Du
Lhut at Kamalastigouia up in Thunder Bay.

Nous embarquâmes, wrote Hennepin, *le troisième Decembre. Avec
trente hommes . . . Dans huit canots.* They were John Boisrondet,
L'Espérance de la Brie, La Rousselière, La Violete, Picard du Gay,
Etienne Renault, Michel Baribault, Bois d'Ardeene, Martin Char-
tier, Noel le Blanc, the nailer called La Forge, the indian guide they
called Oui-Oui-La-Meche, and those with names now known to all
or names now known to none. They took up paddles once again,
prepared to travel on, to shoulder their canoes along the portage
trail if they could find it. Had it been spring, had it been high summer, the fields and woods that lined the river's channel would have
blossomed for them, fruited like the prairies on the east and west of
the Detroit straights when they pulled the Griffin through to Huron
and the priests made wine. And when at last they reached the portage, they would have seen tall cedars, oaks, and water-elms; in a
ravine declining from high ground they would have seen along the
curving trail splashes of the reds and blues of wild forest flowers;
flocks of plovers, snipe, might have flown above the trees to land
beside the standing cranes in fields of wild rice in fens the far side of
the watershed across the prairie with its elk and deer and buffalo
which traders would begin to call one day the Parc aux Vaches. But
it was winter; they saw none of this. They saw the skulls and bones
of animals, a bleak gray plain; they lugged their eight canoes and
forge and iron and anvil up the hill and then along the portage path
behind La Salle who brooded on the Griffin in the melancholy,
willful, isolated silence of his mind, La Salle whose men, with
five exceptions, would forsake his vision and his surrogate at Fort
Crevecoeur—39 degrees and 50 minutes latitude exactly on his fine
Parisian astrolabe—and daub in tar-black letters on the planking of
the half-built river boat: *Nous Sommes Tous Sauvages.*

The man who followed him in many ways was like him, and read
his words, and read the words and followed all the trails of others
who had passed this way before he did himself, but after him who
was the first to come and was the object of his search. Charlevoix he

read, and La Hontan. Tonty's own account, and Hennepin's, and all of La Salle's letters both to Canada and France. Transcripts, depositions. He too knew about insatiable ambition, pride and isolation, subduing all to an inflexibility of purpose. When his chronic and mysterious illness made his head swim and his joints swell, made his eyes so sensitive to light he could not read, his nights so sleepless that he could not even dream his shattered double's thousand mile trek from the lower Illinois back to Montreal, he had his friends read *to* him, tried to comprehend their strange pronunciations of the language of the texts and maps and manuscripts de la France Septentrionale which he followed to the Kankakee or Seignelay and then beyond. . . .

Terres tremblantes, sur lesquelles on peut à peine marcher he read, and wrote how "soon they reached a spot where oozy saturated soil quaked beneath their tread. All around were clumps of alder-bushes . . . pools of glistening water *une espèce de mare* and in the midst a dark and lazy current, which a tall man might bestride . . . twisting like a snake among the reeds and rushes and . . . *il a faut continuellement tourner* . . . They set canoes upon this thread of water and embarked their baggage and themselves and pushed on down the sluggish streamlet looking at a little distance like men who sail on land. . . . Fed by an increasing tribute of the spongy soil it widened to a river *presque aussi large que la Marne,* and they floated on their way into a voiceless, lifeless solitude of boundless marshes overgrown with reeds. . . .

At night they built their fire on ground made firm by frost *quelques mottes de terres glacées*

and bivouacked among rushes . . ."[48]

Notes

1. Morris Dickstein, "'The Very Culture of the Feelings': Wordsworth and Solitude," in *The Age of William Wordsworth: Critical Essays on the Romantic Tradition,* ed. Kenneth R. Johnston and Gene W. Ruoff (New Brunswick and London: Rutgers University Press, 1987), 317.
2. Ibid., 316, 317.

3. John Stuart Mill, *Autobiography,* ch. 5, in *English Prose of the Victorian Era,* ed. Charles Frederick Harold and Willard D. Templeman (New York: Oxford University Press, 1962), 709. Citations from Wordsworth's *Prelude* are from *William Wordsworth: The Prelude, 1799, 1805, 1850,* ed. Jonathan Wordsworth, M. H. Abrams, and Stephen Gill (New York: Norton, 1979).

4. In light of his subsequent career, it is worth noting that the friend was Peter Michelson.

5. The first three capitalized references are of course to the interpretations of Wordsworth in M. H. Abrams, *Natural Supernaturalism: Tradition and Revolution in Romantic Literature* (New York: W. W. Norton, 1971); Geoffrey Hartman, *Wordsworth's Poetry, 1787–1814* (New Haven: Yale University Press, 1964); and James K. Chandler, *Wordsworth's Second Nature: A Study of the Poetry and Politics* (Chicago: University of Chicago Press, 1984). As for the Established Church, W. H. Auden wrote in *New Year Letter* at the end of the 1930s:

> Thus Wordsworth fell into temptation
> In France during a long vacation,
> Saw in the fall of the Bastile
> The Parousia of liberty. . . .
> A liberal fellow-traveller ran
> With Sans-culotte and Jacobin,
> Nor guessed what circles he was in,
> But ended as the Devil knew
> An earnest Englishman would do,
> Left by Napoleon in the lurch
> Supporting the Established Church.

6. Perhaps the angriest recent case against Wordsworth as a poet of place is made by Wendell Berry in his essay "Poetry and Place" in *Standing by Words* (San Francisco: North Point Press, 1983). Working almost entirely with the Prospectus to *The Recluse,* Berry argues that Wordsworth

> affirms the existence both of individual conscience and of a supreme intelligence, but has affirmed no earthly thing between them that can correct his understanding of either or bring the two into harmony. . . . What fills [Wordsworth] with fear and awe is to enter "the Mind of Man." That sets him praying—and well it ought to, considering the arrogance of that mind as represented here. . . . It is hard to tell which is greater, Wordsworth's spiritual presumptuosness or his poetic impudence. . . . This mind, moreover, has no problems with "the external world." It is simply "exquisitely . . . fitted" to it. When the two are "blended," Paradise will be renewed. . . . [This] has behind it all in human arrogance and ambition that speaks in Milton's Satan's determination that "The mind is its own place. . . ." Ahead of it, it has all the propaganda and the works of the scientific romanticism that accompanied the industrial revolution. For if the poetic individual mind can pass unalarmed the heaven of heavens and the whole spiritual order of the universe, why cannot the scientific individual mind do so as well? (174–175)

Given the terminology of Karl Kroeber which I borrow later in this essay, one might say that it is no surprise that a farmer–poet like Berry might be outraged by a predator–poet like Wordsworth.

7. John Matthias, "The Mihail Lermontov Poems," *Crossing* (Athens, Ohio, and London: Swallow Press, 1979), 117. Three sections from this cycle are reprinted in *Northern Summer* (Athens, Ohio, and London: Swallow Press, 1984), 158–168.

8. Karl Kroeber, *Romantic Landscape Vision* (Madison: University of Wisconsin Press, 1975), 25.

9. Ibid., 111.

10. Ibid.

11. Berry, *Standing by Words*, 92.

12. Ibid., 192–193.

13. Kroeber, *Romantic Landscape*, 119.

14. Ibid., 119.

15. Ibid., 119–120.

16. Michael Ignatieff, "An Interview with Bruce Chatwin," *Granta* 21 (Spring 1987), 30–31. Chatwin's book is *The Songlines* (New York: Viking Press, 1987).

17. Kroeber, *Romantic Landscape*, 124.

18. Ibid., 125.

19. Hartman, *Wordsworth's Poetry*, 172 ff.

20. Jeremy Hooker, *Master of the Leaping Figures* (Petersfield: Enitharmon, 1987), 76.

21. Matthias, "Epilogue from a New Home," *Turns* (Chicago and London: Swallow Press, 1975), 104–105. Reprinted in *Northern Summer*, 73–76.

22. Matthias, "Epilogue," 105–106.

23. Chandler, *Wordsworth's Second Nature*, 173–175.

24. Kroeber, *Romantic Narrative Art* (Madison: University of Wisconson Press, 1966), 88.

25. The books are Julian Tennyson's *Suffolk Scene* (London: Blackie and Son, 1939), and Edward Thomas's *The Icknield Way* (1913; repr. London: Constable, 1980). These, along with Norman Scarfe's *The Suffolk Landscape* (London: Hodder and Stoughton, 1972) and Ronald Blythe's *Akenfield* (New York: Pantheon, 1969), were useful in very specific as well as more general ways. Some poems in *Crossing*—"Brandon, Breckland: The Flint Knappers," for example—derive directly from Tennyson. And as I note in my text, Edward Thomas on the Icknield Way is himself a human presence, though not quite a "character," in "An East Anglian Diptych: Ley Lines, Rivers."

26. Matthias, "Poem for Cynouai," *Crossing*, 27; reprinted in *Northern Summer*, 108–116.

27. Cf. Michael G. Cooke on pleasure and play in Wordsworth, "Romanticism: Pleasure and Play," in *The Age of William Wordsworth*, esp. 74–83. Cooke's contrast between Huizinga's apsychoanalytic notion of play and Schiller's concept of "play-drive" in *On the Aesthetic Education of Man* is particularly instructive.

28. Citations here are from two poems in *Turns*: "Double Derivation, Association, and Cliche: from *The Great Tournament Roll of Westminster*," 78–84; and "Clarifications for Robert Jacoby: 'Double Derivation, . . .' part iv., lines

1–10; part vii, lines 1–15, 22–28," 85–89. The poems are reprinted in sequence in *Northern Summer,* 58–67.

29. Hooker, "Crossings and Turns: The Poetry of John Matthias," *The Presence of the Past* (Bridgend, Midglamorgan: Poetry Wales Press, 1987), 103.

30. Hooker, "Poem and Place," *The Poetry of Place: Essays* (Manchester: Carcanet Press, 1982), 181.

31. Ibid., 183.

32. Ibid., 184.

33. Ibid., 186.

34. Part of the problem, of course, is inherent in the act of writing (or, analogously, of painting). John Barrell writes in *The Dark Side of Landscape* (New York: Cambridge University Press, 1980) that the "opposition . . . between a desired closeness and a necessary distance, everywhere apparent in [Constable's] earlier pictures, becomes impossible to conceal in the pictures painted at the end of Constable's life—those in which, as Conal Shields and Leslie Varris have written, the objects are 'glimpsed *through* (my italics) a maelstrom of paint.' The paint neither imitates now, nor creates—it obscures, or as we say it comes between the painter, and the image he is trying to paint, of a social landscape. There is an analogy here, too, with the problems Wordsworth found, in trying to use the language of poetry, purified certainly of poeticisms, to describe a harmonious relationship of man and nature: that the language, however simple, seems to be an unnatural medium which must exclude the articulate poet from the inarticulate community of nature" (159). Cf. James A. W. Heffernan, *The Re-Creation of Landscape* (Hanover, N.H.: University Press of New England, 1984):

> On one level, Wordsworth's account of what he saw and felt at Snowdon can be read as the poet's apotheosis of nature. . . . But Wordsworth's lines on the spectacle at Snowdon are not simply a tribute to the transforming powers of nature or God: they are also a demonstration of what can be done by the language of transformation in poetry—in short, by words. . . . For all his determination to make poetry speak 'the real language of men' and to keep an eye upon natural objects in the act of describing them, Wordsworth here fully exploits the transforming powers inherent in language itself. . . . We do well to ponder the passage with which he concludes book V of *The Prelude.* . . . Wordsworth seems at first to derive the power of language from the power of nature—from 'the motions of the winds.' But essentially he represents the power of language as independently transformative, and he reveals this power in the very language with which he describes it. (158–159)

35. Matthias, "Poetry of Place: From the Kentucky River to the Solent Shore," *The Southern Review* 21:1 (Winter 1985), 183–184.

36. Matthias, "An East Anglian Diptych: Ley Lines, Rivers," *Another Chicago Magazine,* 15:54. To be published, along with "Facts from an Apocryphal Midwest," as *Places/Poems,* by Swallow Press (USA) and Aquila Publishing Ltd. (UK).

37. As it is impossible to account for everything here, I omit any reference to an attempt between 1980 and 1982 to integrate myself with the landscape

and history of Wemyss Castle Estate in Fife, Scotland, where my mother-in-law moved after she was obliged to sell the house in Suffolk. The title poem of *Northern Summer* deals with this ultimately alienating experience.

38. Poets seem to respond to Parkman, even English poets. One cycle which anticipates my own is Donald Davie's "A Sequence for Francis Parkman," *Collected Poems: 1950–1970* (London: Routledge and Kegan Paul, 1972), 119–129. In "A Letter to Francis Bradford," Davie writes, and relevantly indeed to my own situation, "American, / You met with spirits. Neither white nor red / The melancholy, disinherited / Spirit of mid-America, but this, / The manifested copiousness, the bounties."

39. Parkman's romantic credentials, which I have no space to rehearse, have been amply established by many critics, perhaps most impressively by David Levin, *History as Romantic Art* (Stanford: Stanford University Press, 1959).

40. Charles Haight Farnham, *A Life of Francis Parkman,* 3rd ed. (1900, 1901: repr. New York: Greenwood Press, 1969), 196.

41. Ibid., 265–266.

42. For example, Howard Doughty, *Francis Parkman* (New York: Macmillan, 1962), 243, cites this passage from *Pioneers of France in the New World:* "Day dawned. The east glowed with tranquil fire, that pierced with eyes of flame the fir-trees whose jagged tops stood drawn in black against the burning heaven. Beneath, the glossy river slept in shadow, or spread far and wide in sheets of burnished bronze; and the white moon, paling in the face of day, hung like a disk of silver in the western sky. Now a fervid light touched the dead top of the hemlock, and creeping downward bathed the mossy beard of the patriarchal cedar, unstirred in the breathless air; now a fiercer spark beamed from the east; and now, half risen on the sight, a dome of crimson fire, the sun blazed with floods of radiance across the awakened wilderness." There is, admittedly, one Constable-like tree—that "patriarchal cedar"—awash in the Turneresque light.

43. Farnham, 214.

44. Ibid., 196.

45. Doughty, 256, suggests the El Greco connection.

46. Doughty makes the Shakespearian, Miltonic, and Melvillian comparisons in his brilliant chapter on La Salle, 262–283; Otis A. Pease, *Parkman's History* (New Haven: Yale University Press, 1953), 31–33, ranges for comparisons from Homer through Scott, Byron, and Cooper; Levin, 64ff., stresses the Byronic element.

47. Doughty, 224.

48. Matthias, "Facts from an Apocryphal Midwest," *Another Chicago Magazine,* 17:71–77. The final prose paragraph of "The Boat-Maker's Tale," like the end of my essay, leans heavily on Doughty's compelling interpretation of *La Salle and the Discovery of the Great West* and draws upon his terminology to indicate the psychological similarities between La Salle and Parkman. It was inevitable that I too should focus on Parkman's narration of the St. Joseph-Kankakee portage which Doughty treats, 275–276. I thank him for what I have borrowed here, especially passages from the original French of La Salle's *Relations* and the account of the portage written by Father Charlevoix.

The Road of Excess

My William Blake

⤜

Alicia Ostriker

For the purpose of explaining it to others I ask myself: who is my William Blake? Or to put the question differently, more generically: who or what, to a woman poet and critic, is her most significant male precursor? Doubtless many readers believe they already know the answer to such a question. As a feminist I might be expected to feel, with Virginia Woolf, that "it is useless to go to the great men writers for help, however one may go to them for pleasure." According to Sandra Gilbert and Susan Gubar, the primal emotion generated in women by male writers is not even pleasure but the "anxiety of authorship" which follows from masculine dominance of literary history. Still more dispiritingly, were I a good post-modernist I might learn from the master theoreticians of our time, or from their female disciples, that "woman" theoretically does not exist, that "she" is necessarily absence, lack, "the very definition of that which is not representable in language."[1] Each of these three provocative views has some resonance for me, yet none of them quite corresponds to my own experience, in part because William Blake has been so useful to me, in part because my relation to him seems always to be changing. Were the polarities of male and female culturally fixed, or inherent in the nature of language, this would scarcely be possible.

A friend warns me to beware hardening of the categories. I begin then by observing that my relationship with Blake has survived over thirty years, which is slightly longer than my marriage. Like an extended and interesting love affair, it has endured changes. A crude version of the plot would run something like this: I fall in love with the man, I fall deeper in love the better I know him, he fails me, I reject him and walk out, I forgive him and renew my fondness while keeping my distance. Perhaps I love him better at a distance. Or, more truly: Blake to me has been hero, lover, and ally, has been standard-bearer and courage-bringer, has been the chosen teacher to whom I attributed all wisdom, has been an antagonist in that mental fight in which opposition is true friendship, and has latterly become the paternal figure from which I most gratefully deviate. In this essay I will try to suggest what Blake's work has meant to me at various stages of my own development as a critic, then try to show how three poems of my own derive from a Blakean matrix. Throughout, I trust it will be clear that "pleasure" to me is indistinguishable from "help"; that if the Blakean engraving tool is a metaphorical penis it is also a spur; and that my absence from Blake's texts has encouraged me to insert myself in my own. Where Milton's bogey may be daunting to the woman writer, the shade of Blake will speed her on her way.

My romance with Blake began when I was an undergraduate and was primarily a response to his audacity. Any child could see that Blake was audacious about sex, society, politics, religion, and literature. "Exuberance is Beauty," he said;[2] nobody else had ever said that to me. Not even Shakespeare, not even Whitman, though the exuberance which produced their extraordinary human breadth was certainly, I saw it now, also a source of their beauty. And though I already knew I hated social injustice, Blake saw "How the chimney sweepers cry / Every blackening church appals, / And the hapless solder's sigh / Runs in blood down palace walls" (*CP* 128). He was the first man I ever read who seemed to know that sex was about love, not war, breathtaking equality rather than conquest: "What is it men in women do desire? / The lineaments of Gratified Desire. / What is it women do in men desire? / The lineaments of Gratified Desire." Blake called that little quatrain in his notebook "The Question Answered" (*CP* 154), and it was. Another question—about my parents and other men and women of their generation—was answered by the phrase "the marriage hearse" (*CP* 128).

He said: "No bird flies too high if it flies on its own wings." He said: "The road of excess leads to the palace of wisdom" (*CP* 183). I on the other hand was what Garrison Keillor calls a shy person. I was packed with audacious thoughts but very quiet; Blake allowed me to believe that one day I might be less quiet. "When I tell any Truth," he remarks, "it is not for the sake of convincing those who do not believe it, but for the sake of defending whose who do."[3] I was among the ones he was encouraging. Moreover, when Blake proposed seeing the world in a grain of sand, or said things like "For everything that lives is holy, life delights in life" ("America," *CP* 213), he articulated for me a sense of reality which had been inarticulately mine since childhood, in language of which the force and compression, the pattern of sound and cadence, seemed materially to embody that vitality which it advocated. "For we are put on earth a little space / That we may learn to bear the beams of love," he declares in "The Little Black Boy" of *Songs of Innocence* (*CP* 107). A truth lay in the use of "space" instead of time; another truth became manifested through the alliteration of "bear the beams," as if the intensity of the love rushing at us through the cosmos were thereby a shade more passionate. Or, more accurately, it appeared that the cosmic love required those vowels and consonants to express its passion. Again, when the couplet "If the Sun & Moon should doubt / Theyd immediately Go out" ("Auguries of Innocence," *CP* 509) made me snort with laughter, the bold hilarity of the thought was to me inseparable from the unconventional orthography and capitalization. Thus my intuitive adolescent response to Blake was partly a kind of gratitude that he was putting into words what lay at the misty threshold of my own consciousness, partly glee at his transgressions, and partly a recognition that *this* was poetry, this utter fusion of meaning and form.

Now I skip some years. In graduate school when I wrote my doctoral dissertation on Blake's prosody, I discovered more exhaustively what it signifies to say that form in poetry is never more than an extension of content. Pursuing the road of excess and unorthodoxy in his prosody as in his ideology, Blake began by writing the lyric poems for which he is still best known, in lines that sounded like nursery rhymes because he was attempting to produce or reproduce within the reader certain kinds of pure and primitive experiences, at once sensual and spiritual—of joy, of rage—which the throb of a highly regular beat and insistent repetition of key sounds

are uniquely suited to convey. In his middle and late years he came
to write huge mythological poems which out-Milton Milton in line
length as well as every other respect. The pounding, increasingly
irregular septenary Blake uses in *The Four Zoas, Milton,* and *Jerusalem* extended Milton's pentameter by two feet and was intended to
be that much more sublime. Blake justified the outrageousness of
his poetic forms by announcing that "Poetry Fetter'd Fetters the
Human Race" (*Jerusalem* 3, *CP* 637). His larger position was that
technical liberties in any art are the identifying motions of the Human Imagination struggling to realize its own liberation, working
throughout history through the individual artist but on behalf of all
humanity. But was a monstrous and incomprehensible object like
Jerusalem a poem? Brooding over the ideological and prosodic difficulties of Blake's prophecies, I was at first profoundly baffled and
disoriented (after all, I was a bright student; it was a new experience
for me to encounter writing I simply could not understand), but ultimately persuaded. These were poems which competed, as Northrop Frye had pointed out, with the revelation of the Old and New
Testaments. They were designed to imagine a history of the cosmos
and its tyrannical rule by a God of Reason, the psyche of mankind
since it first split into two genders, and the "giant Forms" of human
culture from the moment we erroneously divided body from spirit
until our ultimate recovery of harmony in which all humanity will
be united into a single divine Being after aeons of fury, rage and
madness:

And they conversed together in Visionary forms dramatic which
   bright
Redounded from their Tongues in thunderous majesty, in Visions
In new Expanses, creating exemplars of Memory and of Intellect
Creating Space, Creating Time according to the wonders Divine
Of Human Imagination . . .

                  (*J* 98.28–32, *CP* 845–846)

These were poems, moreover, in which the author was hardly transparent, but periodically foregrounded his epic struggle to "Create a
System or be enslav'd by Another Mans" (*J* 10.20, *CP* 651). As a
prophet and visionary Blake needed to invent poetic forms which
would appear, to most literary sensibilities, unpoetic. Consequently

he has never fitted comfortably into the canon of English poetry, which is overwhelmingly mimetic rather than prophetic. To his contemporaries he was a harmless eccentric. Wordsworth's patronizing remark, "There is no doubt this poor man was mad, but there is something in the madness of this man which interests me more than the sanity of Lord Byron and Walter Scott," was a typical response to Blake in his own time.[4] Among scholars of romanticism today, the canonical romantic is the relatively conservative Wordsworth rather than the poetically and politically radical Blake. To me, laboring at my dissertation, Blake came to seem both the quintessentially sane human being and the quintessential artist.

Some years after the completion of the dissertation and its publication as *Vision and Verse in William Blake,* I was asked to edit Blake's complete poems for Penguin. I undertook this task because I wanted to see if I could write notes which would clarify rather than mystify Blake's thought to the reader—that is, to students like those in my classes who were expressing bafflement not only at the poems but at the explanatory notes in the standard Erdman-Bloom edition. At this point Blake became a sort of guru to me. Laboriously attempting a line-by-line understanding of the text, I found myself awed at every turn by the vastness of his intellect, the power of his moral grasp, the splendor of his art—and the way he illuminated my personal existence. The time was the early 1970s. I had a husband, three children, and my fair share of "the torments of love and jealousy" generated by family life. My students were subject to the draft; one or two were Vietnam veterans, blasted and wasted souls, their hapless sighs running in blood down University walls. Surging around us were the consequences of the sexual revolution, rock and roll, the fumes of marijuana, the vertigo of acid, Black Power and black despair, the deaths of Robert Kennedy, Martin Luther King, Malcolm X. We recalled Woodstock, we entered Watergate. To all the radical impulses of those years Blake was amazingly relevant. For a brief period Blake was spokespoet to a generation; it seemed he knew whatever there was to know about destroying tyranny within the self and within society; from his allegorical method I first discovered the interpenetration of the personal and the political in all our lives. And how transparently obvious all his ideas seemed, once I "got" them! "Truth can never be told so as to be understood, and not be believ'd" (*CP* 185). I had undertaken the task of annotating Blake by telling myself (it was an absurdist private joke which made it possible for me to spend those thousands of hours in the library) that *if* Blake's writing were clear to everyone, why then its truth would convert the world, the millennium would come, cruelty and tyranny would be no more. "I rest not from my great task!" Blake shouted at me from the quiet pages of the illuminated *Jerusalem* at the New York Public Library. From the opening plate of *Milton* he sang at me:

> I will not cease from Mental Fight,
> Nor shall my Sword sleep in my hand:
> Till we have built Jerusalem
> In Englands green & pleasant Land.
>
> (*CP* 514)

The least I could do was lend my hand. Needless to say the millennium has not happened yet, but the reader of Blake learns to think in terms of aeons.

Subsequent to finishing my annotations of Blake, I became engaged both as a poet and as a critic with contemporary women's poetry. During this period, in which I redefined my own writing as feminist, I discovered with pleasure that Blake too was a feminist, and a radical feminist at that. Indeed, it seemed to me that an encounter with women poets was the logical extension of an encounter with Blake. Let me quote from the acknowledgments page of *Stealing the Language,* the book that eventually came out of this work: "To study Blake is to acquire an appetite for the conceptually and emotionally difficult in poetry, and a thirst for the visionary. Reading women poets whose insights are often painful, threatening, and confusing has been a challenge comparable to reading Blake."[5] I have also, with surprise, dismay, and finally satisfaction—perhaps the kind of satisfaction Harold Bloom tells us about, perhaps not—discovered what to my point of view is Blake's chief limitation. "If the doors of perception were cleansed, every thing would appear to man as it is, infinite" (*CP* 188). The quote is from *The Marriage of Heaven and Hell.* It provided Aldous Huxley with the title for his book *The Doors of Perception,* which recorded Huxley's experiments with hallucinogenic substances; it provided a name to one of the best rock groups of the sixties; it provided me personally with a credo. "If the doors of perception were cleansed every thing would appear to man as it is, infinite." The difficulty is that Blake did not really mean to include me in the term "man," just as John Donne did not mean to include me when he said that no man was an island.

It is disagreeable for a woman to come to recognize that the generic "man" with whom she has identified in the works of her favorite authors is a signifier that does not signify her. Yet William Blake was after all an eighteenth-century man, non-generic, whose vision at least in this respect was routinely fogged. Miraculously able to perceive man as infinite, he does not perceive woman as equivalently so. Nor does he in most of his work represent woman as perceiver, woman as creator, woman as imagination, or woman as poet. What does this mean for the doors of my perception?

Let me elaborate somewhat on the Blake who seems my ally, before turning to the Blake who seems my enemy. When we look with feminist eyes at William Blake, his most striking characteristic is his systematic detestation of the works and ways of patriarchal culture, with its glorification of the male principle of Father-God-Priest-King as ruling authority, its institutional privileging of Reason over Passion, its repression of sexuality and sanctioning of war, its victimization of women, children and the poor, its use of "the marriage hearse" to destroy desire and to divide women into private property wives and public property whores, and last but scarcely least, its exploitation of verbal and symbolic mystification to justify and disguise its power. Blake's anti-patriarchal principles are already firmly in place by the time he composes the *Songs of Innocence & Experience, The Marriage of Heaven and Hell,* and *The Song of Liberty.* In his earliest sketch for a prophetic poem, *Tiriel,* we already see the male principle as blindly and obsessively tyrannical. In the prophetic poems of Blake's middle years and in his first great epic *The Four Zoas,* the figure of Urizen—whose name amalgamates "your reason" and "horizon"—becomes Blake's parody patriarch, a "Selfish Father of men," "Father of Jealousy," cosmic lawgiver, and punitive superego within each of us, constantly imaged as icy, rigid, megalomaniac. Urizen wields his phallic sceptre crying "Am I not God," his chains and "mind-forg'd manacles" enslave us, his "Books of brass" are our scriptures and laws, his deadening "number weight and measure" are our pretensions to objective rationality. Blake conceived of Urizen partly as the crystallization of all that opposed political change in England during the French Revolution and the Napoleonic Wars, but he remains as depressing as today's news. Here for example is Urizen as politician, a Moral Majoritarian advising his children:

> So shall you govern over all let Moral Duty tune your tongue
> But be your hearts harder than the nether millstone . . .
> Compell the poor to live upon a Crust of bread by soft mild arts
> Smile when they frown frown when they smile & when a man
> looks pale
> With labour & abstinence say he looks healthy & happy
> And when his children sicken let them die there are enough
> Born even too many & our Earth will be overrun
> Without these arts
>
> (*FZ* 7.80.2–14, *CP* 376–377)

Blake in this passage was probably reacting to the Bread Bill debate of 1800 during which William Pitt as Lord of the Treasury countered complaints of scarcity and proposals for lowered prices with the argument that the poor should be encouraged to "diminish the consumption." His understanding of how oppressed classes internalize the ideologies of their oppressors has hardly been exceeded even today. See, for example, in *Visions of the Daughters of Albion* the heroine's initially self-punishing response to having been raped, or in *The Four Zoas* the reduction of the imprisoned Orc from a figure for birth to a force of destruction, or the two-line summary of the futility of armed revolt in a poem in the Pickering manuscript: "The iron hand crushd the tyrants head / And became a tyrant in his stead" ("The Grey Monk," *CP* 506).

Yet the question of female character and of gender roles fallen and redeemed in Blake is a thorny one. On the one hand Blake in his prophetic phase consistently identifies the Fall of Man with the splitting of an original whole being into gendered fragments; he consistently depicts the war of the sexes throughout human history as a "torment" which is devastating to our Humanity; the victimization of females is a motif that runs from his very earliest prophetic book, *Tiriel,* to his final great visionary work, *Jerusalem;* and he always imagines human redemption as a state in which all divisions are healed—Reason and Passion, Man and God, Man and Nature, man and man are reunited as one. In Blake's culminating visions "sexes vanish" as well. Moreover, female figures make several of the poet's most eloquent speeches, from Oothoon's attack on masculine possessiveness in *Visions of the Daughters of Albion,*

> I cry, Love! Love! Love! happy happy Love! free as the mountain wind!
> Can that be Love, that drinks another as a sponge drinks water?
> (*VDA* 7.15–16, *CP* 205)

to Enion's threnody of compassion in *The Four Zoas,*

> It is an easy thing to triumph in the summers sun
> And in the vintage & to sing on the waggon loaded with corn
> It is an easy thing to talk of patience to the afflicted
> To speak the laws of prudence to the houseless wanderer
> To listen to the hungry ravens cry in wintry season
> When the red blood is filled with wine and with the marrow of lambs. . . .
> It is an easy thing to rejoice in the tents of prosperity
> Thus could I sing & thus rejoice, but it is not so with me!
> (*FZ* 35.16–36–13, *CP* 320)

The problem, as several women critics have observed, is that Blake's most sympathetic female characters are victims, while his most monstrous ones represent a devouring and destructive "Female Will" which as he grew older he represented as more and more frightening and abhorrent. Nature for Blake was female, female was Nature, to be born was to be maternally entrapped and even crucified by her:

> Thou Mother of my mortal part
> With cruelty didst mould my Heart,
> And with false self-deceiving tears
> Didst bind my Nostrils Eyes & Ears.
> ("To Tirzah," *CP* 132)

> And if the Babe is born a Boy
> He's given to a Woman Old
> Who nails him down upon a rock

Catches his shrieks in cups of gold
("The Mental Traveller," *CP* 499)

Or it was to be sexually entrapped, seduced and paralyzed:

The Maiden caught me in the Wild
Where I was dancing merrily
She put me into her Cabinet
And Locked me up with a golden Key
("The Crystal Cabinet," *CP* 504)

When Blake wants to attack the military ethos of Greek and Latin epic he does so through a female muse who announces her pleasure in "War & Princedom & Victory & Blood." When he wants to lament the narrowness of fallen human perceptions, the fault is feminized:

The nature of the Female Space is this: it shrinks the Organs
Of Life til they become Finite & Itself seems Infinite
(*Milton,* 10.6–7 *CP* 531)

When he wants to protest our self-alienation from divinity, the cruel seductiveness of the female is to blame:

What may Man be? Who can tell! But what may Woman be?
To have power over man from Cradle to corruptible Grave.
There is a Throne in every Man, it is the Throne of God
This Woman has claim'd as her own & Man is no more!
(*J* 30.25–28, *CP* 693)

"In Eternity," as Blake puts it emphatically in "Vision of the Last Judgment," "Woman is the Emanation of Man she has No Will of her own There is no such Thing in Eternity as a Female Will" (*PP* 552).

Susan Fox in 1977 was the first commentator to recognize Blake's inconsistency, noting that he "conceives of a perfection of humanity defined in part by the complete mutuality of its interdependent genders" but represents one of those equal genders as either powerless and virtuous or as unnaturally and disastrously dominant. Thus females in Blake come to represent either "weakness" or "power-hunger" and "Blake's philosophical principle of mutuality is . . . undermined" by metaphors of femininity which are all too stereo-typic, in which he trapped himself and could not escape.⁶ Anne Mellor's essay on his female imagery examines gender-defined divisions of labor in Blake, noting that female work is always secondary and contingent: "Men forge, engrave, draw . . . women then add water-colors, weave coverings." Man is human form, woman is garment. Men are intellect, women are emotional mediators. The Eternal Prophet is a male much resembling William Blake, his muse is a female rather like Catherine Blake. "Blake's imagery . . . insists that the masculine principle is prior to the feminine principle and that the female depends upon, serves, and reflects the man." Mellor also argues that Blake's ideal female is presented as subordinate to the ideal male in his visual art.⁷

As my students motivated me to annotate the poems, so it was my students who dragged me reluctantly to view the feet of clay. I reacted, as one does to the discovery that one's parents are imperfect, with incredulity succeeded by anger. For some time I neither taught Blake nor read him. In retrospect this looks to me like a rather post-adolescent sulk. In some sense I wanted Blake already to *know* what a woman knows, to *have done* the work which can only be done by women. I wanted him in fact to have already done my thinking and feeling for me. Now, like a child sullen at growing up (what was I by this time? forty-odd?), I would have to do it myself. So in my own essay on Blake and sexuality I propose a contradiction between the Blake who celebrates free human sexuality and avoids polarization of the sexes, and a Blake who fears sex as a snare, who invents a set of ever more cosmic enclosure-entrapment images to represent female will, and who can ultimately imagine human unity only by imagining that the female is re-absorbed by the male. More important (to me, at any rate), I propose that like any parent figure, Blake is perhaps more interesting when we see him as human, defective, inconsistent, than when we see him as perfect. He of course reminds us himself that "Unity is the cloke of Folly" and "Without Contraries is no Progression." As a critic—indeed as a feminist critic—I find myself at present increasingly fascinated by the great inconsistencies of the greatest poets, whom I suspect we should see as exemplifying, rather than solving, the contradictions from which each of us suffers insofar as we belong to a contradictory culture. We can thread Blake's ambivalence back at least as far as St. Paul, for whom there was neither male nor female in Christ, and for whom nonetheless man was created for God, woman for man. Does any of us—any American alive today—*not* feel profound ambivalence concerning sex? To borrow from Brecht, the man or woman who is laughing has not heard the news. Blake then is a conduit and mirror of our own perplexities.[8]

My own conclusions in this regard are confirmed by Leopold Damrosch's vastly learned study *Symbol and Truth in Blake's Myth* (1980). For Damrosch, "potent contradictions lie at the heart of Blake's system" and "the never-ending struggle to reconcile them" is the heart of his genius. He was all his life a dualist who strove to be a monist "by constantly defining one half of the duality out of existence." Blake's ambivalence toward the body, nature, femaleness and sexuality "simply develops two perennial themes of Western civilization [sex as liberation, sex as prison], emphasizing each with his own characteristic intensity, but not inventing any paradox that was not already there."[9]

In all of Damrosch's arguments I find little to quarrel with save a single point which, however, is a crucial one. The dualism Damrosch delineates in Blake, and in the entire course of Western philosophy, may be neither natural nor culturally inevitable. What if it derives in whole or in part from Man's desire to alienate and subordinate Woman? If indeed "Philosophy is constructed on the premise of woman's abasement" and logocentrism derives from phallocentrism, then masculine subordination of the female (and the body) may be the root cause of all philosophical dualism.[10] To state such a possibility is not to demonstrate it. Yet once I begin to entertain this position even as a possibility I must question Damrosch's description of "the heroic ambition with which [Blake] tackled unresolvable tensions at the heart of Western thought." I must question, that is, the "unresolvable;" I must wonder whether what appears to be a surrender to the philosophically inevitable is not rather an unwillingness to solve it. And although to argue for anything like a monistic universe today seems almost unthinkable, I must let Blake himself remind me that "what is now proved was once only imagined" (*CP* 184).

Can I, then, imagine the world non-dualistically? Frankly, I cannot. But I am working on it. Can I imagine a "Divine Humanity" in which men and women, male and female principles are equally alive, equally active, equally embodiments of the Energy which Blake says is Eternal Delight? Not really, but I am working on that too.

At this point let me turn from critical commentary, remove the critic's hat, and put on the poet's. For Blake's importance to me as a poet has continued throughout the dozen years or so I have spent immersing myself in Sylvia Plath, Anne Sexton and Adrienne Rich, Margaret Atwood and Maxine Kumin, Audre Lorde, June Jordan, Ntozake Shange and Lucille Clifton, H. D. and Marianne Moore, Anne Bradstreet and Emily Dickinson—to name a few of the scores of women poets who have transformed my life and thought. Paradoxically enough, I suspect I have become more indebted to Blake subsequent to defining myself as a woman poet than before. Blake was a writer without a censor, and as I try to defy or deflect the censor in myself, I feel increasingly like his daughter; he continues to propel me along the road of excess though ceasing to accompany me.

Three examples will have to suffice to suggest the Blakean premises within poems that are plainly in a woman's voice—poems that Blake could not himself have written yet which could not have existed without the example and inspiration of his passion, humor, and vision.

Among the recurring themes in Blake is the struggle between Reason and Energy—repressive Reason and passionate Energy—which enacts itself within the self of any individual as well as within culture and history. In *The Marriage of Heaven and Hell,* Blake argues that these contrary principles are "necessary to human existence" and declares that "what the religious call Good and Evil" are simply the principles of Reason and Energy in action (*CP* 181). In his prophetic poems Blake represents these principles as living beings: the Urizenic tyrant is repressive Reason inscribed in our superegos and our cultural institutions, while the compelling figure of Orc—portrayed in Blake's poems and designs as a fiery adolescent—is Desire, Energy, or Libido within the self, Revolution throughout the drama of history. From the perspective of Reason, Passion is of course always horrifyingly destructive. *Paradise Lost* tells that tale; but Blake reminds us that "the Devils account" is different. In Blake's view, the destructiveness of Passion is not intrinsic to it, nor is it to be curtailed by repression. On the contrary, the more repression, the more ultimate destruction.

An early and striking version of the evil effects of repression is "The Poison Tree," one of the lyrics of *Songs of Experience*. In Blake's Notebook draft the poem is ironically called "Christian Forbearance":

> I was angry with my friend:
> I told my wrath, my wrath did end.
> I was angry with my foe:
> I told it not, my wrath did grow.
>
> And I waterd it in fears,
> Night & morning with my tears:
> And I sunned it with smiles.
> And with soft deceitful wiles.
>
> And it grew both day and night.
> Till it bore an apple bright.
> And my foe beheld it shine.
> And he knew that it was mine.
>
> And into my garden stole,
> When the night had veiled the pole;
> In the morning glad I see;
> My foe outstretchd beneath the tree.
> (*CP* 129–130)

In thinking about writing this paper I realized for the first time the parallel between "A Poison Tree" and a poem which I wrote during a painful period of my marriage, called "The Exchange":

> I am watching a woman swim below the surface
> Of the canal, her powerful body shimmering,
> Opalescent, her black hair wavering
> Like weeds. She does not need to breathe. She faces
>
> Upward, keeping abreast of our rented canoe.
> Sweet, thick, white, the blossoms of the locust trees

Cast their fragrance. A redwing blackbird flies
Across the sluggish water. My children paddle.

If I dive down, if she climbs into the boat,
Wet, wordless, she will strangle my children
And throw their limp bodies into the stream.
Skin dripping, she will take my car, drive home.

When my husband answers the doorbell and sees
This magnificent naked woman, bits of sunlight
Glittering on her pubic fur, her muscular
Arm will surround his neck, once for each insult

Endured. He will see the blackbird in her eye,
Her drying mouth incapable of speech,
And I, having exchanged with her, will swim
Away, in the cool water, out of reach.[11]

I wrote "The Exchange" because this fantasy played itself out in my imagination—a private horror movie—one fine day when I was, in fact, canoeing with my three children. What it told me was that I did not know myself. The woman I identified as myself was a *good* person, a *good* wife and mother. Resentful, of course (of the misbehavior of others which she was powerless to alter), but virtuous, generous, reasonable . . . in short, a martyr. Yet here was this powerful and attractive murderess who was, plainly enough, also myself. My will, my desire, literally submerged (by me, by the cultural prohibition against feminine assertiveness which I had internalized), ready to wreak massive damage precisely because she *was* submerged and didn't like it. A female version of repressed wrath, repressed energy, a female Orc. That she bears a strong family resemblance to Blake's cruel and threatening Vala is obvious. That I had to accept this woman into my soul, integrate her amoral power into my daily life, and surrender my image of myself as virtuous victim (tasks easier defined than done, tasks requiring years), was my conclusion but probably would not have been Blake's. Yet it was Blake who gave me the paradigm of the divided self which can be made whole only by uniting its parts. Thus my debt and thus my deviation.

A theme related in Blake to the struggle between Reason and Energy is his critique of western religion and its conception of God. In *The Marriage of Heaven and Hell* and many of Blake's Notebook poems, critique takes the form of comedy. Consider the tidy Notebook couplet "An Answer to the Parson:"

> Why of the sheep do you not learn peace
> Because I don't want you to shear my fleece
> (*CP* 155)

Or the untitled Notebook poem which begins

> I rose up at the dawn of day
> Get thee away get thee away
> Prayst thou for Riches away away
> This is the throne of Mammon gray
>
> Said I this sure is very odd
> I took it to be the throne of God.
> (*CP* 629)

In the ensuing verses Blake explains that God takes care of all his needs except the financial ones, which are the responsibility of the devil. But Blake's liveliest and most extended comic treatment of his differences with organized Christianity is "The Everlasting Gospel," an unfinished poem existing in several fragments composed in his late fifties or early sixties. Here is a portion:

> The vision of Christ that thou dost see
> Is my Visions Greatest Enemy
> Thine has a great hook nose like thine
> Mine has a snub nose like to mine
> Thine is the friend of All Mankind
> Mine speaks in Parables to the Blind
> Thine loves the same world that mine hates
> Thy Heaven doors are my hell Gates
>
> . . . .
>
> Both read the Bible day & night
> But thou readst black where I read white.
> (*CP* 851)

Subsequent sections of "The Everlasting Gospel" open with questions like "Was Jesus Chaste?" "Was Jesus gentle?" "Was Jesus humble?" "Was Jesus Born of a Virgin pure / With narrow Soul and looks demure?" Each is answered emphatically in the negative, with evidence drawn from the gospels. This theological project is one I have myself engaged in, taking my cue both from Blake's self-trusting conviction that "God only Acts and is, in existing Beings or men," and from his use of humor as a weapon against the sanctimonious. Blake's inclination to collapse the boundary between the sacred and the profane is also very much mine. Yet my own versions of the sacred are rather different from Blake's, or from what I would expect any man to produce. The following poem is called "Everywoman Her Own Theology":

> I am nailing them up to the cathedral doors
> Like Martin Luther. Actually, no,
> I don't want to resemble that *Schmutzkopf*
> (See Eric Ericson and N. O. Brown
> on the Reformer's anal aberrations
> Not to mention his hatred of Jews and peasants)
> So I am thumbacking these ninety-five
> Theses to the bulletin board in my kitchen.
>
> My proposals, or should I say requirements,
> Include at least one image of a god,
> Virile, beard optional, one of a goddess,
> Nubile, breast size approximating mine,
> One divine baby, one lion, one lamb,
> All nude as figs, all dancing wildly,
> All shining. Reproducible
> In marble, metal, in fact any material.
>
> Ethically, I am looking for
> An absolute endorsement of loving-kindness.
> No loopholes except maybe mosquitos.
> Virtue and sin will henceforth be discouraged
> Along with suffering and martyrdom.
> There will be no concept of infidels;
> Consequently the faithful must entertain
> Themselves some other way than killing infidels.

And so forth and so on. I understand
This piece of paper is going to be
Spattered with wine one night at a party
And covered over with newer pieces of paper.
That is how it goes with bulletin boards.
Nevertheless it will be there,
Like an invitation, like a chalk pentangle,
It will emanate certain occult vibrations.

If something sacred wants to swoop from the universe
Through a ceiling, and materialize,
Folding its silver wings,
In a kitchen, and bump its chest against mine,
My paper will tell this being where to find me.[12]

A third related theme in Blake is the theme of visionary experience. As we well know, though our critical discourse grows ever less capable of dealing with visionary artists as it grows ever more infatuated with pseudo-scientific postures and jargons, William Blake's most important single attribute was his lifelong capacity to see (his habitual word) images and events in the realm of the sacred:

> What, it will be Question'd, When the Sun rises do you not see a round disk of fire somewhat somewhat like a Guinea? O no no, I see an Innumerable company of the Heavenly host crying Holy Holy Holy is the Lord God Almighty. ("Vision of the Last Judgment," *PP* 555)

"On a cloud I saw a child," says the Piper at the opening of *Songs of Innocence* (*CP* 104). "And all this Vegetable World appeard on my left Foot," says Blake in *Milton* (21.12, *CP* 554). We know the anecdotes. At eight or ten Blake saw a tree filled with angels on Peckham Rye; when he told his parents, his father threatened to thrash him for lying but his mother intervened. When his beloved brother Robert died, William Blake saw Robert's spirit rise through the ceiling clapping its hands for joy. He taught his wife Catherine to see visions with him, and when in old age he was visited by his young disciple George Richmond, who complained of a creative block and wondered whether Blake ever suffered such a thing, Blake turned to his wife and remarked, "It is just so, is it not, for weeks together, when the visions forsake us? What do we do then, Kate?" "We kneel down and pray, Mr. Blake."[13] *Milton* and *Jerusalem* contain extensive analyses of visionary perception; "A Descriptive Catalog" and "A Vision of the Last Judgment" contain spirited defenses of it, claiming that all his art derived from imaginative visions which were "organized and minutely articulated beyond all that the . . . perishing mortal eye can see." Blake's letters often refer to the visions which inspired his poems and designs, sometimes very specifically as in the verses sent to his friend and patron Thomas Butts describing the apparition at Felpham of "Los in his might" which later became the core of *Milton*. At the climax of this experience, which begins "With happiness stretchd across the hills" and ends apocalyptically as "The heavens drop with human gore," Blake announces:

> Now I a fourfold vision see
> And a fourfold vision is given to me
> Tis fourfold in my supreme delight
> And three fold in soft Beulahs night
> And twofold Always. May God us keep
> From single vision and Newtons sleep.
>   (*CP* 487)

Single vision and Newton's sleep is of course what you and I experience as normality and what Blake called Ulro—a hellish region of dark despair and delusion. How to escape it? Where else is there? According to Blake, we are being called to night and morning by a savior to whom we are deaf: "Awake! awake O sleeper of the land of shadows, wake! expand! / I am in you and you in me, mutual in love divine." (*J* 4.6–7, *CP* 638). Blake spent his life attempting "To open the Eternal Worlds, to open the immortal Eyes / Of Man inwards into the Worlds of Thought: into Eternity / Ever expanding in the Bosom of God, the Human Imagination" (*J* 5.17–19, *CP* 640).

Something like what habitually and recurrently happened to Blake has happened on a few occasions to me. These occasions have been mere glimpses—eyeblinks—unworthy of being called "visions." They have been neither sustained nor organized. They have by no means cohered to form, for me, a sense of an alternative region in which my mind might permanently dwell—no Beulah, no Eden. Nor do they point to a specific philosophy, politics, or theology. I have heard better stories from friends, I have read better stories in William James's *Varieties of Religious Experience*. Nevertheless, my flashes of altered consciousness have in some sense informed the rest of my life. They have been intense and powerful enough to let me know that a divine (or demonic) world does exist, and that my ordinary conscious life is a kind of sleeping, or disease, or death (all Blakean metaphors). They have also made it clear to me that the distinction we habitually assume between reality and the imagination is essentially a false one, since for the brief duration of the moments I'm speaking of I know I am perceiving something supremely real and at the same time that I am "imagining" it. In Shaw's *Saint Joan* there is a dialogue which approaches this apparent paradox:

JOAN.   I hear voices telling me what to do. They come from God.
ROBERT.   They come from your imagination.
JOAN.   Of course. That is how the messages of God come to us.[14]

It appeals to me that Shaw's version of vision contains the dimension of humor just as it appeals to me when Blake's does. Though I cannot even begin to guess at the sources of those moments of which I'm the grateful recipient—and if they are "Beings" I cannot imagine their motivations—I have a distinct sense that within the solemnity of all that is sacred is a grain of comedy. Dimly it occurs to me that beyond my earshot, all around me, is laughter. Benign, as when adults watch a child take its first stumbling steps. Condescending, as when a drunkard plays the fool. Cruel, very possibly, since my existence is of negligible importance in this sphere. What do they want of me? Let me end with "What You Want":

> A half a dozen times in my existence
> You have permitted me to glimpse
> Some portion of you:
>
> The morning I lay in the bathtub
> Very pregnant, and my body was
> Mount Moriah, before the people
> Or the goat, or the god.

The afternoon my infant son
Waking up from his nap was the divine
Baby, hurtling
Coldly toward me from the other world
Where everything is lightning.

The night my father
Let me know he wasn't gone
Just because he was dead, and the night
I was driving happy, and saw a woman
In a white gown, dancing
Where my windshield was, and so on.

I could say
I've been alive a half a dozen moments
        but that's not true
        I've been alive my entire time on this earth
        I've been alive

That's what you want me to say, isn't it.[15]

Notes

1. Virginia Woolf, *A Room of One's Own* (New York and London: Harcourt Brace, 1957), 79. Sandra M. Gilbert and Susan Gubar, *The Madwoman in the Attic: The Woman Writer and the Nineteenth Century Imagination* (New Haven and London: Yale University Press, 1979), Ch. 2. Margaret Homans, "'Her Very Own Howl': The Ambiguities of Representation in Recent Women's Fiction," *Signs* 9:2 (Winter 1983): 187.

2. William Blake, *The Complete Poems,* ed. Alicia Ostriker (Harmondsworth and New York: Penguin Books, 1977), 185. Hereafter *CP.*

3. "Public Address," *The Poetry and Prose of William Blake,* ed. David V. Erdman, commentary by Harold Bloom (Garden City, N.Y.: Doubleday, 1965), 567. Hereafter *PP.*

4. Henry Crabb Robinson, "Reminiscences," in Arthur Symons, *William Blake* (New York: E. P. Dutton, 1907), 28.

5. Alicia Ostriker, *Stealing the Language: The Emergence of Women's Poetry in America* (Boston: Beacon Press, 1986), ix.

6. Susan Fox, "The Female as Metaphor in William Blake's Poetry," *Critical Inquiry* 5 (Spring 1977): 507.

7. Anne Mellor, "Blake's Portrayal of Women," *Blake Quarterly* 16, no. 3 (Winter 1982–83): 148–155.

8. Alicia Ostriker, "Desire Gratified and Ungratified: Blake and Sexuality," *Blake Quarterly* 16, no. 3 (Winter 1982–83): 156–165.

9. Leopold Damrosch, Jr., *Symbol and Truth in Blake's Myth* (Princeton: Princeton University Press, 1980), 3, 165–168, 194.

10. Hélène Cixous, "Sorties," in Hélène Cixous and Catherine Clément, *The Newly Born Woman,* trans. Betsy Wing (Minneapolis: University of Minnesota Press, 1986), 65. See Jean Grimshaw, *Philosophy and Feminist Thinking* (Minneapolis: University of Minnesota Press, 1986), Ch. 2, "The 'Maleness' of Philosophy," for a brief survey of these issues.

11. Alicia Ostriker, "The Exchange," *A Woman Under the Surface* (Princeton: Princeton University Press, 1982), 7.

12. Alicia Ostriker, "Everywoman Her Own Theology," *The Imaginary Lover* (Pittsburgh: University of Pittsburgh Press, 1986), 64–65.

13. G. E. Bentley, *Blake Records* (Oxford; Clarendon Press, 1969), 7, 32, 293–294.

14. G. B. Shaw, *Complete Plays* (London: Paul Hamlyn, Ltd.), 967.

15. Alicia Ostriker, "What You Want," *Green Age* (Pittsburgh: University of Pittsburgh Press, 1989).

Continuity

"The Man Freed from the Order of Time"

Poetic Theory in Wordsworth and Proust

❧

Louis Simpson

One can hardly imagine two writers who seem less alike than William Wordsworth and Marcel Proust—one a poet living in the Lake District of England at the beginning of the nineteenth century, the other a Parisian of the twentieth, essayist and novelist, habitué of salons. But they had the same theory of literary creation: they believed that it originates in certain experiences that give the mind a sense of its own creative power. I wish to consider the theory, for it was realized in poems and novels that have influenced and continue to influence our thinking. If faith can be justified by works, the ideas of these writers have been justified.

Wordsworth states his belief in a passage that will be familiar to many. But though it is familiar the questions it raises have not been settled. It occurs in Book Twelve of *The Prelude:*

> There are in our existence spots of time
> That with distinct pre-eminence retain
> A renovating virtue, whence—depressed
> By false opinion and contentious thought,

Or aught of heavier or more deadly weight,
In trivial occupations, and the round
Of ordinary intercourse—our minds
Are nourished and invisibly repaired;
A virtue, by which pleasure is enhanced,
That penetrates, enables us to mount,
When high, more high, and lifts us up when fallen.
This efficacious spirit chiefly lurks
Among those passages of life that give
Profoundest knowledge to what point, and how,
The mind is lord and master—outward sense
The obedient servant of her will. Such moments
Are scattered everywhere, taking their date
From our first childhood.[1]

Here, as in "Lines Composed a Few Miles above Tintern Abbey,"
Wordsworth says that memory has a power to nourish and repair
the mind. He speaks of extraordinary experiences, "spots of time"
when we perceive the workings of a supreme intelligence and know
that we are like it, and that the mind makes use of the senses for a
purpose of its own. The passage is followed by a description of two
incidents in the early life of the author. I shall consider the first of
these—the second repeats the impression made by the first and is
less striking.

Once, he tells us, when he was a small boy, he was riding toward
the hills accompanied by a servant, and they became separated. As
he was afraid he dismounted and led his horse across the moor. At
the foot of a slope he came to a place where a murderer's body had
been hung in chains. The gibbet and bones were gone, but the murderer's name was cut in the turf, and out of superstition people had
kept the grass cut and name visible. He fled from the place, then, as
he climbed again, he came upon a pool beneath the hills, a beacon
on the summit, and

A girl who bore a pitcher on her head,
And seemed with difficult steps to force her way
Against the blowing wind.

It was, he says, an ordinary sight, but he would need

Colours and words that are unknown to man,
To paint the visionary dreariness
Which, while I looked all round for my lost guide,
Invested moorland waste, and naked pool,
The beacon crowning the lone eminence,
The female and her garments vexed and tossed
By the strong wind.

Note that the impression made by the scene is described as "visionary," and that this vision lies beyond the reach of language to describe. In view of some current theories of literature, the point needs to be made. A witty remark by Mallarmé to Degas, "Poems are made with words, not ideas," has been the cornerstone of a theory that separates language from meaning and, in effect, denies that there is any reality outside language—words relate to other words, not to objects. But Wordsworth's theory of imagination posits a set of sense-impressions that cannot be done justice to by words. Poetry is an attempt to reproduce the effect of a powerful experience, one so strong that it seizes upon the senses and stamps them with a configuration of objects. Poetry such as this is not made with words alone—it is made by a force acting through nature to impress the mind with a sense of power. The mind so impressed retains the power. Poems are made not with words but feelings and ideas.

The description of the scene on the moor is followed by reflections of a kind that readers of "Tintern Abbey" will recognize. On returning to the scene years later, with his lover at his side, every day roaming the same dreary scene, the poet felt "A spirit of pleasure and youth's golden gleam." The pleasure was greater because he could look back upon the experience of childhood and recollect the strong impression, "the power / They had left behind."

This is not all—it is only part of the explanation. There follows a description that goes beyond anything the poet might actually have seen or heard and shows the difference between memory and imagination. Wordsworth is often quoted as having said that poetry is "emotion recollected in tranquillity"—the *Everyman History of English Literature* tells us that he said so. But he said nothing of the kind—he said that "poetry . . . takes its origin from emotion recollected in tranquillity," which is a different thing altogether. The emotion that creates a poem is not the emotion you had when you were having the experience, but the emotion you are having now, as you write. The poem is *poema,* a made thing.

Imagination is already at work in the description of the moor, the pool, the beacon, the girl whose garments are tossed by the wind. These objects have been arranged by the poet to produce a certain effect, and the thoughts we have as we read the passage will be different from the thoughts of the child on the moor. As we read about the child's being frightened we are not frightened but take pleasure in the sight and arrangement of objects and the language and movement of verse. This is the "tranquillity" Wordsworth meant. If he had done no more than describe what was actually there, in this order of seeing and these words, he would have done much. He would have shown, as he says in "Ode: Intimations of Immortality," that though the man has lost the habit of losing himself in sense-impressions he has gained a "philosophic," that is, poetic mind. The complex of sensations and thoughts that arise from our reading the poem is more interesting than anything memory itself could have produced.

If Wordsworth had only done this he would have shown the mind's power to make poetry out of experience, but he did more: he passed beyond the selection and arrangement of received images to make a new thing:

> I am lost, but see
> In simple childhood something of the base
> On which thy greatness stands; but this I feel,
> That from thyself it comes, that thou must give,
> Else never canst receive. The days gone by
> Return upon me almost from the dawn
> Of life: the hiding-places of man's power
> Open; I would approach them, but they close.

"The hiding-places of man's power / Open. . . ." This image is a pure invention. In this writing the mind appears to be "lord and master—outward sense / The obedient servant of her will."

I am reminded of Ferdinand Alquié's observation about the Surrealists: "If surrealism wishes to bring together in images the most distant realities, is it not because of its unlimited confidence in the powers of the spirit? . . . Surrealism would justify the axiology of Raymond Polin, for whom man is the creator of values, which have their sense only from him and relative to him."[2]

The memory of the moor, the pool, the beacon, and the girl in the wind, through a process of meditation, has made a sudden opening into an order of reality that does not depend on memory: a surreal vision of "the hiding-places of man's power." What I have called "pure invention" is a product of mind and seems to reflect an order that lies beyond human experience. On this point we shall divide into separate parties. Those who believe that invention reflects a reality beyond this world will take their leave, waving to the majority who stay on shore. There have been poets who did not venture beyond the first stage of imagining, making aesthetically pleasing objects out of their experiences. Keats, I would say, was one. Blake comes to mind as an example of the other kind; he would have preferred to break all ties with nature and inhabit a world of his invention.

Some works of art, like some lives, are unlike anything in experience. Are these intimations of immortality? We shall surely disagree about this. But I think we can agree that certain works of art seem to display an absolute power of mind. The image of "the hiding-places of man's power" has this effect. I am not surprised that the poet who created the image would feel that the mind is "lord and master—outward sense / The obedient servant of her will"—that he would feel, in a word, immortal.

*   *   *

I am suspicious of influences. As Coleridge remarked, there are those who think that everyone draws water from the same well—they don't conceive of its being in streams and fountains. Besides, when you have established that a poem or novel has been influenced by someone else's ideas, are you better able to read it? I am not so much concerned to show that Wordsworth influenced Proust as to show that they had similar ideas. Indeed, I could wish there were no trace of influence, that ideas could be shown to rise by their own force, like water in a fountain.

But Wordsworth did influence Proust, indirectly. In 1899 Proust ended work on his novel, *Jean Santeuil,* feeling that the attempt was a failure. His mother encouraged him to read Ruskin, and in October he was reading *The Seven Lamps of Architecture*. In the following year he published some pieces on Ruskin in periodicals. "I admire him," Proust wrote, "listen to him, and make a greater effort to understand him than I do a good many of the living."[3] He continued to read Ruskin, and in 1904 published a translation of *The Bible of Amiens*. In a long preface to his translation he explains his ideas, not only about Ruskin but literary criticism. The first task of the critic is to familiarize himself with the works of the author and so seize upon the salient traits of his genius. The next task is "to reconstitute what could have been the singular spiritual life of a writer haunted by realities of such a special kind, his inspiration being the measure in which he had the vision of those realities, his talent the measure in which he could recreate them in his work."[4]

Proust's "realities of such a special kind" that haunt the author are Wordsworth's "spots of time." And his remark about inspiration, that it is strong or weak according to the impression made by a "vision of those realities," evokes Wordsworth's theory of poetic composition.

John Ruskin, whose works Proust studied so carefully, was a devoted reader of Wordsworth and shared Wordsworth's enthusiasm for nature. In *Praeterita,* the account of his early years, Ruskin says, "A snowdrop was to me, as to Wordsworth, part of the Sermon on the Mount." Kenneth Clark, in his comments on Ruskin, observes that he "approached art through nature . . . Nature could be read like a holy book, which it was his privilege to interpret. He often spoke of himself as nature's priest. In this he was to some extent the successor of Wordsworth, and a quotation from *The Excursion* was printed on the title page of each of the five volumes of *Modern Painters*":

> Accuse me not
> Of arrogance
> If, having walked with Nature,
> And offered, far as frailty would allow,
> My heart a daily sacrifice to Truth,
> I now affirm of Nature and of Truth,
> Whom I have served, that their divinity
> Revolts, offended at the ways of men.

Clark observes that "Wordsworth is not often as Ruskinian as this," by which he means that Wordsworth is not so given to telling us what Nature thinks or Truth is. Clark draws a distinction between the poet and the factotum: "Ruskin's encyclopedic intelligence was not satisfied by Wordsworth's immediate delight, and his strict religious upbringing made it impossible for him to accept the pantheism of the Immortality ode, which he refers to as 'absurd.' As a child, however, he had responded to nature with almost Wordsworthian intensity."[5]

The child is father of the man, and Ruskin continued to respond to nature with an almost Wordsworthian intensity. As Proust read Ruskin he encountered this, his Wordsworthian side. But, as I have said, I am not so much concerned to show the influence of Wordsworth on Proust as to show that Proust developed a theory of imagination that is remarkably similar to Wordsworth's. To read Proust's *A la Recherche du Temps Perdu* is to encounter Wordsworth's "spots of time," moments of contact with "realities of a special kind" in which Proust finds, as did Wordsworth, the meaning of existence and the organizing principle of his work.

Proust, like the mature, "philosophic" Wordsworth, was no simple lover of nature—he was always looking for the principle it embodied. "There is no particular form in nature," he observes, "however beautiful it may be, that has value other than by the share of infinite beauty that has been able to embody itself in that form."[6]

At this point we had better drop the word "nature," for it has a meaning in Wordsworth it does not have in Proust. Or if we do refer to nature, the word must have its widest meaning, as the whole visible world. It may refer to nature in the Wordsworthian sense, but it may also mean human society: it includes the Guermantes' drawing room as well as the hawthorns of Combray. It applies to a fashionable courtesan as well as a peasant girl, and to the searchlights over Paris seeking out the raiding Gothas.

For Wordsworth nature is the mask of a power that manifests itself in terror and beauty. The decaying woods of the Alps, the waterfalls, winds, torrents, and rocks, are

> all like workings of one mind, the features
> Of the same face, blossoms upon one tree;
> Characters of the great Apocalypse,

The types and symbols of Eternity,
Of first, and last, and midst, and without end.

In "Tintern Abbey" nature is a power that rolls through all things and through the mind that observes them. In Proust, also, nature is the mask of a power that we glimpse at certain moments, but not in winds and torrents; it is manifest in the rapid walk of one man, the wandering speech of another. Inexorable laws are working themselves out in these characters. It is the task of the novelist to grasp the reality and show how it manifests itself in speech and gesture, as the sculptor shows it in stone. The characters of fiction are a Bible, just as much as the figures of Vices and Virtues—of Courage, Cowardice, Patience, Anger, Gentleness, Rudeness, and Love—that one sees in the central porch of the Cathedral at Amiens.

Proust, like Wordsworth, placed his most deeply revolved ideas about art in the artwork itself. It is to *A la Recherche* that we must turn if we wish to discover Proust's aesthetics, especially the concluding volume, *Time Regained (Le Temps Retrouvé)*. "There was in me," says the narrator, "a personage who knew more or less how to look, but it was an interrupted personage, coming to life only in the presence of some general essence common to a number of things, these essences being its nourishment and its joy."[7] In *Time Regained* the intermittent personage is brought to the front and given a thorough examination. Proust, like Flaubert, had a medical man for a father.

The narrator of *Time Regained* returns from a second sojourn in a sanatorium where he has been confined for a nervous disorder. He is disillusioned, especially with nature. "'Trees,' I thought, 'you no longer have anything to say to me. My heart has grown cold and no longer hears you. I am in the midst of nature. Well, it is with indifference, with boredom that my eyes register the line which separates the luminous from the shadowy side of your trunks. If ever I thought of myself as a poet, I know now that I am not one.'"

The day following these reflections the narrator is on his way to an afternoon party at the house of the Princesse de Guermantes, and is looking forward to it, for, as he can hope for nothing better, why deprive himself of such frivolous pleasures? He reflects on his situation, that he has given up all hope of being a writer. But, he tells us, it is just at the moment when we think that everything is lost that "the intimation arrives which may save us." And so it happens now. (I do not wish to delay the appearance of the "intermittent personage," but there is a striking resemblance between this train of thought and that of Wordsworth in "Resolution and Independence.") In the courtyard outside the Guermantes' mansion the narrator fails to see a car approaching—the chauffeur shouts a warning and as the narrator moves out of the way he trips on a paving stone. Recovering his balance he steps on a stone that is lower than its neighbors, whereupon, he says,

> All my discouragement vanished and in its place was that same happiness which at various epochs of my life had been given to me by the sight of trees which I had thought that I recognized in the course of a drive near Balbec, by the sight of the twin steeples of Martinville, by the flavour of a madeleine dipped in tea, and by all those other sensations of which I have spoken and of which the last works of Vinteuil had seemed to me to combine the quintessential character. Just as, at the moment when I tasted the madeleine, all anxiety about the future, all intellectual doubts had disappeared, so now those that a few seconds ago had assailed me on the subject of the reality of my literary gifts, the reality even of literature, were removed as if by magic. . . . The emotion was the same; the difference, purely material, lay in the images evoked.

"A profound azure," says the narrator, "intoxicated my eyes, impressions of coolness, of dazzling light, swirled around me." As he repeats the motion of staggering in order to recapture his feeling of happiness, to the amusement of the chauffeurs, he recognizes the source of his vision of "profound azure." It is Venice, where, in St. Mark's, he once stood on two uneven paving stones. This sensation is restored to him now "complete with all the other sensations linked on that day to that particular sensation, all of which had been waiting in their place—from which with imperious suddenness a chance happening had caused them to emerge—in the series of forgotten days. In the same way the taste of the little madeleine had recalled Combray to me." But why, the narrator asks, and it is the important question, "why had the images of Combray and of Venice, at these two different moments, given me a joy which was like a certainty and which sufficed, without any other proof, to make death a matter of indifference to me?"

This question is left unanswered while the narrative continues. The narrator is in the Guermantes' sitting room waiting for a piece of music to finish when a servant knocks a spoon against a plate. This evokes the train journey on which he saw the trees that failed to arouse his interest. While the train was stopped near a wood a railway workman struck one of the wheels with a hammer. Returning to the present . . . the narrator drinks some orangeade and wipes his mouth with a napkin. The rough texture of the cloth evokes the sea—it has the same stiff texture as a towel he used to dry his face at Balbec. It evokes "the plumage of an ocean green and blue like the tail of a peacock." The happiness he feels is caused not by the colors but by an instant of his life at Balbec that had "aspired" toward happiness but had been prevented by some fatigue or sadness. But now, freed from the sensations of the moment, the instant has caused him to be happy.

Happiness is enclosed within our sensations and perceptions, a thousand "sealed vessels" that are separated by time and space, "a colour, a scent, a temperature." When two such identical moments are brought together by some physical accident—uneven paving stones, a napkin, the sound of a spoon on a plate, the taste of a madeleine—the time between is removed and one sees that, concealed by temporal circumstances, there lives a being whose nature it is to be happy. This is the "intermittent personage" or true self, perceived only outside time and therefore existing outside time. "This being made its appearance only when, through one of these identifications of the present with the past, it was likely to find itself in the only medium in which it could exist and enjoy the essence of things, that is to say: outside time."

The "true self" cannot be captured by an effort of the will. "In the observation of the present, where the senses cannot feed it with this food, it languishes, as it does in the consideration of a past made arid by the intellect or in the anticipation of a future which the will constructs with fragments of the present and the past . . . But let a noise or a scent, once heard or once smelt, be heard or smelt again in the present, and at the same time in the past, real without being actual, ideal without being abstract," then the true self is revealed. "A minute freed from the order of time has re-created in us, to feel it, the man freed from the order of time."

We have arrived with Proust at the point we have reached before with Wordsworth:

> This efficacious spirit chiefly lurks
> Among those passages of life that give
> Profoundest knowledge to what point, and how,
> The mind is lord and master . . .

Wordsworth says that the mind, having realized its own independent existence, can make use of the senses—"outward sense" being "The obedient servant of her will." The narrator of *A la Recherche* will take this step too by writing a novel. He decides to find the fragments of real time, his true happiness, that are dispersed among the scenes and acts of his life. If he succeeds in his task he will have recovered his immortal part, "the man freed from the order of time."

*   *   *

Both Wordsworth and Proust argue that there is a reality outside the world that is perceived at certain moments and that it is the task of the poet to capture and make visible. The argument stands on sensations and feelings and therefore, from one point of view, is no argument at all. All theories of art rest on sensations and feelings. It is only science that claims to operate in a realm of pure logic—and perhaps it no longer does, not since Werner Heisenberg and his Principle of Uncertainty. There is no longer, we are told, any such thing as a "scientific fact."

The proof of an artistic theory is in the results. Wordsworth follows his statement about the "efficacious spirit" by composing two incidents in which the spirit showed itself—to him as a child and to the present reader. Proust's explanation of the true self comes toward the end of a novel that has already shown, in numerous passages, the happiness of this "intermittent personage." How has it been shown? In the writing, the style of the passages.

The argument for immortality is in those passages of literature that seem immortal. This is what the poet and novelist seem to say. And this is the argument for reading their works. But how? Should we practise "close reading"? Analyze the choice and use of words? The structure of sentences? Should we search for symbols and see what they mean? The method is certainly tempting. I might, for example, choose these lines by Wordsworth and attempt to explain the symbolism:

> the hiding-places of man's power
> Open; I would approach them, but they close.

Think what a Freudian analyst might make of this! But to do so would be to destroy the larger effect of the image. As it stands it radiates outward to the furthest reaches of imagining. Explained by the analyst it is immediately reduced to a symptom of the author's personality.

To dissect, Wordsworth tells us, is to murder, and this is no mere figure of speech. Though we may gain information when we dissect, it is certain that the subject must be dead. The style of a writer does not consist of logic but a felt reality. What Proust says of nature is true of style: "There is no particular form in nature, however beautiful it may be, that has value other than by the share of infinite beauty that has been able to embody itself in that form."

It is for want of contact with the infinity Proust speaks of that the theory of literature is, at the present time, in such a confused and dreary state. Theoretical critics have attempted to bring logic to bear on literature, whereas they are two quite different things. The theorists have had no experience of the "special realities" of which Proust speaks—they have had no visions, and spin their ideas out of themselves. One theorist tells us that institutions are only verbal agreements; another, that words have no real meanings—they only relate to other words. Theorists such as these have never experienced the "spots of time" of which Wordsworth writes, nor Proust's moments of intuition into a reality that is more enduring than the life of the individual. For such theorists the only reality is society, and its voice is rhetoric, a way of manipulating language so that it means what one wants it to mean.

How then, if we do not read like surgeons dissecting a cadaver, are we to read? I think we should drop all pretense to a scientific objectivity, which is not objective anyway. I am not asking for a suspension of intelligence: there is a way of reading intelligently but not analytically. Proust, in a passage I have quoted, gives us the method: it is to grasp the salient ideas and reconstitute "what could have been the singular spiritual life of a writer haunted by realities of . . . a special kind." In short, one surrenders to the writer's vision of things. Unfortunately, surrendering is quite beyond the ability of most theorists, attached as they are to their theories.

To reconstitute the spiritual life of a writer one would have to read the works widely and in depth—one would have, in a sense, to become the writer. Then one would be able to see the truth, the amount of "infinite beauty," contained in a passage of the text. One would be able to read as the author wrote, feeling that one has done justice, or failed to do justice, to the subject. This is close reading, not the mechanical exercise that frequently passes by that name in graduate schools. Reading requires the same intuitive intelligence that is used in writing. Everything depends, as Proust says, on the amount of "infinite beauty" that has been able to embody itself in the particular form, and on the reader's ability to perceive it.

But, does an "infinite beauty" exist or is this only a manner of speaking? Wordsworth refers to

> all the mighty world
> Of eye, and ear,—both what they half create,
> And what perceive . . .

Consciousness, then, is an amalgam of ideas and sense-perceptions. Here the analyst rushes in to say that sense-perceptions are just that: there's no intelligence behind them. The external world does not stamp the mind, as I have said it does, with a "configuration of objects." The mind alone can do this: out of some psychic need the poet fastens on certain objects and so composes his poem.

The same argument could be made about Proust. If, jarred by a paving stone, his mind flashed back to Venice, this was no more than an association of ideas, and the ideas can be accounted for. The rest of it—a reality "aspiring" to make itself known, a "pure and disembodied" reality—was only a fantasy born of some inner need. Indeed, one could discover the writer's "true self"—this is what psychoanalysis does. But it is nothing that cannot be explained by science.

We cannot disprove this way of thinking. We can only say that the writers had a different idea; they believed there were powers external to the mind that acted upon it at certain moments to bring it to a higher level of consciousness. They would not have denied that writers are peculiarly constituted—as Wordsworth says, the poet is "finding everywhere objects that immediately excite in him sympathies which, from the necessities of his nature, are accompanied by an overbalance of enjoyment." But they also believed that nature acts upon the poet—it is sending him messages. The poet "considers man and nature as essentially adapted to each other, and the mind of man as naturally the mirror of the fairest and most interesting properties of nature."

There was a time when the belief I have been describing was the common belief of all peoples. Homer and Dante assumed that it was so. By the time of Wordsworth the idea had to be argued on the basis of the poet's experience—it was no longer held by a community. Proust represents perhaps the last stage of the great tradition. And now, so far have we come from having experiences of the kind that we are inclined to think that poets never had them and their testimony is merely figurative. We think that when Homer described the acts and speeches of the gods, and Dante related the appearance of Eros in a dream, they did not believe in the reality of the things they were saying. The balance of belief in our time has swung overwhelmingly towards scientism and away from any line of thought that could be called "spiritual."

I do not think, however, that the prejudice will continue to have things all its own way. I think that the rapid advances in technology in our time do not entail a surrender of the imaginative to the calculating side of life, but a reification of scientific beliefs so that we shall see, once and for all, what their limits are, and that poetry and the arts proceed from

> those passages of life that give
> Profoundest knowledge to what point, and how,
> The mind is lord and master—outward sense
> The obedient servant of her will.

* * *

WORDSWORTH, PROUST, AND "THE NEW HISTORY"

At the present moment in English studies there is talk of "the new history" and an "interdisciplinary approach" to the teaching of literature. William E. Cain—I choose his book because it appears to be an accurate account of trends in literary criticism—recommends an interdisciplinary approach. "I am not," he says, "recommending simply that the literary critic and teacher become more 'historical' in attitude and orientation. Nor am I proposing (as might be suspected) that critics should transform themselves into historians." (From his treatment of Booker T. Washington's *Up from Slavery* one might indeed have the suspicion.) He hastens to reassure us that the literary critic will be retained, for "The literary critic . . . possesses skills that the historian does not." What are these skills? The ability "to grasp the workings of figurative language in texts as his colleagues in other disciplines cannot." The raison d'être of the critic is to "elucidate texts and probe inter-textual configurations."[8]

It seems that the literary critic is a sort of mechanic. It does not seem to have occurred to this author that literary criticism may be something more than finding hidden meanings and pointing out figures of speech, that it may be based in a belief that is just as real as his belief in history. If the thought occurred to him he must have rejected it as not being to his purpose. The "interdisciplinary" study of literature is based on the assumption that literature is produced by conditions. But many writers have believed something quite different: that their thoughts are original and do not merely report conditions, that which is already known.

Though he disclaims any intention of trying to replace the study of literature with the study of history, Cain says, "Whether we are studying the canonical texts, counter-traditions, children's novels, translations of the Bible, or some other grouping, we should direct discussion towards history, society, and culture." What is this but substituting the study of history, society, and culture for the study of literature? Directing the discussion towards history means discussing history, especially when those who direct the discussion have no bias in favor of literature. Indeed, some of them are positively eager to deny that "the canon" has any particular merit. The kind of literary criticism we may expect from those who are oriented toward history is shown in Cain's discussion of a passage from *Up from Slavery*. He says that he is explicating the language but all his discussion brings forth is Washington's ideas about culture and society. This is the historical approach to literature—it has everything to do with history and little to do with literature.

I would have no objection to relating English studies to the other disciplines if it were understood that there is an essential difference between literature and the other disciplines. But whenever the attempt is made to study the other relations of literature, we see that the interest is in those other relations and in making literature serve them. From the point of view of the historian, a sentimental novel of the year 1850 is as rewarding to study as *The Scarlet Letter*—indeed, more rewarding, for the ideas are simpler and set forth more plainly. What is omitted from such considerations is the power of the writing of great authors. In "interdisciplinary" studies of literature the only discipline that seems to be missing is the discipline of literature.

The more sentimental and clumsy the writing, the more it lends itself to be studied as something else. But when we are dealing with imaginative writing of the quality of Proust's fiction or Wordsworth's poetry, what does history have to tell us? The better the writing the more clearly we see that it proceeds from the mind of an individual and not from social conditions. The works of Wordsworth and Proust do have something to say about society and do cast a light on history, but to make that the focus of our study would surely be a mistake. The message of such writing is set forth in images of a reality that has been perceived by the mind at moments of extraordinary experience. The mind that creates such works is not the handmaid of history. With Joyce's Stephen Dedalus it says, "Non serviam."

A long time ago Thomas De Quincey explained the difference between the "Literature of Knowledge" and the "Literature of Power." The kind of interdisciplinary study that is being recommended would deny that there is an original power in literature. The approach of the historian would make literature the servant of economics, of sociology, or anything that might be called knowledge. But poetry is the expression of power, and power is always original. The only reason for literary criticism is to show the workings of this power and show, if it can, from where the power proceeds.

Notes

1. William Wordsworth, *The Prelude, Selected Poems and Sonnets* ed. Carlos Baker (New York and Toronto: Rinehart, 1948). All subsequent quotations from Wordsworth are from this text.

2. Ferdinand Alquié, *The Philosophy of Surrealism* (Ann Arbor: The University of Michigan Press, 1969), 101–102.

3. *Marcel Proust: Selected Letters 1880–1903,* ed. Philip Kolb (Garden City, N.Y.: Doubleday, 1983), 212.

4. John Ruskin, *La Bible d'Amiens,* trans. Marcel Proust. "Préface du Traductuer." (Paris: Mercure de France, 1947), 10–11. The translation into English is mine.

5. Kenneth Clark, ed., *Ruskin Today* (Harmondsworth, England: Penguin, 1982), 22.

6. Proust, "Préface," *La Bible d'Amiens,* 88.

7. Marcel Proust, *Remembrance of Things Past,* vol. 3: *The Captive, The Fugitive, Time Regained* (London: Chatto and Windus, 1981), 737–738.

8. William E. Cain, *The Crisis in Criticism* (Baltimore and London: The Johns Hopkins University Press, 1984), 270.

Romancing the (Native) Stone

Yeats, Stevens, and the Anglocentric Canon

❦

George Bornstein

In November of 1892 the young Douglas Hyde, later to become the first president of Ireland, delivered a speech called "The Necessity for De-Anglicising Ireland" which remains famous in his native country. His audience was the newly-founded Irish Literary Society, which he had helped to establish, and the crowd included the principal organizer, the poet William Butler Yeats. Yeats thought that the speech opened a new epoch in Ireland. Hyde began this way:

> When we speak of 'The Necessity for De-Anglicising the Irish Nation,' we mean it, not as a protest against imitating what is *best* in the English people, for that would be absurd, but rather to show the folly of neglecting what is Irish, and hastening to adopt, pell-mell, and indiscriminately, everything that is English, simply because it *is* English.[1]

Hyde aimed principally at recuperating a national culture, and particularly at the preservation and fostering of the native Irish language. But his point applied (and continues to apply) to national and colonial writers reacting against a dominant foreign culture. We may recontextualize his remarks for all non-English poets writing in the English language who seek to recuperate romanticism. Their project involves "The Necessity of De-Anglicising Romanticism." I take their desire to de-Anglicize romanticism not only as a defensive trope against anxieties of influence but also as a positive strategy for original literary creation.

The response of Yeats and Wallace Stevens, among others, to English romanticism should not surprise us in 1990, nearly a century after Hyde's speech. It forms part of the contemporary expansion of canons which displaces England as the center of twentieth-century literature in English. In his article "English Department Geography," Reed Way Dasenbrock has recently reminded us that "Parts of the national literature of some thirty countries form a vital part of contemporary literature in English."[2] Those countries include not only former colonies with predominantly white populations, like Australia and Canada, but large numbers of those populated primarily by people of color, such as India, Nigeria, or those of the Caribbean. The geographic decentering of English literature is matched by a decentering in class, gender, race, and—theme little heard of this among contemporary theorists—religion as well. As the cultural critic Raymond Williams has noticed, romanticism coincided with the expansion of the class origins of major English writers—Keats's livery-stable background being perhaps the best known—which has continued ever since.[3] Similarly, the nineteenth century saw the rise of increasing numbers of major female writers, and contemporary feminism has taught us to look at neglected earlier ones as well. Race and religion show analogous patterns. Unable like Carlyle's Diogenes Teufelsdröckh to be a professor of Allerleiwissenschaft, or everything at once, I focus here on nationality and defer the other categories to other occasions.[4]

Appropriately, the first two literatures to decenter England's hegemony were those of her oldest colony, Ireland (granted by the Pope to Henry II of England in 1172), and her first to win independence, the United States. With his typical iconoclasm, the American poet Ezra Pound declared in the 1920s that "the language is now in the keeping of the Irish (Yeats and Joyce); apart from Yeats, since the death of Hardy, poetry is being written by Americans. All the developments in English verse since 1910 are due almost wholly to Americans. In fact, there is no longer any reason to call it English verse, and there is no present reason to think of England at all."[5]

The boast of an American like Pound was possible only because of the long struggle against English literary hegemony waged by nineteenth-century American writers, particularly against that of their contemporary English counterparts. In that respect literary independence lagged behind political liberation by a century. The closest modern student of the literary struggle, Robert Weisbuch, has discriminated two strands of opposition: a "party of mimesis" urging the substitution of American for European places (the Hudson for the Thames, or the Catskills for Mount Olympus) and a "party of consciousness" urging instead the creation of a new sensibility rather than merely new material.[6] The two parties come together in the work of the strongest writers, like Whitman or even Henry James. Throughout the nineteenth century Americans raised the cry that would be echoed later for Ireland by Douglas Hyde and others. For example, in 1838 Orestes Brownson laments that "we write as Englishmen, not as Americans. We are afraid to think our own thoughts, to speak our own words, or to give utterance to the rich and gushing sentiments of our own hearts. And so it must be so long as we rely on England's literature as exclusively as we have hitherto done." In the next decade Nathaniel Willis and George P. Morris asked, "What more natural than that we should tire of having our thinking done for us in London, our imagination fed only with food that is Londonish. . . . The country is tired of being *be-Britished*." And in 1869 James Russell Lowell declared, "We are worth nothing except so far as we have disinfected ourselves of Anglicism."[7]

Disinfecting oneself of Anglicism posed a particular problem for poets like Yeats and Stevens who on the one hand saw themselves as modern-day romantics but on the other hand claimed a national status as poets of Ireland and America. They thus sought to de-Anglicize English romanticism itself, following instead the parties both of mimesis and of consciousness. The first step was to attach romanticism to their local landscapes, with Ben Bulben or Chocorua in place of Mount Snowden or Tintern Abbey and Cuchulain or Andrew Jackson in stead of Albion or Napoleon. But romancing their native stone turned out to involve more than geography; it involved consciousness as well. In becoming modern romantics they changed the conception of romanticism itself. Thus, when Yeats in "Coole and Ballylee, 1931" makes the famous avowal "We were the last romantics," he immediately turns to Irish tradition ("chose for theme / Traditional sanctity and loveliness; / Whatever's written in what poets name / The book of the people") and then to a broader consciousness ("whatever most can bless / The mind of man or elevate a rhyme").[8] Similarly, even before he called for a "new romanticism" in the 1930s Stevens had reworked romantic quest in his poem "The Comedian as the Letter C." There the hero Crispin first learns not only that "man is the intelligence of his soil" but also and conversely that "his soil is man's intelligence" before going on to proclaim:

> Exit the mental moonlight, exit lex,
> Rex and principium, exit the whole
> Shebang. Exeunt omnes. Here was prose
> More exquisite than any tumbling verse:
> A still new continent in which to dwell.
> What was the purpose of his pilgrimage,
> Whatever shape it took in Crispin's mind,
> If not, when all is said, to drive away
> The shadow of his fellows from the skies,
> And, from their stale intelligence released,
> To make a new intelligence prevail?[9]

The new intelligence pertained to the individual author as well as to the development of national literature. With both Yeats and Stevens, ontogeny recapitulates phylogeny as each enacts in his own career his aspirations for a national literature. Both poets started out as cosmopolitan, derivative romantics writing the enfeebled verse typical of late nineteenth- and early twentieth-century aesthetes. So, indeed, did most of the major modernist poets, like Ezra Pound, T. S. Eliot, William Carlos Williams, Hilda Doolittle, or Robert Frost. But where poets like Pound or Eliot reacted against English romanticism by embracing a modernized cosmopolitanism, more rooted writers like Yeats, Stevens, or Frost reacted by creating a modern romanticism issuing in what Stevens once called the poems of their climates.

The decisive turn in Yeats's case came from his meeting the exiled Irish patriot John O'Leary shortly after O'Leary's return to Dublin in 1885, when Yeats was twenty. Aged but still ardent, idealistic, and full of moral fervor, the white-bearded O'Leary became the chief mentor to the young poet on anything involving Irish national-ism and inspired his quest to unite that nationalism with a specifically Irish version of romanticism. In his autobiography Yeats recalled:

> From these debates, from O'Leary's conversation, and from the Irish books he lent or gave me has come all I have set my hand to since. I had begun to know a great deal about the Irish poets who had written in English. I read with excitement. . . . I who had never wanted to see the houses where Keats and Shelley lived would ask everybody what sort of place Inchedony was, because Callanan had named after it a bad poem in the manner of *Childe Harold*.[10]

The best place to see O'Leary's influence on Yeats's literary views is in *Letters to the New Island,* a collection of newspaper columns that Yeats wrote for Irish immigrants in America from 1888 to 1892. O'Leary himself turns up ubiquitously in the essays, and his sister Ellen's newly published volume of poems—*Lays of Country, Home, and Friends*—receives extended discussion. Yeats declares, "We of the younger generation owe a great deal to Mr. John O'Leary and his sister. What nationality is in the present literary movement in Ire-land is largely owing to their influence. . . . He, more clearly than any one, has seen that there is no fine nationality without literature, and seen the converse also, that there is no fine literature without nationality."[11] That formula became something of a slogan for Yeats, who closed another column with it as well (*LNI* 30).

Throughout *Letters to the New Island* Yeats's formulation of the relation between literature and nationality reflects O'Leary's doc-trines. He declares in one column that "Creative work has always a fatherland"; in another that "Ireland is the true subject for the Irish"; and in still another that Irish writers must have "Irish themes and Irish feeling" (*LNI* 12, 21, 30). Conversely, he condemns cosmo-politanism as "one of the worst" distractions for Irish writers; he denounces "cosmopolitan literature" as "at best, but a poor bubble, though a big one"; and he deplores writers who "have read much English literature, and have taken from it, rather than from their own minds and the traditions of their own country, the manner and matter of their poetry" (*LNI* 32, 12, 47). These sentiments pointed to a clear and advantageous direction for young Irish writers. Yeats concluded one column exhorting Irish writers to take Irish subjects with the ringing declaration: "The literature of Ireland is still young, and on all sides of this road is Celtic tradition and Celtic passion crying for singers to give them voice. England is old and her poets must scrape up the crumbs of an almost finished banquet, but Ireland has still full tables" (*LNI* 60).

To some extent Yeats was preaching to himself. O'Leary's impact had already changed the direction of Yeats's own poetry. Before he met O'Leary, Yeats set his cosmopolitan, derivative verse indifferently in India, Arcadia, or vaguely romantic landscapes. His previous major work, *The Island of Statues,* dramatized an Arcadian quest of the young Keatsian hunter Almintor for his ideal lady Naschina, whose mastery of occult arts rivalled that of Shelley's heroines; the verse itself derived from the English line running from Spenser through the great romantics and on to their Pre-Raphaelite imitators. In contrast, his next major work after meeting O'Leary, *The Wanderings of Oisin,* dramatized the quest of the ancient Irish Fenian poet and warrior Oisin, lured on by the supernatural temptress Niamh, in a plot derived from both Irish legends and the Patrick-Oisin dialogue poems.

Yet Yeats desired not so much to reject English romanticism as to marry it to the rock and hill of Ireland. Oisin or Ben Bulben presaged a de-Anglicized romanticism, as Yeats made clear in one of his periodic ponderings of his relation to one of his two favorite English romantics, Shelley:[12]

I could not endure, however, an international art, picking stories and symbols where it pleased. Might I not, with health and good luck to aid me, create some new *Prometheus Unbound;* Patrick or Columcille, Oisin or Finn, in Prometheus' stead; and, instead of Caucasus, Cro-Patrick or Ben Bulben? Have not all races had their first unity from a mythology that marries them to rock and hill? (*A* 193–194)

So far Yeats sounds rather like a member of the American "party of mimesis." His concept of mythology, however, allowed him to stand with the "party of consciousness" as well. He made that clear in an essay on his other favorite English romantic, Blake, where he wrote:

[Blake] was a symbolist who had to invent his symbols; and his counties of England, with their correspondence to tribes of Israel, and his mountains and rivers, with their correspondence to parts of a man's body, are arbitrary. . . . He was a man crying out for a mythology, and trying to make one because he could not find one to his hand. Had he been a Catholic of Dante's time he would have been well content with Mary and the angels; or had he been a scholar of our time he would have taken his symbols where Wagner took his, from Norse mythology; or have followed . . . that pathway into Welsh mythology . . . or have gone to Ireland and chosen for his symbols the sacred mountains, along whose sides the peasant still sees enchanted fires, and the divinities which have not faded from the belief . . . and have been less obscure because a traditional mythology stood on the threshold of his meaning.[13]

In those terms, the story of Oisin allowed Yeats not just a ready-made, national mythology in old Irish myth but also an entree into an heroic sensibility predating English romanticism (indeed, all of English literature) and yet capable of altering that romanticism to its own uses. The question was which would absorb which: would the Irish materials remake English romanticism or only reecho it?

Yeats remained ambivalent about the outcome in his early verse. For all the nationalist bravado, he clearly owed a double allegiance both to his native land and to English literary tradition. His ambitious sequence of Rose lyrics revealed the dichotomy. On the one hand, the Rose offered a multi-faceted symbol, replete with Christian, hermetic, and Irish national associations. Yeats particularly stressed the extent to which "the Rose is a favourite symbol with the Irish poets" and listed its association with religion and female beauty in Gaelic tradition and its use as an Irish national symbol in poems like James Clarence Mangan's "My Dark Rosaleen" (itself derived from the Gaelic) and Aubrey de Vere's "The Little Black Rose."[14] On the other hand, the particularly national consciousness which Yeats found in the Rose tended to merge with Intellectual Beauty, a Platonic concept which Yeats found particularly in the English poets Spenser and Shelley, though he tried to demarcate his usage from theirs (*VP* 842).

The early ambivalence reached a troubled resolution in the last poem of the section of Yeats's poems denominated *The Rose,* "To Ireland in the Coming Times." Its original title in 1892, "Apologia

addressed to Ireland in the coming days" (*VP* 137), revealed its aspirations as a defense of its author's nationalist credentials even more
clearly. Yeats began by invoking his claim to be a national poet and
then denying that his allegiance to the Rose as Intellectual Beauty
undercut it:

> *Know, that I would accounted be*
> *True brother of a company*
> *That sang, to sweeten Ireland's wrong,*
> *Ballad and story, rann and song;*
> *Nor be I any less of them,*
> *Because the red-rose bordered hem*
> *Of her, whose history began*
> *Before God made the angelic clan,*
> *Trails all about the written page.*
> (*VP* 137–138)

By asserting that Intellectual Beauty was in fact the core of Irish tradition before its Anglicization, Yeats seeks to be counted one with
national poets like "*Davis, Mangan, Ferguson.*" In this respect he belongs to an Irish "party of consciousness" as well. That approach
has lately been contested both in this country and in Ireland, on the
grounds that the consciousness it represents belongs to a kind of
Gaelic "essentialism" obscuring the particulars of Irish history, including the bourgeois component of the modern Irish revolution;
less tolerant critics contend that Yeats, as an Anglo-Irish Protestant,
has in any case a dubious claim to speak for such a tradition.[15]

But I do not think that such merely philosophic arguments reach
the core of Yeats's problematic early effort to de-Anglicize English
romanticism. The problem lies rather in Yeats's being primarily a
poet, and in writing up until the turn of the century with the verse-
craft—diction, rhythms, and other techniques—created by the great
English romantics as filtered through their later admirers like Rossetti and Morris. In that way, whatever the struggle between Irish
and English cultures in his work, the outcome would always be
shaped by the dominant mode of expression being English. Yeats
might write of Niamh and Oisin, and even use Irish words like
"findrinny" or "firbolg," but the *way* he wrote inevitably recalled
the English tradition.

Even so overtly national a poem as "The Dedication to a Book of Stories selected from the Irish Novelists" exemplifies the dilemma. Yeats first published the poem in 1891 as the dedication of his own selection of *Representative Irish Tales,* reprinted it often, and subjected it to major revision in 1924. For all its nationalist content, the 1891 version seems enfeebled by the clichés of a different tradition:

> I tore it from green boughs winds tossed and hurled,
> Green boughs of tossing always, weary, weary,
> I tore it from the green boughs of old Eri,
> The willow of the many-sorrowed world.
>
> Ah, Exiles, wandering over many lands,
> My bell branch murmurs . . .

In contrast, the 1924 version speaks in a truly independent voice not compromised by its substitution of savage indignation for sentimental invocation:

> I tore it from green boughs winds tore and tossed
> Until the sap of summer had grown weary!
> I tore it from the barren boughs of Eire,
> That country where a man can be so crossed;
>
> Can be so battered, badgered and destroyed
> That he's a loveless man . . .
>
> (*VP* 130)

The contrast lies not just in content but in technique, particularly the substitution of an impassioned speaking voice ("battered, badgered and destroyed") for a dreamy, over-literary one ("The willow of the many-sorrowed world"). Yeats's celebrated thematic "movement downwards upon life"[16] after 1906 was matched by a technical one as well. He later recalled, "I tried to make the language of poetry coincide with that of passionate, normal speech" and "as I altered my syntax I altered my intellect" (*E&I* 521, 530). The new diction and syntax replaced the derivative, strongly English patterns of fin-de-siècle verse with those we now associate with modernism. Ezra Pound described the pre-modern, turn of the century poetry this way: "The common verse of Britain from 1890 to 1910 was a horrible agglomerate compost, not minted, most of it not even baked, all legato, a doughy mess of third-hand Keats, Wordsworth, heaven knows what, fourth-hand Elizabethan sonority blunted, half melted, lumpy" (*LE* 205). In the present context, I emphasize that the modernist patterns replacing those described by Pound are predominantly Irish and American rather than British—the patterns of Yeats, Pound, Eliot, Frost, Williams, and Stevens. They help account for why the diverse language of literary modernism appeals so strongly to English-language poets around the world today: it has already de-centered England and prepared the ground for further such enterprises.[17] In Yeats's case, the new way he wrote poetry enabled him to renegotiate the relation between Ireland and England in his poetry, and to de-Anglicize his own romanticism.

We can see the results in a poem from the middle of Yeats's career like "September 1913." Caught up in the controversies surrounding the greatest labor upheaval in Dublin history and looking backward to the death of John O'Leary six years earlier, the poem begins:

> What need you, being come to sense,
> But fumble in a greasy till
> And add the halfpence to the pence
> And prayer to shivering prayer, until
> You have dried the marrow from the bone;
> For men were born to pray and save:
> Romantic Ireland's dead and gone,
> It's with O'Leary in the grave.
>
> (*PNE* 108)

Here Yeats writes of specifically Irish matters in a language no longer redolent of English romanticism. It is not so much that phrases like "fumble in a greasy till" or "dried the marrow from the bone" belong to Irish speech rhythms but that they no longer echo the diction and cadences of the English romantics. Instead, they belong to literary modernism, and that modernism itself no longer displays an Anglo-centrism. Indeed, Yeats calls up an explicit counter ideal to English romanticism in "Romantic Ireland," which he associates particularly with O'Leary. The coincidence between stanza and syntax builds as the stanza moves toward the powerful refrain

"Romantic Ireland's dead and gone, / It's with O'Leary in the grave." The very power of the poem and the refrain suggests that Romantic Ireland is not dead after all: it lives on, incarnated in the speaker of those lines. Yeats's later career would feature him as both elegist and celebrater of Romantic Ireland. In that phrase, Ireland as noun was primary and Romantic as adjective was secondary. He de-Anglicized English romanticism by establishing Ireland as center and assimilating romanticism to it rather than it to romanticism (as he had done in the early verse), not less in style than in subject. The creation of modernism rendered that reversal one of consciousness as much as of mimesis. "It is myself that I remake," wrote Yeats (*PNE* 548).

Yeats's mature deployment of his tower symbol serves as synecdoche for the entire enterprise. The tower appears in many major poems from "In Memory of Major Robert Gregory" through "Coole and Ballylee, 1931." The most important aspect of the tower for the present argument is its physicality. Yeats's tower is not merely a literary device but also, and equally importantly, an actual physical building in Ireland—specifically, a later medieval Norman tower in County Galway with two attached cottages. Yeats bought it in 1917, restored and furnished it extensively, and spent summers there for a decade beginning in 1919. Its very name proclaimed its Irishness. The tower Yeats purchased was known as "Ballylee Castle"; he renamed it "Thoor Ballylee," thoor being his version of the Irish word Tor (tower). The new name thus recapitulates both political and poetic processes, in which Yeats re-appropriates for Ireland (and the soon to be born Irish Free State) a castle previously so thoroughly assimilated to English hegemony that he has to de-Anglicize even its name.

Thoor Ballylee functions in the poetry analogously to the renaming of the physical tower: it enables Yeats to de-Anglicize English romanticism and assimilate it instead to Romantic Ireland. Yeats himself remained keenly aware of the literary associations of towers, particularly the English poetic ones. In a note to his own *Collected Poems* (1933) he remarked:

In this book and elsewhere, I have used towers, and one tower in particular, as symbols and have compared their winding stairs to the philosophical gyres, but it is hardly necessary to interpret what comes from the main track of thought and expression. Shelley uses towers constantly as symbols . . . Part of the symbolism of 'Blood and the Moon' was suggested by the fact that Thoor Ballylee has a waste room at the top. (*PNE* 597)

The poems could be even more explicit. "Blood and the Moon" mentions the towers of ancient Alexandria and Babylon as well as of Shelley's *Prometheus Unbound,* and Robartes in "The Phases of the Moon" says that the tower's owner has "chosen this place to live in / Because, it may be, of the candle-light / From the far tower where Milton's Platonist / Sat late, or Shelley's visionary prince" (*PNE* 163). Yet the very physicality of Thoor Ballylee, its solidity as an Irish structure, meant that in this case Milton's and Shelley's towers would be assimilated into Yeats's, not his absorbed into their usage. In writing of Thoor Ballylee he would be romancing his native stone.

Yeats's strategies stand forth most prominently in "The Tower," the title poem from the volume *The Tower,* itself one of the great achievements of poetic modernism. The first section of that poem identifies the speaker confronting his old age as an Irishman, one who in boyhood "climbed Ben Bulben's back" (*PNE* 194). In the great second section the speaker "send[s] imagination forth" to re-create images of passionate intensity associated with the particular landscape around the tower—Mrs. French and the serving-man, the poet Raftery and his beloved Mary Hynes, Yeats's own hero Hanra-han, and finally the "ancient bankrupt master" of the tower. As Yeats emphasized in a note, "The persons mentioned are associated by legend, story and tradition with the neighbourhood of Thoor Ballylee or Ballylee Castle, where the poem was written" (*PNE* 595). Yet had Yeats stopped there, he would have belonged merely to the party of mimesis. The modernist rhythms and diction of the poem joined him to the party of consciousness as well:

> What shall I do with this absurdity—
> O heart, O troubled heart—this caricature,
> Decrepit age that has been tied to me
> As to a dog's tail?

Secure in his modernist style and Irish materials, Yeats could go on in the second section of "The Tower" to rework one of the principal forms of the English romantics, the Greater Romantic Lyric, without fear of lapsing back into Anglo-centrism. That section adapts the typical romantic three-part sequence in which a particularized speaker in a definite landscape moves from description through vision to evaluation, as in Coleridge's "Aeolian Harp," Wordsworth's "Tintern Abbey," or Keats's "Ode to a Nightingale."[18] Unlike the romantics, Yeats devalues nature and centers his poem not on the mind's interaction with nature but on its relation to its own summoned images of passionate human questing. Those images turn out to be Irish, and the language that expresses them a modernist one created by an Irishman.

Yeats could never go so far as Douglas Hyde and thoroughly de-Anglicize his verse by writing in Gaelic. He thought the point important enough to raise at length in the late essay "A General Introduction for my Work." Recalling a discussion with writers from India, he admitted, "I could no more have written in Gaelic than can those Indians write in English; Gaelic is my national language, but it is not my mother tongue" (*E&I* 520). The continued use of a language originating from England, no matter how modified, meant that a love-hate relationship with the English tradition would pervade his work:

> I remind myself that though mine is the first English marriage I know of in the direct line, all my family names are English, and that I owe my soul to Shakespeare, to Spenser and to Blake, perhaps to William Morris, and to the English language in which I think, speak, and write, that everything I love has come to me through English; my hatred tortures me with love, my love with hate. (*E&I* 519)

Yet if he could not de-Anglicize his work totally by writing in a different language, he could at least de-Anglicize it to the extent of de-centering England in it and from it. He aspired to become one of the last romantics but not one of the last English romantics. The antinomy between England and Ireland would become one of the great dialectics of his verse, one never capable of a final synthesis but always beckoning toward a continual quest.

If Irish literature sponsored the first modernist de-Anglicizing of romantic poetry, American verse promoted the second. Ironically, Yeats had articulated some of his crucial stances in *Letters to the New*

Island, newspaper essays aimed at the Irish–American readers of the Providence *Sunday Journal* and Boston *Pilot.* But those readers, and their descendents, would eventually shed their Irish identity for an American one. As Wallace Stevens remarked in a letter glossing his long poem *The Man With the Blue Guitar,* "Things imagined . . . become things as they are. This is pretty much the same thing as to say that in the United States everyone sooner or later becomes an American."[19] The remark refers not so much to an homogenizing "melting pot" theory of a sort receiving sharp questioning nowadays, but rather a pluralistic conception of American society tied partly to place. Regionalization would play an important part in Stevens's own efforts to de-Anglicize English romanticism.

While Stevens thought of himself as adapting romanticism from his first book, *Harmonium* (1923), onwards, he articulated his stance with particular care in the early 1930s. He called in particular for a "new romanticism."[20] The introductory poem of the first edition of *Ideas of Order* (1935) announced:

> It is the word *pejorative* that hurts . . .
> Mon Dieu, hear the poet's prayer.
> The romantic should be here.
> The romantic should be there.
> It ought to be everywhere.
> But the romantic must never remain,
>
> Mon Dieu, and must never again return.
> (*CP* 120)

He explained his meaning further in a letter to one of his publishers, Ronald Lane Latimer: "When people speak of the romantic, they do so in what the French commonly call a *pejorative* sense. But poetry is essentially romantic, only the romantic of poetry must be something constantly new and, therefore, just the opposite of what is spoken of as the romantic. Without this new romantic, one gets nowhere . . . " (*L* 277). Stevens's development of a new romanticism throughout his work bore some resemblances to Yeats's strategies. He sought to de-Anglicize English romanticism by fastening it to American landscapes in a fusion of the parties of mimesis and of consciousness, by seeking to absorb and refashion English tradition rather than being absorbed by it, and by developing a markedly non-English modernist style as a guarantee of that independence.

Like Yeats, Stevens regularly attacked cosmopolitanism as a chief antithesis of his own stance. In writing to his Irish friend Thomas McGreevy about the 1953 selection of his poems published in England by Faber and Faber, he wondered about his reception in a foreign country. "After all, England is not the United States," he pointed out. "And social ideas and attitudes are as completely different as those in Hartford are from those in the capital of the moon. . . . Under such circumstances a man that is himself always seems to do very much better than, say, the cosmopolitan. Whatever I have comes from Pennsylvania and Connecticut and from nowhere else."[21] The anywhere else could in any case have consisted of very few direct experiences. Stevens's entire foreign travel amounted to two trips to Cuba, a cruise through Mexican waters and the Panama Canal, and a brief vacation in British Columbia.[22] The regionalism resulting from a keen sense of a personal past formed part of Stevens's defensive dismissal of romantic influence: "While, of course, I come down from the past, the past is my own and not something marked Coleridge, Wordsworth, etc. . . . My reality-imagination complex is entirely my own even though I see it in others" (*L* 792). Chief among poets in whom Stevens would have seen his dialectic between imagination and reality were, of course, the English romantics.

Readers often forget how thoroughly American place names pervade the poetry of Stevens. Over twenty poems feature American places even in their titles, among them "In the Carolinas," "Stars at Tallapoosa" [a river flowing through Georgia], "New England Verses," "Two at Norfolk," "Indian River," "Farewell to Florida," "The Idea of Order at Key West," "Loneliness in Jersey City," "Arcades of Philadelphia the Past," "Of Hartford in a Purple Light," "Dutch Graves in Bucks County," "Chocorua to its Neighbor," "An Ordinary Evening in New Haven," "The River of Rivers in Connecticut," and even "Arrival at the Waldorf." In a controversial aphorism from his *Adagia* notebook, Stevens wrote that "for me life is an affair of places."[23] The most important places lay not simply in America but, as the remark against cosmopolitanism suggests, in Pennsylvania and Connecticut. From eastern Pennsylvania

came Tulpehocken, Ephrata, Tinicum, the Oley Valley, the Dutch
cemetery at Feasterville, Perkiomen Creek, and the Swatara and
Schuylkill Rivers, while from Connecticut came Hartford, Farm-
ington steeple, Haddam, New Haven, and others.[24] Stevens might
write of foreign places, but always underscoring their foreignness.
In "Our Stars Come from Ireland," for example, he wrote, "He
stayed in Kerry, died there. / I live in Pennsylvania" and went on to
invoke "the puddles of Swatara / And Schuylkill" (*CP* 455).

Yet had Stevens stopped with mere geography, he would have belonged only to the party of mimesis in America. His de-Anglicizing
of English romanticism meant a change in consciousness as well.
"Nothing could be more inappropriate to American literature than
its English source since the Americans are not British in sensibility,"
he declared (*OP* 176). That sensibility depended partly on place was
one of his most characteristic ideas. As early as "The Comedian as
the Letter C" he wrote that "The natives of the rain are rainy men"
(*CP* 37). Men were the intelligence of their soil and, more importantly, their soil was their intelligence. Their productions came from
their places and from themselves. Hence, as late as the 1951 essay
"Two or Three Ideas," he argued "that the gods of China are always
Chinese; that the gods of Greece are always Greeks and that all gods
are created in the images of their creators" (*OP* 211). Stevens extended such ideas beyond his own country to include third-world
poets striving to dislodge Europe from their work. For example, he
entered into a long correspondence with the young Cuban poet José
Rodriguez Feo. When illness kept Feo from accepting the offer of a
teaching job at Princeton, Stevens wrote:

> Providence has, as I say, probably invented colitis so that you could
> sit on the front porch and respond to Cuba and make something of it,
> and help to invent or perfect the idea of Cuba in which everyone can
> have a being. . . . Your job is to help to create the spirit of Cuba.
> Every one of your friends who writes a poem, whether or not it is
> about Cuba which nevertheless is a thing of the place . . . is doing
> just what you ought to be doing somehow or other. (*L*654–655)

Such geographic rootedness would influence not only content
and consciousness but also technique. In "The Comedian as the

Letter C," Stevens had his hero Crispin journey from Bordeaux via Yucatan to Carolina. There he imagined the proper relation between place and poetry for a future America:

> The man in Georgia waking among pines
> Should be pine-spokesman. The responsive man,
> Planting his pristine cores in Florida,
> Should prick thereof, not on the psaltery,
> But on the banjo's categorical gut,
> Tuck, tuck, while the flamingoes flapped his bays.
>
> (*CP* 38)

The language itself acts out its content (particularly in the "Tuck, tuck" of the banjo), and the passage instantly identifies itself as Stevensian.

It also identifies itself as non-English. Like Yeats, Stevens used poetic modernism as a way of de-Anglicizing his poetry. The result is readily apparent not just to American readers but also to English ones. Here is the most distinguished English critic to have written a book on Stevens, Frank Kermode:

> Large borrowings from French are part of the general fantastication of English which goes on in Stevens; they take their place beside all the archaisms and neologisms that critics like to make lists of. . . . Why is he so clearly at home with his speech? The answer is simple but not to be neglected: Stevens is fully American. . . . The truth of this is evident from the relation that has come to exist between English and American poetry . . . the intercourse between the two is very much what it might be as between two literatures in different but mutually intelligible languages. . . . English readers . . . can see that Stevens is a profoundly American, to them a very foreign, poet.[25]

Like Yeats, Stevens particularly used modernism to de-Anglicize English romanticism even while recasting the dialectic between imagination and reality into his "new romanticism." Far from supporting European (including English) hegemony, poetic modernism instead undermines it at every turn in the name of liberation. In that ongoing enterprise Stevens had one great American forerunner, Walt Whitman, whom he memorialized in lines that apply equally well to himself:

In the far South the sun of autumn is passing
Like Walt Whitman walking along a ruddy shore.
He is singing and chanting the things that are part of him,
The worlds that were and will be, death and day.
Nothing is final, he chants.

(*CP* 150)

But Whitman's striding and chanting were not to be Stevens's mode. Part of the problem lay in the modern American poet's difficulty finding a poetic stance to confront the contemporary world at all, let alone one as confident as Whitman's. Stevens addressed that issue in the opening question of "The American Sublime":

How does one stand
To behold the sublime,
To confront the mockers,
The mickey mockers
And plated pairs?

(*CP* 130)

In the poem, Stevens takes for his icon of such difficulties Clark Mills's statue of Andrew Jackson facing the White House across Lafayette Square in Washington, D.C. ("When General Jackson / Posed for his statue / He knew how one feels"). The persistent questions of "The American Sublime" are partly illuminated by Stevens's meditation on the same statue in his 1941 Princeton lecture, "The Noble Rider and the Sound of Words." There he views the statue as neither mimetic of reality nor expressive of the imagination, but rather as cobbled together by fancy and hence "unreal."[26] That result was not really Mills's fault. Without a coherent inherited mythology, he tried to invent his own for Jackson. This is the same situation that Yeats attributed to Blake, of being "a symbolist who had to invent his symbols . . . a man crying out for a mythology and trying to make one because he could not find one to his hand" (*E&I* 114). It was also the situation of Stevens himself, more talented than Mills if not than Blake.

In his campaign of de-Anglicization to romance his own native stone, Stevens thus lacked a principal component of Yeats's analogous enterprise. Yeats could and did strive to recuperate a native

Celtic mythology once central to Irish identity and capable of becoming so again as a replacement for mere Anglicism. That option was not open to Stevens. On the one hand, European settlers in America had brought the native population even closer to annihilation than the English did the Irish and had suppressed their culture even more thoroughly. It seemed futile and hypocritical for a descendant of those settlers to try to recuperate Indian lore as the basis of a national culture, and Stevens never made more than incidental use of it. Further, in a country the size of a continent there was in any case no one Indian culture as dominant and pervasive as Celtic culture had been in Ireland. (The situation is quite different in parts of Latin America.) On the other hand, to return to the ancestral myths of the white settlers would have meant returning to the very European roots which Stevens thought he had to leave behind in his creation of an American sublime.

Stevens addressed the difficulties of a resultant lack of mythology in his very late poem, "A Mythology Reflects Its Region":

> A mythology reflects its region. Here
> In Connecticut, we never lived in a time
> When mythology was possible—But if we had—
> That raises the question of the image's truth.
> The image must be of the nature of its creator.
> It is the nature of its creator increased,
> Heightened. It is he, anew, in a freshened youth
> And it is he in the substance of his region,
> Wood of his forests and stone out of his fields
> Or from under his mountains.
>
> (OP 118)

He still believed in the link between place and myth which the comedian Crispin had discovered more than three decades earlier. Yet the poem dismisses the realization of such mythology in modern Connecticut as not "possible." The interrupted clause "But if we had" carries a full burden of frustrated yearning in miming the very predicament toward which it gestures: not only can the poet not specify what such a mythology and its effects would have been like, but he cannot complete the thought because the syntax here would require a shift to that mythic language which has just been declared impossible. Instead, the poem retreats from mythology to imagery, from myth to image. The image was always primary in Stevens. "The Sense of the Sleight-of-Hand Man," for example, had declared that "The wheel [the initial image] survives the myths [the systematic elaborations of the image]" and that "the fire eye in the clouds survives the gods" (*CP* 222). In that way, re-conceiving initial and fecund images provided the first step toward creating a new mythology. And "A Mythology Reflects Its Region" can take that initial step even if not the final one. It offers an image "of its creator . . . in a freshened youth" embodying his native stone and substance. That was as far as Stevens got in romancing his native stone, and as an act of (American) mind it sufficed him.

Notes

1. *Irish Literature: A Reader,* ed. Maureen O'Rourke Murphy and James MacKillop (Syracuse: Syracuse University Press, 1987), 137.

2. Reed Way Dasenbrock, "English Department Geography," in *Profession 87* (New York: Modern Language Association, 1987), 57.

3. Raymond Williams, "The Social History of English Writers," in *The Long Revolution* (Harmondsworth: Penguin Books, 1965), 254–270.

4. The present essay thus follows up on one of the "Four Gaps in Post-romantic Influence Study" identified in the introductory chapter of my recent *Poetic Remaking: The Art of Browning, Yeats, and Pound* (University Park and London: Penn State University Press, 1988).

5. Ezra Pound, "How To Read," reprinted in *Literary Essays of Ezra Pound,* ed. T. S. Eliot (New York: New Directions, 1968), 34. Hereafter cited as *LE.*

6. Robert Weisbuch, *Atlantic Double-Cross: American Literature and British Influence in the Age of Emerson* (Chicago: University of Chicago Press, 1986), ix–x and passim.

7. As quoted in Weisbuch, 4–5, along with other examples.

8. W. B. Yeats, *The Poems: A New Edition,* ed. Richard J. Finneran (New York: Macmillan, 1983), 245. Hereafter cited as *PNE.*

9. Wallace Stevens, *Collected Poems* (New York: Alfred A. Knopf, 1968), 27 and 36–37. Hereafter cited as *CP.*

10. W. B. Yeats, *Autobiographies* (London: Macmillan, 1966), 101. Hereafter cited as *A.*

11. William Butler Yeats, *Letters to the New Island: A New Edition,* ed. George Bornstein and Hugh Witemeyer (London and New York: Macmillan, 1989), 12. Hereafter cited as *LNI.*

12. I have discussed Yeats's relation to Shelley more fully in *Yeats and Shelley* (Chicago: University of Chicago Press, 1970); in relation to the present subject see particularly chapter 5.

13. *Essays and Introductions* (New York: Macmillan, 1961), 114. Hereafter cited as *E&I*.

14. *The Variorum Edition of the Poems of W. B. Yeats,* ed. Peter Allt and Russell K. Alspach (New York: Macmillan, 1957; rev. 3rd printing, 1966), 798–799 and 811–812. Hereafter cited as *VP*.

15. See, for example, Seamus Deane, "Yeats and the Idea of Revolution," in his *Celtic Revivals: Essays in Modern Irish Literature* (London: Faber and Faber, 1985), and Denis Donoghue, "Yeats, Ancestral Houses, and Anglo-Ireland," in his *We Irish: Essays on Irish Literature and Society* (New York: Alfred A. Knopf, 1986). For a "New Historicist" view of the general relation of literature and nationalism in nineteenth-century Ireland see David Lloyd, *Nationalism and Minor Literature: James Clarence Mangan and the Emergence of Irish Cultural Nationalism* (Berkeley: University of California Press, 1987).

16. W. B. Yeats, *The Letters of W. B. Yeats,* ed. Allan Wade (London: Rupert Hart-Davis, 1954), 469.

17. Hugh Kenner has recently noted the decentering of the English language from England, though his emphasis on cosmopolitans like Pound and Eliot leads him to view the language of International Modernism as free from any particular nationhood. In *A Sinking Island: The Modern English Writers* (New York: Alfred A. Knopf, 1988), which appeared after the present article was written, he says: "English by about 1930 had ceased to be simply the language they speak in England. It had been split four ways. It was (1) the language of International Modernism, having displaced French in that role. And it was (2) the literary language of Ireland, and (3) of America, and yes, (4) of England, countries which International Modernism bids us think of as the Three Provinces" (pp. 3–4).

18. See M. H. Abrams, "Structure and Style in the Greater Romantic Lyric," in *From Sensibility to Romanticism,* ed. Frederick W. Hilles and Harold Bloom (New York: Oxford University Press, 1965), 527–560. I have discussed Yeats's adaptation of Greater Romantic Lyric from a point of view less centered on de-Anglicizing in "Yeats and the Greater Romantic Lyric," in *Romantic and Modern: Revaluations of Literary Tradition,* ed. George Bornstein (Pittsburgh: University of Pittsburgh Press, 1977), 91–110.

19. Wallace Stevens, *Letters of Wallace Stevens,* ed. Holly Stevens (New York: Alfred A. Knopf, 1970), 360. Hereafter cited as *L*.

20. I have discussed Stevens's "new romanticism" from a different point of view in *Transformations of Romanticism in Yeats, Eliot, and Stevens* (Chicago: University of Chicago Press, 1976), chap. 4. See also A. Walton Litz, "Wallace Stevens's Defense of Poetry: *La poésie pure,* the New Romantic, and the Pressure of Reality," in *Romantic and Modern,* ed. Bornstein, 111–132.

21. Wallace Stevens, *Poems,* sel. Samuel French Morse (New York: Vintage Books, 1959), vi–vii.

22. James Baird, *The Dome and the Rock* (Baltimore: Johns Hopkins Press, 1968), 232.

23. Wallace Stevens, *Opus Posthumous,* ed. Samuel French Morse (New York: Alfred A. Knopf, 1969), 158. Hereafter cited as *OP.*

24. On the Pennsylvania names see Milton J. Bates, "Stevens as Regional Poet," *Wallace Stevens Journal* 5 (1981): 32–35.

25. Frank Kermode, *Wallace Stevens* (New York: Grove Press, 1961), 12–13.

26. Wallace Stevens, *The Necessary Angel* (New York: Vintage Books, 1965), 10–11.

The Gazer's Spirit

Romantic and Later Poetry on Painting and Sculpture

❧

John Hollander

Questions of ekphrastic poetry no longer seem peripheral to the matter of romanticism. Poems addressed to silent works of art, questioning them; describing them as they could never describe— but merely present—themselves; speaking for them; making them speak out or speak up (as the Greek verb *ekphradzein* implies)—all engage the otherness of the image. They look with longing on images themselves perhaps of erotic longing. They seek to break open the self-absorption with which all images seem to be veiled. They manifest, as W. J. T. Mitchell has suggested, interpretive anxiety.[1] Such poems are prone to their own mode of self-absorption, incorporating the gazer and even the act of gazing into the purported object. Their rhetorical and formal structures can be variously developed as troped responses to graphic and plastic ones, or even to those of the story of the act of scanning or reading a picture or sculpture. Their two-way mirrors have lamps behind them.

Ekphrastic poems are also, inevitably, transumptive of prior texts, as their object-images necessarily allude to and engage prior images. The whole past tradition of this sort of poetry is rooted in what is purely notional—all early poetic ekphrasis, that is, describes or invokes purely fictional objects. Homer's shield of Achilles and Hesiod's Herakleian one; the carved ivory cup in Theocritus' first *Idyll;* Aeneas' armor and the images in the Temple of Juno; the carved images that seem to generate their own discourse in *"visibile parlare"* of the tenth canto of Dante's *Purgatorio;* the many ekphrastic descriptions in Ariosto; the remarkable paired sets of erotic tapestries past which—and through whose meanings—Britomart must move in Malecasta's and Busirane's houses at the beginning and end of Book 3 of *The Faerie Queene;* the differently remarkable dramatic scene of reading the "piece of skillful painting" in whose story Shakespeare's Lucrece construes her own plight, and which contrasts four modes of interpreting images. These are all what I have elsewhere called "notional ekphrasis," in that the linguistic account invents a fictional visual object, the description of which constitutes its creation.[2] It is important to observe this, I think, because these notional ekphrases are the paradigms and templates for all subsequent ones.

Actual ekphrastic poetry—the text of which speaks to, or of, or for an image to which the reader of the text has like access—is largely confined in Renaissance England to emblem verse. It might be argued that this is a limited and reductive form of ekphrasis, for the Alciatian impresa can be redrawn and reengraved many times (as it indeed was, over two centuries), but the reading given it by the moralizing verses will only cut through to the bare iconographic essentials: Occasion's forelock, Cupid's blindfold, Temperance's pouring of water into a cup of wine. The nature, quality, structure, and ancillary visual material of the image might as well not exist. The relation of picture—corpo—to interpreting language—anima—conventionally adduced, is misleading to the degree that, in emblems, the corpo is itself only an abstracted iconographic anima of the particular engraving or woodcut, with its particular graphic realizations of the icon. By the seventeenth century, actual ekphrastic poetry is more common on the continent. Well-known examples are the poems of Giambattista Marino's *La Galeria,* the Dutch poet Vondel's sonnets on paintings, and so forth. But whereas Marino, for instance, will address Caravaggio's head of Medusa on a shield (in the Uffizi) by directing his little poem to its owner, the Grand Duke of Tuscany, asking what foes there could possibly be who would not turn into cold marble on seeing the shield, and concluding that, in actual war, "*la vera Medusa è il valor vostro*" ("the true Medusa is your own valor"), a famous romantic counterpart is another matter entirely.[3]

Shelley's (if it is indeed all his own) poem "On the Medusa of Leonardo da Vinci in the Florentine Gallery" typifies the kinds of displacement which can occur in modern as well as in romantic poems of this sort. (The painting, about which Pater also wrote, is now thought to be a seventeenth-century copy, perhaps of a lost Leonardo, or after Vasani's description.) Its five stanzas start out with literal description—"It lieth, gazing on the midnight sky / Upon the cloudy mountain-peak supine" (where the mountain-peak is not in the picture, but in Shelley's memory of the myth). By the second stanza, the gazer has become Medusa's victim: "Yet it is less the horror than the grace / Which turns the gazer's spirit into stone . . . ," and the terror has become petrifying loveliness. Finally, there is the gazer through the text of the poem at the invoked image. (I am reminded of the fact that from the sixteenth through the early nineteenth centuries, the noun "gaze," in *OED* sense 1, designated the *object* of the concentrated stare, rather than the stare itself—much as, today, something is said to have a "look" if ar-

1. *Leonardo da Vinci (attribution),* The Head of Medusa, *Uffizi Gallery, Florence. Alinari / Art Resource, New York.*

ranged to appear to a fashionably conscious and thereby beclouded act of looking, or "look.")⁴ The matter of the harmonization of horror and beauty pervades the rest of the poem's *ascriptive description*—for so one might call all poetic ekphrasis—until, at the end, the gaze is turned upon the victor-victim herself. Perseus' mirror protected him from the Gorgon's literally petrifying stare, but, in Shelley's last stanza, the mirroring is revised; the very air becomes a mirror of the beauty and the terror, and the sublimity leaps out of the conceptual scheme of the image and the myth:

> 'Tis the tempestuous loveliness of terror;
>   For from the serpents gleams a brazen glare
> Kindled by that inextricable error,
>   Which makes a thrilling vapour of the air
> Become a [dim?] and ever-shifting mirror
>   Of all the beauty and the terror there—
> A woman's countenance, with serpent-locks,
> Gazing in death on Heaven from those wet rocks.⁵

The issue of the organic harmonization of elements that involves an implicit inclusion of the picture-reading subject in the pictorial object is raised in another romantic poem I have discussed in detail elsewhere. It is quite unfamiliar, but rather important, I think. The American painter Washington Allston, while in England where he was in close contact with Coleridge and Wordsworth, had written some time before 1811 a sonnet on one of the frescoes, high on the walls of the loggie in the Vatican, known as "Raphael's Bible." The painting is of the three angels before the tent of Abraham at Mamre. Allston's sonnet not only reads the frescoed scene, but also the acts both of gazing from below, and of construing a picture structurally and hermeneutically, for the "subtle mystery" of "unity complete":

> O, now I feel as though another sense,
> From heaven descending, had informed my soul;
> I feel the pleasurable, full control
> Of Grace, harmonious, boundless, and intense.
> In thee, celestial Group, embodied lives
> The subtile mystery, that speaking gives
> Itself resolved; the essences combined

2. *Raphael, Vatican, Rome. Alinari / Art Resource, New York.*

> Of Motion ceaseless, Unity complete.
> Borne like a leaf by some soft eddying wind,
> Mine eyes, impelled as by enchantment sweet,
> From part to part with circling motion rove,
> Yet seem unconscious of the power to move;
> From line to line through endless changes run,
> O'er countless shapes, yet seem to gaze on One.

The painter's eye reads as much for graphic structure as for scriptural interpretation here (finding the presence of God—who finally breaks forth into anger at Sarah's laughter—among the three "men" who appear to him). This poem must have impressed Coleridge, who in his essays *On the Principles of Genial Criticism Concerning the Fine Arts* (1814) discusses Allston and Raphael together under the rubric of beauty defined as "Multeity in Unity," and seems to echo in his own prose ekphrases (of, among other pictures, a painting of Allston's) the latter's invocation of the scanning process, eyes moving "from part to part with circling motion," yet which "seem unconscious of the power to move."[6] Allston's few sonnets on pictures are closer in power to Rossetti's than to, say, the verses Turner attached to some of his paintings or wrote for catalogues.

In the following discussion, I shall not consider notional ekphrases, nor poems to, or about, artists, nor examples of what might be called the capriccio of allusions to various images (as a modern instance, one might suggest that W. H. Auden's famous "Musée des Beaux Arts" is actually one of these, representing a sort of gallery walk past several Breughels, only finally alighting on *The Fall of Icarus*). But one other interesting category of ekphrastic poem might be remarked upon here, the kind of iconic poem for which the original object of poetic gaze actually present for the poet, has since gotten lost, making the ekphrasis notional for purposes of comparative reading.[7] Most of the actual paintings addressed by poems in Marino's *La Galeria,* for example, are now missing. But the poet's mode of invocation and further troping of image is consistent enough so that not too many interpretive puzzles remain. And yet with romantic and later poetry, this is another matter. We can all contemplate, as an interpretive set piece, the relation of Wordsworth's "Elegiac Stanzas" to Sir George Beaumont's painting of Peele Castle in a storm, and observe the unfolding of the anecdote of reading and misreading the scene in the painting, followed by the correction effected by adducing scenes (in another sense) of reading the picture. (The poem is in this respect transumptive of the gaze at, and through, landscape in "Tintern Abbey".) The "Elegiac Stanzas" are so familiar that I shall not discuss them here; I mention their literal ekphrasis only to contrast it with Wordsworth's later (1811) sonnet "Upon the Sight of a Beautiful Picture, Painted by G. H. Beaumont," that begins

> Praised by the Art whose subtle power could stay
> Yon cloud, and fix it in that glorious shape;
> Nor would permit the thin smoke to escape,
> Nor those bright sunbeams to forsake the day,
> Which stopped that band of travellers on their way
> Ere they were lost within the shady wood . . .

The painting is lost. We know from a letter that the smoke, and the travellers, were "in the picture" but that two later lines were purely notional (Wordsworth writes that other details "were added")—

"And showed the Bark upon the glassy flood / For ever anchored in her sheltering bay."[8] J. A. W. Heffernan has interestingly discussed the relation of this poem to the earlier one,[9] and we ourselves might add that the tranquillity of the bark on the glassy flood undoes the horror of depicted storm and adduced shipwreck, drowning and loss of a beloved brother, in the earlier poem-painting pair, "Ah, THEN if mine had been the Painter's hand" in the "Elegiac Stanzas" is figuratively completed in a future "THEN" when the poet's hand paints his own peace and reconciliation into Beaumont's benign scene, even as he had twice re-construed the earlier, stormy one. But—we don't have the later painting, and we can only guess at what the smoke was like, and whether the travellers were headed into a painted shady wood of Beaumont's—or rather into Spenser's, or Dante's textually shadowed ones.

One more instance of this virtually notional state is iconographically tantalizing. D. G. Rossetti's 1847 sonnet "For an Annunciation" is directed to an unidentified early German painting he had seen in an auction room.[10] Even a general acquaintance with Northern art allows one to visualize the objects of the opening description—"The lilies stand before her like a screen / Through which, upon this warm and solemn day, / God surely hears . . ." But the scene of the sestet, with the obliquely identified angel, and particularly the two last lines, remains mysterious:

> So prays she, and the Dove flies in to her,
>> And she has turned. At the low porch is one
>> Who looks as though deep awe made him to smile.
> Heavy with heat, the plants yield shadow there;
>> The loud flies cross each other in the sun;
>> And the aisled pillars meet the poplar-aisle.

How could flies, whether making a sign of the cross, or merely glossed as doing so, be legible at all? And what, if any, is the structural and perspectival pattern that is invoked—and troped—in the graceful chiasm of the last line, in which "the aisled pillars meet the poplar-aisle" and, perhaps, the designs of text meet the textures of design? But unless the painting is ever identified, we cannot know.

It should also be remarked that partial, or oblique, ekphrastic moments often occur in poetry from the eighteenth century on.

Ces pauures gueux pleins de bonaductures
Ne portent rien que des Choses futures.

3. *Jacques Callot,* Les Bohémiens, *one of a series of four, etching.*

Keats is full of these passing references to pictorial prototypes in specifically identifiable works of art, although his one great ekphrastic poem on the Greek pot is as purely notional as Homer's shield or Dante's intaglio carvings. Often a poet, though, having been struck by an image in a picture, will provide an indirect reading of that image, writing a text for which the picture might serve as an illustration, although not a slavish one. Charles Baudelaire, having in his mind's eye a number of etchings of gypsies on the road done by Jacques Callot around 1621, was perhaps affected by the inscription on one of them ("These poor vagabonds, full of good adventures, bear with them only things to come"),[11] as well as by the figures themselves and their deep and darkening shadows. The cricket and the earth-goddess, Cybele, are both his additions to the scene, the poet's own *"chimères absents;"* but the element of heroic and mysterious questing that makes the caravan into a sort of allegorical chariot of spiritual journeying is already in Callot's etching, in the structures of line and shadow which point so strongly out of the picture, into a future which itself is like a homely goal.

BOHÉMIENS EN VOYAGE

La tribu prophétique aux prunelles ardentes
Hier s'est mise en route, emportant ses petits

Sur son dos, ou livrant àleurs fiers appétits
Le trésor toujours prêt des mamelles pendantes.

Les hommes vont à pied sous leurs armes luisantes
Le long des chariots où les leurs sont blottis,
Promenant sur le ciel des yeux appesantis
Par le morne regret des chimères absentes.

Du fond de son réduit sablonneux, le grillon,
Les regardant passer, redouble san chanson;
Cybèle, qui les aime, augmente ses verdures,

Fait couler le rocher et leuris le désert
Devant ces voyageurs, pour lesquels est ouvert
L'empire familier des ténèbres futures.

GIPSIES ON THE MOVE

The prophet tribe with burning eyes took to the road yesterday,
    bearing their babes on their backs, or offering to their proud
    hungers the ever-ready treasure of their full breasts.

Carrying their gleaming weapons, the men walk alongside the
    carts wherein their people are huddled, their eyes heavy with
    dull regret for absent visions.

From deep in his sandy covert, the cricket, observing them go
    by, redoubles his song; Cybele, who loves them, amasses her
    greenery,

Makes the rocks run with water and the desert bloom before
    these travellers from whom the familiar empire of future
    shadows opens out.

(*Les Fleurs du mal,* 1857)

I have been speaking of paintings and prints so far. Actual ekphrases of sculpture extend from Hellenistic epigrams, Jacobus

Sadoletus' early sixteenth-century poem on the newly discovered
Laocoön, up through modernity. Summary mention can be made
of Rilke's "Archäische Torso Apollos," which struggles with the
stony silence of the *kouros* in the Louvre to get it figuratively to
utter its famous "*Du muss dein Leben ändern*" (by now, almost as
proverbial as the "Beauty is Truth, Truth Beauty" of Keats' purely
notional urn); Randall Jarrell's poem on "The Bronze David of Do-
natello;" James Merrill's splendid "The Charioteer of Delphi," with
its complex allusive relation to the Rilke poem. I have discussed
some of these elsewhere; here I should like to consider some lines of
Byron, from the visionary travelogue of Canto 4 of *Childe Harold,*
on the subject of one of the most famous and paradigmatic sculpted
images since the quattrocento. But first, one might well look at two
instances of what Byron is going far beyond. Samuel Rogers addressed another one of the Vatican marbles, the famous Torso
Belvedere thought to be of Hercules, in a most unromantic sonnet
(after a conventional quatrain, it degenerates into five couplets, in
fact).[12] It commences with a conventional ekphrastic query, but a
rather empty one—a question rhetorical rather than, despite the
echo of Milton, poetic:

> And dost thou still, thou mass of breathing stone
> (Thy giant limbs to night and chaos hurled)
> Still sit as on the fragment of a world;
> Surviving all, majestic and alone?

—*Well, yes* is the answer; we realize that only the old issue of fragmentation and ruin has been addressed, and we are closer to the
prose of Gibbon than to the hearsay, notional ekphrasis of "Ozyman-
dias." But the death of antiquity is followed nonetheless by the res-
urrections of art, and it is no sentimental meditation on yet another
antique fragment that we are left with. The marble arises in the Renaissance, and has its consequences for the art of the cinquecento:

> What tho' the Spirits of the North, that swept
> Rome from the earth when in her pomp she slept,
> Smote thee with fury, and the headless trunk
> Deep in the dust mid tower and temple sunk;
> Soon to subdue mankind 'twas thine to rise,

Still, still unquelled thy glorious energies!
Aspiring minds, with thee conversing, caught
Bright revelations of the Good they sought;
By thee that long-lost spell in secret given,
To draw down Gods, and lift the soul to Heaven!

The "aspiring minds, with thee conversing" are neoplatonic artists like Michelangelo (who praised the piece, and drew from it for the Medici tombs), Raphael, and others. The direct echo is of Eve addressing Adam in *Paradise Lost* (Book 4.638) ("With thee conversing, I forget all time"). With their spousal address to the fragment, all time is forgotten and new art is born. After this one poetic moment, the epigrammatic cliché—a piece of rhetorical filigree from baroque poetry mass-produced in a later century—reminds us that the form of this poem is in no way engaged in an act of representation, and that the somewhat reductive reading of the object—as a fragment of what once was Hercules—signifies not ruin but recreation.

But Byron's lines on the Apollo Belvedere are a different matter. This celebrated and influential piece had been previously described by James Thomson in Part 4 of his *Liberty* (1736) as one of Sculpture's "marble race" that the Renaissance had seen "spring to new light." There is little doubt that an electrifyingly elegant and powerfully canonical marble is being invoked:

All conquest-flushed from prostrate Python came
The quivered God. In graceful art he stands,
His arm extended with the slackened bow:
Light flows his easy robe, and fair displays
A manly-softened form. The bloom of gods
Seems youthful o'er the beardless cheek to wave:
His features yet heroic ardour warms;
And sweet subsiding to a native smile
Mixed with the joy elating conquest gives,
A scattered frown exalts his matchless air.

("Scattered" here is used in the sense "dropped negligently," *OED* 3b.) But aside from the change of tense in the first two lines, this reading might as well be a Hellenistic one. Its inferences are psycho-

4. *Apollo Belvedere, Vatican, Rome. Alinari / Art Resource, New York.*

logical in re the beautiful boy; there is nothing truly revisionary about it, no ad hoc mythmaking occurs, and the consciousness of the gazer does not inhere in the object in any way.

But here is the first of Byron's stanzas:

> Or view the Lord of the unerring bow,
> The God of life and poesy and light,—
> The Sun in human limbs array'd, and brow
> All radiant from his triumph in the fight;
> The shaft hath just been shot—the arrow bright
> With an immortal's vengeance; in his eye
> And nostril beautiful disdain and might
> And majesty flash their full lightnings by,
> Developing in that one glance the Deity.

This glosses the nature of what Thomson had called "the quivered God" and reads back onto the piece the bow, not slackened, but just having loosed an avenging arrow (but at what or whom?). Thomson's "scattered" frown is replaced by the rhythmic energy with which the "beautiful disdain and might / And majesty flash their full lightnings by"; Byron adds, with a sort of meta-mythopoeia, that through such lightnings disdain, might, and majesty are "Developing in that one glance the Deity."

But in the next stanza the mythmaking is quite explicit, and the relations among bodily beauty, desire, and an ideal of *to kalon* are revealed as complex:

> But in his delicate form—a dream of Love,
> Shaped by some solitary nymph, whose breast
> Long'd for a deathless lover from above
> And madden'd in that vision—are exprest
> All that ideal beauty ever bless'd
> The mind with in its most unearthly mood,
> When each conception was a heavenly guest—
> A ray of immortality—and stood,
> Starlike, around, until they gather'd to a god!

This is no Ovidian story, but more of the post-Spenserian sort one might encounter in Shelley. And there is a theogony parallel to, but

revisionary of, the one in the previous stanza. Here it is not univer-
sals, but the conceptions of desire—themselves emanations of immortality—that coalesce into deity. Here, too, a *furor poeticus* is
invoked, and a vision of those conceptions standing "starlike,
around"—almost as if they were gazers, like Childe Harold, star-
struck at the image of godhead as "life and poesy and light."

And the poesy is what it comes down to. The refigured light,
glancing off and modelling the carved marble as if in an immortal animation, becomes further refigured in the fire of art and
imagination:

> And if it be Prometheus stole from Heaven
> The fire which we endure, it was repaid
> By him to whom the energy was given
> Which this poetic marble hath array'd
> With an eternal glory—which, if made
> By human hands, is not of human thought;
> And Time himself hath hallow'd it, nor laid
> One ringlet in the dust; nor hath it caught
> A tinge of years, but breathes the flame with which 't was
>   wrought.

This is the last of the poem's topographical visions, save for a glance
of the lake at Nemi, and the sea. The phases of its mythography,
unfolding from stanza to stanza, are indeed slightly Spenserian. Yet it
is not the picturesque, eighteenth-century Spenserianism of Thomson we see here, but a more dialectical, romantic version of it.

Still, the most important and influential ekphrastic poems in English in the nineteenth century are directed to paintings. Dante
Gabriel Rossetti's sonnets on pictures are so central to the modern
tradition that one could easily confine this discussion to several of
these alone. That Rossetti used the sonnet form as a strong and flexible framework for his tropes of picturing emerges clearly from a
study of any one of them. Perhaps the greatest of these sonnets is
the one for Leonardo's famous madonna in the National Gallery in
London, written, purportedly, "in front of the picture." Leonardo's
image (Rossetti calls it "Our Lady of the Rocks") is of the madonna
and child with the young John the Baptist and the Angel Gabriel,
right, witnessing the fact that Jesus is blessing his older precursor.

5. *Leonardo da Vinci,* The Virgin of the Rocks, *by permission of the Trustees, The National Gallery, London.*

(In the version of this painting in the Louvre, he literally points it out.) The celebrated background has to this day not been given an authoritative iconographic interpretation, and it is with the looming, dark enigma of the landscape, the complex background with its structures of rocks, that this poem seems most concerned. It starts out with a question, as do so many modern ekphrases and, indeed, some more of Rossetti's own. (Three poems on paintings—two on Memling, one on his own *Astarte Syriaca*—begin with a grammatical absolute, the propounding word "Mystery:" and *Pandora, A Sea-Spell,* and the end of the one on Botticelli's *Primavera* are all interrogative.) But here, the inquiry is directed neither at the painting nor the painter, but instead at the figure of the madonna herself, wondering at the meaning of the darkness, the shadows and the distant, gleaming ocean:

> Mother, is this the darkness of the end,
>> The Shadow of Death? and is that outer sea
>> Infinite imminent Eternity?
> And does the death-pang by man's seed sustained
> In Time's each instant cause thy face to bend
>> Its silent prayer upon the Son, while He
>> Blesses the dead with His hand silently
> To his long day which hours no more offend?
>
> Mother of grace, the pass is difficult,
>> Keen as these rocks, and the bewildered souls
>>> Throng it like echoes, blindly shuddering through.
>> Thy name, O Lord, each spirit's voice extols,
>>> Whose peace abides in the dark avenue
> Amid the bitterness of things occult.

The octave of this sonnet is all questions; the sestet comprises two dark assertions, one addressed to the "Mother" invoked in the opening word of both octave and sestet, the other to the child. Is this a picture of death, rather than of the childhood of Eternal Life? The very phrase, "Shadow of Death" (ultimately from the English translations of Psalm 23), is a complex one, grammatically and tropologically, given the dense history of the term "shadow" in the Renaissance and after (it can mean *shade, cast shadow, image or picture of any kind, verbal trope, anti-type in an interpretive figural relation, version,* etc.). The shadow of death can be a literal darkness cast by an occluding presence, a shaded region in which death lurks, the shadow or hypostasization that "Death" is, the frightening but ultimately fictive stuff—given the ransom paid by the Christian sacrifice—of which it is made, and so forth. The mother in the painting seems, like the other figures in it, to be unaware of the landscape. But the poet reads a consciousness of its meaning into her gesture and, more outrageously, adduces the matter of death in regard to the Son's blessing, which transcends his mother's knowledge of mortality—even as a probable pun here on "ours/hours" frees "his long day" from the tincture of fleeting human instants. "The darkness of the end" in the opening line, and "that outer sea," both guide the scanning eye rapidly into the pictorial space toward the ultimate clefts in the rocks through which far distant light thrusts itself.

Whether it has heard answers to these questions, whether it has propounded its own, or even deemed them to be unanswerable as put, the sestet moves deep into the background of the painting. In cadences that sound like lines from Eliot's "Ash-Wednesday" written eighty years later, ("Mother of grace, the pass is difficult / Keen as these rocks . . . "), the sestet calls attention to its own passages, to the poem's "pass" from octave to sestet, from question to answer, from foreground figure to background place, and to rhymes not on "He" and "outer sea" and "Eternity," but on the bracketing of "difficult" and, ultimately, "occult." The ways through the rocks are of life's entrances and exits—the pass of the birth canal, or, conversely, with the narrow room of dying. These lead to or from the maternal, oceanic spaces through which "the death-pang by man's need sustained" causes us all to move and move again, "blindly shuddering through."[13] The opening to the sea on the left is balanced by the cleft on the right, filled with a towering phallic rock. The ambiguous syntax (*whose* peace is it that "abides in the dark avenue?" the Lord's? that of "each spirit?") makes for no dark puzzle. But the poem's one remarkable omission is another matter.

The angel Gabriel gazes at the infant John, while the younger Son seems to follow the indication with his gaze and benedictional hand. But Gabriel looks out at the viewer, for whom the act of pointing-at is more generally one of pointing-out. Gabriel serves as what the history of art calls a *Sprecher*—a figure in a narrative scene who looks out of it, figuratively speaking to a viewer—for the picture's meaning. George Hersey, in a fascinating unpublished commentary on this poem, suggested a decade ago that it is the Dante Gabriel (indeed, called "Gabriel" at home) who replaces the angelic one as a speaker. The whole poem, with its recasting of foreground events in the dark light of the background, its radical poetic misprision of the matter of shadow (for Leonardo, shadow was never a matter of death), its obscure lesson about deaths and entrances, and its insistence on nature rather than grace, after all, is a triumphantly audacious replacement for the direct, at most two-fold, ostension of the undiscursive Gabriel in the painting.[14]

Ekphrasis, then, its own sort of dangerous supplement, has stood in for, represented, the image of a figure. Starting with a question, it ends in a hermeneutic realm of difficulty, darkness, and occulted light. As such, it is paradigmatic of the modern iconic or pictorial poem in its troping of its own formal scheme and rhetorical structure in representation of something spatial and structural it sees in the picture, as well as in the way it looks to other texts—here, the Psalm—as a filter through which the light of the painting is read, and, finally, in the way it regards its own breaking of silence, its own usurpation of the realm of image, speaking for it because it will not speak for itself.

Another superb example of the way in which an interpretive poem can affirm the complexity of an image by making it even more problematic is to be found in Swinburne's "Before the Mirror," ambiguously subtitled "Verses Written under a Picture" (composed there? inscribed there?). Whistler's *The Little White Girl: Symphony in White* in the Tate Gallery is a portrait of Jo Heffernan, the artist's model and mistress, done in 1864. The picture was marked by its affinities with French painting in the formal structures of its design, its loose treatment of surface, and in its allusions to Japanese art in the fan, the porcelain, and the placement of the flowers. Swinburne's ekphrasis moves its attention beyond these questions and addresses, in the first of its three sections, the theme of whiteness which had been privileged in Whistler's typical, polemically abstract title, allowing the anecdotal and pictorial only a secondary role:

> White rose in red rose-garden
> Is not so white;

6. *James Abbot McNeill Whistler,* The Little White Girl: Symphony in White, *no. 2, 1864, Tate Gallery. Art Resource, New York.*

Snowdrops that plead for pardon
   And pine for fright
Because the hard East blows
Over their maiden rows
   Grow not as this face grows from pale to bright.

Behind the veil, forbidden,
   Shut up from sight,
Love, is there sorrow hidden,
   Is there delight?
Is Joy thy dower or grief,
White rose of weary leaf,
   Late rose whose life is brief, whose loves are light?

Soft snows that hard winds harden
   Till each flake bite
Fill all the flowerless garden
   Whose flowers took flight
Long since when summer ceased,
And men rose up from feast,
   And warm west wind grew east, and warm day night.

The second section of the poem gives voice to the girl herself, or perhaps—and here the problem is part of the meaning—the mirrored image. It answers, obliquely and subtly, the questions in Part I about joy or grief by transcending those two alternatives, and allowing the meditation to sink into a contemplation of its own beauty:

"Come snow, come wind or thunder
   High up in air,
I watch my face, and wonder
   At my bright hair;
Nought else exalts or grieves
The rose at heart, that heaves
   With love of her own leaves and lips that pair.

"She knows not loves that kissed her
   She knows not where.

Art thou the ghost, my sister,
　　White sister there,
Am I the ghost, who knows?
My hand, a fallen rose,
　　Lies snow-white on white snows, and takes no care.

"I cannot see what pleasures
　　Or what pains were;
What pale new loves and treasures
　　New years will bear,
What beam will fall, what shower,
What grief or joy for dower;
　　But one thing knows the flower; the flower is fair."

Finally, the last section focusses on the mirror itself, rather than on the girl's relation to her own image, her other self, revealed in it; the poem moves inside the girl's reverie to the traces of the past that must inevitably emerge from its depths, even as the internal rhymes emerge in the ultimate line of each strophe. Swinburne's extravagant phonological patterning is never more effective—"Old loves and faded fears / Float down a stream that hears / The flowing of all men's tears beneath the sky"—and his characteristic semantic pairings and oppositions resonate delicately in this context of reciprocity and mirrored replication. The last resonance of the poem's title is that the text, ending in a fictive sound, itself holds up a mirror to the nature of picturing.

Glad, but not flushed with gladness,
　　Since joys go by;
Sad, but not bent with sadness,
　　Since sorrows die;
Deep in the gleaming glass
She sees all past things pass,
　　And all sweet life that was lie down and die.

There glowing ghosts of flowers
　　Draw down, draw nigh;
And wings of swift spent hours
　　Take flight and fly;

She sees by formless gleams,
She hears across cold streams,
    Dead mouths of many dreams that sing and sigh.

Face fallen and white throat lifted,
    With sleepless eye
She sees old loves that drifted,
    She knew not why,
Old loves and faded fears
Float down a stream that hears
    The flowing of all men's tears beneath the sky.

From being the engine of narcissistic contemplation, the mirror has become that of the seer of truths beyond that of the gazer's own beauty, like the mirror of the Lady of Shalott, like the glass of art itself.

Rossetti's strong misreading of Leonardo commits no empirical mistakes, save one crucial one of omission. But occasionally, through the same sort of ignorance that causes scholars to misattribute pictures or to title them in trivial error, a poem on an image may entail a mistaken reading, whether received or ad hoc. In Book III of *The Testament of Beauty* (1929), Robert Bridges calls up the image of the famous Titian in the Galleria Borghese usually called *Sacred and Profane Love*. Erwin Panofsky correctly identified the two figures: the nude one (not, as we might distinguish the terms, *naked*) is that of a heavenly Venus, *Venere Celeste,* and the other, clothed in fashionable Venetian dress, *Venere Volgare,* her allegorical complement.[15] (Panofsky suggested that the painting should be retitled *The Twin Venuses.*) Bridges gets this quite wrong—as well he might, given the received misinterpretation of the painting—and all the more so since his language too literally employs the interpretive modes of the iconographer. He evokes

        the great picture of the two Women at a Well,
    where Titian's young genius, devising a new thing,
    employ'd the plastic power to exhibit at once
    two diverse essences in their value and contrast;
    for while by the aesthetic idealisation of form
    his earthly love approacheth to celestial grace,

7. *Titian,* Sacred and Profane Love, *Borghese Gallery, Rome. Alinari / Art Resource, New York.*

his draped Uranian figure is by symbols veil'd,
and in pictorial Beauty suffereth defeat:
Yea, despite all her impregnable confidence
in the truth of her wisdom, as there she sitteth
beside the fountain, dazzlingly apparel'd, enthroned,
with thoughtful face impassiv, averting her head
as 'twer for fuller attention so to incline an ear
to the impartial hearing of the importunat plea
of the other, who over-against her on the cornice-plinth
posturing her wonted nakedness in sensuous ease,
leaneth her body to'ards her, and with imploring grace
urgeth the vain deprecation of her mortal prayer.

Giorgione, his master, already had gone to death
plague-stricken at prime, when Titian painted thatt picture,
donning his rival's mantle, and strode to higher fame—
yet not by this canvas; he who had it, hid it;
nor won it public favour when it came to light,
untill some mystic named it in the Italian tongue
L'AMOR SACRO E PROFANO, and so rightly divined;
for tho' ther is no record save the work of the brush
to tell the intention, yet what the mind wrought is there;
and who looketh thereon may see in the two left arms

the symbolism apportioning the main design;
for while the naked figure with extended arm
and outspredd palm vauntingly balanceth aloft
a little lamp, whose flame lost in the bright daylight
wasteth in the air, thatt other hath the arm bent down
and oppositely nerved, and clencheth with gloved hand
closely the cover'd vessel of her secret fire.
    Thus Titian hath pictured the main sense of my text,
and this truth: that as Beauty is all with Spirit twined,
so all obscenity is akin to the ugliness
which Art would outlaw; whence cometh thatt tinsel honour
and mimicry of beauty which is the attire of vice.

In seizing upon the mistaken reading of nudity as profane and clothed as sacred, Bridges still contrives, in the final lines, to trope against his own conception, by speaking of the "mimicry of beauty which is the attire of vice," and allowing an archaistic bit of personifying machinery to trip him up.[16] For the profane love is indeed attired in the painting. Nevertheless, Bridges is able to conclude his disquisition with a fecund poetic fable that reads more deeply and imagines more fully than in the more literary, polemical, and erroneous account of the female figures. I quote the end of Book 3, still on the Titian:

    Allegory is a cloudland inviting fancy
to lend significance to chancey shapes; and here
I deem not that the child, who playeth between the Loves
at Titian's well, was pictured by him with purpose
to show the first contact of love with boyhood's mind;
and yet never was symbol more deftly devised:
Mark how the child looking down on the water see'th
only a reflection of the realities—as 'twas
with the mortals in Plato's cave—nor more of them
than Moses saw of God; he can see but their backs,
save for a shifty glimpse of the pleading profil
of earthly Love (which also is subtle truth); and most
how in his play his plunged hand stirreth to and fro
both images together in a confused dazzle
of the dancing ripples as he gazeth intent.

Even Panofsky cannot do as well as this, writing over thirty-five years later of how "Cupid, stirring, and, as it were, homogenizing the water, may be presumed to symbolize the principle of harmonization of virtue of which the two forms of love represented by the two Venuses, though different in rank, are one in essence."[17]

Modernist poetry, in its revisionary stance against the whole nineteenth century, avoided ekphrastic genres. We might except Yeats, an overt Rossettian, and William Carlos Williams who, after some remarkable meditations on the consequences of cubism for poetics like those in *Spring and All,* produced a good many rather humdrum ekphrastic poems on Brueghel, and a more interesting meditation on the so-called Unicorn Tapestries at the Cloisters in New York. Wallace Stevens is full of notional ekphrasis: it is one of his canonical rhetorical modes (one has only, for example, to consider the opening stanza of "Sunday Morning" in this context to hear it as evocative catalogue copy for an exhibition catalogue, and the problematically identified "She" falls into place). But I should like to dwell in some detail on one powerful and original confrontation with an image which, with considerable audacity, makes that image speak up, and yet recursively meditates upon the poetic imagination's capacities for moralizing.

Marianne Moore's poem on an emblematic tapestry in the Burrell Collection in Glasgow propounds a moral riddle lurking both about and within its hermeneutic one. A late fifteenth-century representation of "Charity Overcoming Envy" (the title of Moore's poem) in a millefleurs setting elicits immediate questions of any viewer: Who is this Charity mounted on a triumphal elephant and armed with a sword, menacing an enemy she has already chopped at and is now, brightly and coolly, about to cut again? Where is her usual flame, candle, flaming heart, or cornucopia? Why is she not in the process of doing one of the six works of mercy (attending to the hungry, the thirsty, the stranger, the naked, the sick, the prisoner [Matt. 25:35–37])? And what sort of envy is manifest in this male figure?—*Invidia,* from Ovid on, is usually a nasty looking woman (because of the gender of the noun in Latin), feeding on snakes or proverbially "eating her heart out." Even Spenser's male and malicious "Envie [who] rode / Vpon a rauenous wolfe, and still did chaw / Betweene his cankred teeth a venomous toad," his clothing "ypainted full of eyes" and maturing in his bosome secretly a snake,

8. *Late fifteenth century,* Charity Overcoming Envy, *tapestry, The Burrell Collection, Glasgow.*

is not this personage.[18] His dog, rejoicing in the evil befalling him even as his rider does, according to the Latin inscription,[19] is familiar from other images. Charity has scratched him: is he now about to lose his right hand?

Moore's poem asks none of the usual ekphrastic questions of the mute Other of the image, so conventional but yet imaginatively forceful, in poems of this kind. Instead, she questions the reader in indirect rhetorical fashion: "Have you time for a story / (depicted in tapestry)?" she asks, in a seven-syllable rhyming couplet she will not return to in the poem—almost as if this prominently-framed utterance were her version of the *titulus* in the tapestry. She then proceeds to tell her own tale, starting out with an echo of the kind of workaday ekphrastic prose one finds in an exhibition catalogue, occasionally almost literally quoting from curatorial comment. Yeats, in "Lapis Lazuli," evokes this sort of prose:

> Two Chinamen, behind them a third,
> Are carved in lapis lazuli,
> Over them flies a long-legged bird
> A symbol of longevity;
> The third, doubtless a serving-man,
> Carries a musical instrument.[20]

(The "doubtless" is wonderful here.) And so, Moore:

> Charity, riding an elephant,
> on a "mosaic of flowers," faces Envy,
> the flowers "bunched together, not rooted."

But then her story-telling takes over, with its radical moral analysis of envy coming at once:

> Envy, on a dog, is worn down by obsession,
> his greed (since of things owned by others
> he can only take *some*). Crouching uneasily
> in the flowered filigree, among wide weeds
>   indented by scallops that swirl,
> little flattened-out sunflowers,
> thin arched coral stems, and—ribbed horizontally—
> slivers of green, Envy, on his dog,
>   looks up at the elephant,
> cowering away from her, his cheek scarcely scratched.
>   He is saying, "O Charity, pity me, Deity!
>   O pitiless Destiny,
>   what will become of me,

maimed by Charity—*Caritas*—sword unsheathed
over me yet? Blood stains my cheek. I am hurt."
In chest armor over chain mail, a steel shirt
to the knee, he repeats, "I am hurt."
The elephant, at no time borne down by self-pity,
    convinces the victim
that Destiny is not devising a plot.

The problem is mastered—insupportably
tiring when it was impending.

Deliverance accounts for what sounds like an axiom.
    The Gordian knot need not be cut.[21]

The final Gordian knot, in its echo of negation, seems to have been tied by, and with, the poem itself, the latter half of which is purely Moore's story of what Envy cries out. It is marked by extravagant diction, strange, sporadic, and cumulative rhyming, the invocation by the invidious knight of Destiny—a goddess not shown in the tapestry because she may or may not have been among its weavers—and the ad hoc pattern of attributes, of Envy "worn down by obsession" and the Elephant, "at no time borne down by self-pity." That elephant, with its own version of a gaze out of the picture, at first anomalous in its iconography, on second thought emblematic of both temperance and douceur,[22] has a charming unnaturalness for a modern viewer. Yet Moore's story has it "convincing the victim"—with her typical wordplay she enacts a victory with the etymon of conquest in the gentler "convince" only morally equivalent of the warlike.

And yet the elephant, startling and lovely to our gaze, had, for Moore, reflective weight and substance as well. Her early "Melancthon" (originally entitled, with its translation, "Black Earth" in *Observations*) is hardly a white elephant, but rather a figure of power, who observes

    nevertheless I
    perceive feats of strength to be inexplicable after
    all; and I am on my guard; external poise, it

has its centre
well nurtured—we know
   where—in pride; but spiritual poise, it has its centre where?[23]

And in "Elephants" from *Nevertheless,* she had read the positions of
the elephant's trunk almost as a Renaissance impresa or emblem
might have:

With trunk tucked up compactly—the elephant's
sign of defeat—he resisted, but is the child
of reason now. His straight trunk seems to say: when
what we hoped for came to nothing, we revived.
As loss could not ever alter Socrates'
tranquillity, equanimity's contrived

by the elephant . . .[24]

But the trunk of Charity's mount signals another condition entirely,
and there is something at once winsome and sad-eyed about him.
Patricia Willis, who has provided so much interesting information
about Moore's many allusions to pictures, has suggested that the
death of e.e. cummings in 1962, while Moore was abroad working
on the tapestry poem, may have reminded her of the elephant as
cummings's personal totem, in which case the victim to be con-
vinced "that Destiny is not devising a plot" could seem to be the
mourning friend, the poet herself, who immediately submits, like
Wordsworth in the "Elegiac Stanzas," to "a new control."[25]

    But then the poem continues past the picture, to an allegory of its
own. Mastering a steed, or a canonical enemy, is a matter *in* the tapestry, but mastering a conceptual problem is a matter *of* the tapestry
and the image with its own clearly labelled parable. Interpretive
problems such as the reading of the tapestry with its Latin and its
profusion of flowers and tiny enigmas—like that of the sword's
point being lost behind the inscription (just about at *"hoc nephas"*)
succumb to the engagement of a sword-like pen mounted on meditative reading. What sounds like an axiom—"charity overcomes
envy"—is revealed as the product of an etiological story after all.
Yet the picture is nonetheless timeless in that the action portrayed in
it is continual, being wrought anew in every human instance. Each

of Moore's last three tiny struggles (a couplet and then two single lines, all isolated like strophes) glosses the text above it, in a sequence of moralizations allusive of the medieval *applicatio* tacked on to an exemplum or tale. The very last line proclaims the general triumph of poetry, not over image or picture, but over the sword of the conqueror—Alexander, or even Charity—a triumph of *over-coming* at the hands of *becoming*, neither particularly charitable nor envious, but distanced nobly in the way in which Moore's own actual moral tone always remains. The mastery is achieved without agon; rather than poetry killing falsehood at some risk to its own truthfulness—so Bellerophon on Pegasus contra the Chimera—instead, the deliverances of language itself. The poem's very structure of *titulus,* ekphrasis, reading of spoken language into the world of flowers, and layers of inscription at the end, is itself a trope of the tapestry's orders of woven lines, rubrics, and images. Plucking out of the realm of the tapestry the internal rhymes of the ultimate line of the ekphrasis proper—"Destiny is not devising a plot"—the whole, poem's final line, as was observed before, puns insouciantly on the name of the emblematic figure of the problem: "The Gordian knot need not be cut." And, by final implication (inevitable for a poet who had alluded so often to painting and sculpture and photography), anima of text need not struggle with *corpo* of image in some perverse psychomachia. The deliverance has been one of protecting *corpo* from itself, and rescuing the very personhood of allegory from captivity by the reductive language of its own inscriptions. The poem generates an ultimate parable about ekphrasis itself. And in answer to its opening question—have we time for a story?—a reader can return a strong "Yes." We have gotten several stories for the price of one; that is to say, this has been a real poem.

Ekphrastic poetry has become so conventional a genre in contemporary verse that almost every manuscript I have been shown in recent years has included the obligatory poem on a Brueghel or Hopper or Magritte; like most conventional literature in verse, they are of little interest. But there are remarkable poems on specific images by Elizabeth Bishop, Robert Lowell, Delmore Schwartz, Anthony Hecht, Daryl Hine, and others. Particularly interesting are James Merrill's (mentioned earlier) and Randall Jarrell's poem on Dürer's *The Knight, Death and the Devil,* and Richard Howard's wonderful, willful misreading of Caspar David Friedrich's *The Chalk*

Cliffs of Rügen. Howard knowingly substitutes for the established identities of the three figures in the painting (the artist, his wife, and brother) a fictional trio of "Ottilie," "Walther," and "Franz." The poem's rambling dramatic monologue reconstructs the event, what the figures have just been and are now doing, and their remarks on art and life in conversation during a sort of high-minded picnic. Then, after 115 lines, it concludes with a reading of the landscape in which the narrator—one of Friedrich's typical *Rückfiguren,* or figures seen from behind facing the scene as a surrogate for the viewers of the painting—finally deals with his own identity:

> There are two boats
> on the Hiddensee. The sun,
> hewing the cliffs, is mighty now. Perhaps
> we have discovered what their shape, sharp
> against the water beyond,
> reminds us of: it is a womb, a birth,
> a spanning of the earth no longer
> just a grave, delivering
> Ottilie splayed against her alder-stump,
> and Walther sprawled at the verge, and Franz
> under his birch. So we are
> born, each alone, in chaos while that waiting
> silence glows.
> And you will never know
> which of us has told you this.[26]

We are reminded at one instant that we have suspended the question of who the narrator has been and that we are not to find out, and the poem ends up by leading us back into the major problem of those Friedrich figures with their faces—and their identities—always averted from our knowledge and our gaze. It is at once a fine dramatic and a brilliant ekphrastic stroke.

Howard has written several fine iconic poems, including a long series addressing photographs by Nadar; David Ferry's poems on photographs by Eakins are also memorable. W. D. Snodgrass has some meditative poems on paintings by modern French masters, including an unusually powerful one on Matisse's *Le Studio rouge* of 1911. Douglas Crase has a splendid poem on Jackson Pollock's *Blue*

Poles. It enters the painting so totally—even in the opening act of seeming to have left it behind—that its reading of where the present place of description in fact is remains totally figurative. Crase opens with an obvious point about scale (the vastness of the painting is indeed initially most prominent), analogous to Swinburne's topic of whiteness in the Whistler painting. But then his poem moves into its unrelenting trope of mapped landscape:

> What we bring back is the sense of the size of it,
> Potential as something permanent is, the way a road map
> Of even the oldest state suggests in its tangled details
> The extent of a country in which topography and settlement
> Interrupt only at random into a personal view . . .[27]

Crase's poem implicitly connects the relation of reading (an image) and painting with that of mapping a place, and its narrative unfolding entails going off into a mapped landscape even as the voluble text wanders into the silent painting, particularly this vast one, like a huge map of a landscape it is at one with.

But there is little time left, and I shall conclude these observations with a return to a romantic text, fascinatingly problematic in its form and in the contemporary theoretical questions it raises. A profound and amusing romantic undoing of the merely picturesque, it nevertheless avoids any touch of the older sublime. It is from a series of prose poems by Leigh Hunt (published in *The Keepsake*, 1828) called "Dreams on the Borders of the Land of Poetry."[28] The seventh one, "An Evening Landscape," opens with a question suggesting that what follows will be a sort of shaped poem, an emblem or impresa whose image is made up of its own motto, as it were. But Hunt's fancy raises more interesting questions for ekphrastic poetry. Here it is entire:

> Did any body ever think of painting a picture in writing? I mean literally so, marking the localities as in a map.
>
> The other evening I sat in a landscape that would have enchanted Cuyp.
>
> Scene—a broken heath, with hills in the distance. The immediate picture stood thus, the top and the bottom of it being nearly on a level in the perspective:

> Trees in a sunset, at no great distance from the foreground
> A group of cattle under them, party-coloured,
> principally red, standing on a small landing place;
> the Sun coming upon them through the trees.
> A rising ground   A rising ground
>   Broken ground.
> with trees.   with trees.
> Another landing place, nearly on a level
> with the cows, the spectator sitting and looking at them.

The Sun came warm and serious on the glowing red of the cattle, as if recognizing their evening hues; and every thing appeared full of that quiet spirit of consciousness, with which Nature seems rewarded at the close of its day labours.

This "picture painted in writing" frames a good, deep joke about ekphrasis, to which I'll return in a moment. But first, it may be observed that the larger issue of art inventing nature is proleptic here of Wilde and Whistler (Wilde, in "The Decay of Lying" when he observes that English sunsets had learned to imitate Turner; Whistler, when to someone remarking that an evening walk along the Embankment has revealed a prospect just like one of his Thames *Nocturnes,* he replied "Ah yes, madam, Nature is creeping up.")that Nature had crept up to Cuyp—probably by the mid-eighteenth century in England, is figuratively confirmed by the sun's coming "warm and serious on the glowing red of the cattle, as if recognizing their evening hues." And as if recognizing their kinship in pigment.

The little lesson about ekphrasis, on the other hand, is less outrageous but more original. The typographic "scene" is not, indeed, a *calligramme* of the notional painting itself: Cuyp would have had a lot of sky, and to correct for this, we should have had to double the height of the ruled borders and fill the top with something like

---

A   Dutch   Sky   with

Bunched and

L a y e r e d
C l o u d s

- -

Instead, we have what is unambiguously *text*. The largest objectified visual masses—the trees—come first in an order of catalogu-
ing, extending verse-like down the page. Then too, word-and-line
order can only momentarily serve as troped figures for the visual
images their words designate. Trees, cattle and "landing place," in
the first three "lines" are all named in lines of text correspondingly
layered, and the phrase "under them" is self-descriptive. But in line
four, the sun is no longer "under," and the two extensions of "rising
ground / with trees" on either side require something like Miltonic
verse: something like "And, with other trees, / A rising ground"
would map them more appropriately. (It would be irrelevant, however, to demand that Hunt anticipate Apollinaire, and have the type
set up as "Br$_{ok}$en gr$_o$und," or the like." The non-functional,
counter-productive "enjambment" of "nearly on a level / with the
cows," while probably so arranged for the trivial symmetry of a
traditional inscription-patern,[29] would have been far more effective
in a pseudo-pictorial way had the line broken at "level with / the
cows," thus "nearly" placing the cows on—*in*—the same line of
type as the spectator's viewpoint. We may also observe that the
ruled box includes said spectator, as if C. D. Friedrich-like, from
behind, as a Dutch landscape would not. The presence in and outside of the scene of the spectator—the painter-poet—is finally connected with "that quiet spirit of consciousness with which Nature
seems rewarded at the close of its day labours"—the consciousness
itself ambiguously bestowed upon the scene, and thus to inhere in
it, until darkness falls. And what can so reward nature but poetry
itself, pretending to do the more obviously but less eternally rewarding work of painting?

Ekphrasis ordinarily purports to speak up for the silent picture,
to make it speak out in some way. But poems are writing, and what
"speaks" in iconic poems is their use of a complex set of generic,
schematic, formal, and other rhetorical conventions. These can
range from the elemental way in which lines of verse follow by
being stacked under each other, and having to be read downwards
in sequence, to the intricate sort of allegorizing of sonnet structure
as foreground-background, event and interpretation, letter and ana-
goge, that we saw in the parable of octave-sestet in Rossetti's sonnet
on the Leonardo painting. All ekphrastic writing must exploit rhetorical design as well as, more obviously: the scale of writing as well

as of reading the image (Horace's *ut pictura poesis* first applied to *scale*); the identification—and thereby, often, the invention—of parts or elements; selection among these; ascriptions of primariness and secondariness, of relative importance or prominence; the emergence of some explanatory or interpretive agenda, and so forth. But whether one starts out one's analytic or critical writing with what would be, interpretively speaking, "the bottom line," or else gradually argues toward it, the structure and form of poetic argument are another matter. There the text's own schemes and tropes elicit or insinuate meanings from or in the image, and the moment of gazing at—and being gazed at by—any work of art becomes an authentic poetic occasion, as ennobling for poetry from Wordsworth and Coleridge to our own time as any epiphanic flash of transcendence from the surfaces of the ordinary, focussed and empowered by one's own depths. An ekphrastic poem is not occasional in the way a hireling laureate's birthday ode might be, but rather, for a true poet, the scene of the occurrence of some internal occasion. The silence of images may constitute anything from a Gorgon's deadly stare to the wondrous labyrinth of a Gordian knot, from an erotic object to be possessed by language, to a rebuking one, from a virginal object untouched yet by interpretation to a noble but fallen captive, ill-used by false expositors. In any case, the poem engaged in an encounter with the presence of such otherness—such an absence of the body of discourse—can always touch upon the problematic nature of its own language, of its own consciousness. I conclude by glossing this observation with some lines that Coleridge appended (and, later on, misquoted) to a scene of his play, *Remorse,* in praise of Titian,

Who, like a second and more lovely Nature,
By the sweet mystery of lines and colours
Changed the blank canvas to a magic mirror,
That made the absent present; and to shadows
Gave light, depth, substance, bloom, yea, thought and motion.[30]

But they apply as well at one remove, to the figurative painting of verse, turning the blank page to a mirror of the nature of art.

Notes

1. W. J. T. Mitchell, *Iconology: Image, Text, Ideology* (Chicago: University of Chicago Press, 1986), 47–150 explores the groundwork of text-image relations. In an unpublished essay he has concentrated on the stance of poems toward visual images.

2. John Hollander, "The Poetics of Ekphrasis," *Word and Image* 4:1 (1988), 209–19. Also see my preliminary investigation of a number of poem-picture pairings in "Words on Pictures," *Art and Antiques* 1:1 (1984): 80–91.

3. Hollander, 210–211.

4. The fashionable use today of "gaze" in critical studies of film and photography as well as of painting of the eighteenth and nineteenth centuries seems to have come, perhaps via Jacques Lacan, from Sartre's pages on "*le regard*" in *L'Être et le Néant*, but originally Englished by Hazel Barnes in her 1956 version as "the look."

5. The text is corrupt, and I have filled a lacuna here with a bracketed suggestion.

6. S. T. Coleridge, "On the principles of Genial Criticism Concerning the Fine Arts" (1814), repr. in W. J. Bate, ed., *Criticism: The Major Texts* (New York: Harcourt Brace Jovanovich, 1970), 364–375. Allston's poem was published in *The Sylphs of the Seasons, and Other Poems* (London, 1813); my text is from his *Lectures on Art* (New York, 1850). I am grateful to paul H. Fry for pointing me to this passage. See also Carl Woodring, "What Coleridge Thought of Pictures," in Karl Kroeber and William Walling, eds., *Images of Romanticism* (New Haven: Yale University Press, 1978), 91–106.

7. Jean H. Hagstrum, *The Sister Arts* (Chicago: University of Chicago Press, 17–18, suggests this description for poems on pictures generally.

8. See *The Letters of William and Dorothy Wordsworth,* 7 vols., ed. C. L. Shaver, M. Moorman, and A. Hill, 2nd ed. (Oxford: Oxford University Press, 1967–1982), 2:506–507.

9. James A. W. Heffernan, in a forthcoming article in *Word and Image*.

10. See W. M. Rossetti's note on this poem in his edition of his brother's *Works* (London, 1911), 661.

11. "*Les pauvres gueux pleins de bonadventures / Ne portent rien que des Choses futures.*" The etching is Lieure no. 374.

12. Samuel Rogers, "To the Fragment of a Statue of Hercules Commonly Called the Torso" (1806), in *Poetical Works* (London, 1892), 170.

13. Hersey has suggested that Rossetti had added the crowd of souls to the ekphrasis of the painting from memories of the *Adoration* by Leonardo in the Uffizi.

14. See, e.g., the discussion in Moshe Barasch, *Light and Color in the Italian Rennaissance Theory of Art* (New York: New York University Press, 1978), 52–55. And yet a passage from the Arundel ms. in the British Library, cited by Robert Payne in his *Leonardo da Vinci* (Garden City, N.Y.: Doubleday, 1978), 75, from an uncompleted *novella* by Leonardo, has its narrator "wandering for

some time among the shadowy rocks" and coming upon a cavern, before which he hesitates, there having been awakened in him "two emotions, fear and longing—fear of the dark, threatening cave, and longing to see whether some marvellous thing lay inside."

15. Erwin Panofsky, *Studies in Iconology* (New York: Oxford University Press, 1939), 150–160; and further, in his *Problems in Titian* (New York: New York University Press, 1969), 110–119.

16. On the significance of the parallel oppositions of drapery/clothing: nudity/nakedness, see Anne Hollander, *Seeing through Clothes* (New York: Viking, 1978), chapters 1 and 2, passim, and particularly, 157–159, 448.

17. Panofsky, *Titian,* 116–117.

18. Edmund Spenser, *The Faerie Queene,* 1.4.30–31. A later, female representation of Envy appears with her sister, Detraction, in Book 5.

19. The somewhat problematic inscription appears to read: INVIDI DOLOR ANIMI DE PROSPERIS EST PROXIMI GAUDENS EIUS DE MALIS [MALO?] UT CANIS SED HOC ELEPHAS NESCIT VINCIT ET HOC NEPHAS CARITAS FRACERI, perhaps to be rendered as "The sorrow of the envious soul is at the prosperity of its neighbor; it rejoices at the evil that befalls him, like the dog. But the elephant does not know this. And Charity conquers that evil [smashing it?]."

20. W. B. Yeats, "Lapis Lazuli," lines 37–42, in *The Poems of W. B. Yeats,* ed. Richard J. Finneran (New York: Macmillan, 1983), 245.

21. Text from Marianne Moore, *The Complete Poems* (Macmillan/Viking: New York, 1981), 216–217. The poem as it originally appeared in *The New Yorker,* March 30, 1963, reads at one point: "daisies, pink harebells, little flattened-out / sunflowers, thin arched coral stems, and— / ribbed horizontally—".

22. As, for example, in the French translation of Valeriano's *Hieroglyphica* by Jean de Montylard (Lyon, 1615), B6v; the elephant is also made to embody temperance, equity, and other virtues in Valeriano's lengthy discussion.

23. Marianne Moore, *Collected Poems* (New York: Macmillan, 1961), 46–47.

24. *Collected Poems,* 130.

25. In her catalogue for an exhibition at the Rosenbach Museum and Library, *Vision into Verse* (Philadelphia, 1987) Willis illustrates a range of allusive—if not all actually ekphrastic—instances in Moore's poetry, including poems that engage Leonardo's St. Jerome, a Giorgione self-portrait, a Bewick wood-engraving, an Isaac Oliver miniature, A. B. Durand's *Kindred Spirits,* and many anonymous photographs and images from advertising, etc. Her comment on the poem under discussion is on p. 87. Moore had been sent a postcard of the tapestry by a friend, Lawrence Scott, and had written to the Burrell Collection for more cards; she received with them two copies of *The Scottish Art Review* (No. 6, 1957) with a color reproduction and a discussion of the tapestry. Moore's mode of direct quotation, elegantly analyzed by Elizabeth Gregory in her 1989 Yale dissertation, often entails the oblique and sometimes fictive use of seemingly direct transcription. William Wells, the author of the *Scottish Art Review* note, refers to tapestries like this one, "characterized by a dark blue ground covered with a dense mosaic of naturalistically drawn

flowers . . . the flowers are not part of a meadow or garden, i.e. they are not rooted in the soil, but are massed together without connection as on a wallpaper or silk fabric . . ." The reader will observe that neither "direct" quotation in the poem is indeed that, and that Moore's "bunched" for the original "massed" is significant.

26. Richard Howard, "The Chalk Cliffs of Rügen," in *Findings* (New York: Atheneum, 1971), 17.

27. Douglas Crase, "Blue Poles," in *The Revisionist* (Boston: Little, Brown, 1981), 69.

28. *The Keepsake* (London, 1828), 234–241. Edmund Blunden, in *Leigh Hunt, A Biography* (London, 1930), 229, remarks that "These are aphorisms and something more." They are, I think, true prose poems (unlike, say, the Ossianic texts, full of accentual-syllabic, often anapestic, cadences—*vers chachés,* as it were). The publication of Hunt's prose poems antedate that of Aloysius Bertrand's *Gaspard de la Nuit* by two years.

29. See John Sparrow, *Line Upon Line* (Cambridge: Cambridge University Press, 1967) for a discussion of this format.

30. Samuel Taylor Coleridge, *Remorse,* in *Complete Poetical Works,* 2 vols., ed. E. H. Coleridge (Oxford: Clarendon Press, 1912), 2:842.

Skies of the City
A Poetry Reading

❧

Robert Pinsky

Some images seem so inexhaustibly rich that a billion appeals to them cannot pound them entirely into cliché. Not all the desperate force and repetition of the movies, and not even the furtive greed for cheap feelings of our own hearts seem quite able to deplete these wells of emotion. Such an image is the city sky: balmy and clear or hung with poison vapors, in fleeting morning calm or the fiery violence of noon, dreamy and sensual at dusk or immense and enigmatically charged at night.

In the quick, skeletal anthology of the city sky which I will present to you, a central perspective will be the view from the bridge. I mean to suggest that the meaning of the sky over the city and the meaning of the city bridge are one meaning, having to do with elevation above the earth and return, the opening up of spatial perspective and the vital compression of a conduit. It is a meaning invented by the romantics, and I think that in the permutations and developments of two centuries it has changed remarkably little.

* * *

First, still in the countryside (but precisely not the wilderness) here is one of the most indelible skies of the period, the sky over the farms near Tintern Abbey, in Wales, in July of 1798:

Five years have passed, five summers, with the length
Of five long winters! and again I hear
These waters, rolling from their mountain-springs
With a soft inland murmur. Once again
Do I behold these steep and lofty cliffs,
That on a wild secluded scene impress
Thoughts of more deep seclusion; and connect
The landscape with the quiet of the sky.
The day is come when I again repose
Here, under this dark sycamore, and view
These plots of cottage ground, these orchard tufts,
Which at this season, with their unripe fruits,
Are clad in one green hue, and lose themselves
'Mid groves and copses. Once again I see
These hedgerows, hardly hedgerows, little lines
Of sportive wood run wild; these pastoral farms,
Green to the very door; and wreaths of smoke
Sent up, in silence, from among the trees!
With some uncertain notice, as might seem
Of vagrant dwellers in the houseless woods,
Or of some Hermit's cave, where by his fire
The Hermit sits alone.

These lines embody, quite purely, one of the two romantic modes of dealing with human artifacts and buildings: momentarily, blessedly, architecture and farming blend imperceptibly into the summer vegetation. On this day, human boundaries and human labor are all but invisible: the hedgerows are hardly hedgerows, they blend into the surrounding green woods, as the orchard blends into a single green because mid-July comes after the great clouds of white blossom, and before the bright red fruit. The farms are green to their very doors, an apparent ease that also reminds us that hedgerows are boundary markers, that orchards have been planned toward harvest, and that doorways bear the wearing scuffle of traffic. The ease and quiet and blending are all presented as temporary or illusory, with a single exception: the quiet of the sky. The relatively quiet landscape is connected to that absolute, literally transcendant quiet by the cliffs that guide the eye upward, providing between the scene of human affairs and the overarching calm of the sky a kind of bridge.

Wordsworth's lines, in other words, remind us that our life can only approach, and never attain, the quiet of the sky. The smoke that repeats the bridging gesture of the cliffs is not, in fact, the smoke of an imaginary houseless hermit, but the smoke of farm-houses, and presumably, since the month is July, the smoke not of heating (even in Wales) but of mundane cooking fires. Appropri-ately as the introduction to a poem of spiritual struggle and doubt, Wordsworth invokes the sky as a supreme natural image of peace, but he evokes it across a gulf. The gulf is nearly bridged, the sky for the moment "connected" to the household doors and hearths.

* * *

Now here is the other, opposite romantic vision of human build-ing and making, also in a familiar example:

LONDON

I wander thro' each charter'd street,
Near where the charter'd Thames does flow,
And mark in every face I meet
Marks of weakness, marks of woe.

In every cry of every man,
In every Infant's cry of fear,
In every voice, in every ban,
The mind-forg'd manacles I hear:

How the Chimney-sweeper's cry
Every blackning Church appalls,
And the hapless Soldier's sigh,
Runs in blood down Palace walls.

But most thro' midnight streets I hear
How the youthful Harlot's curse
Blasts the new-born Infant's tear
And blights with plagues the Marriage hearse.

The forces of revolution and repression, overt here, are doubtless behind or beneath Wordsworth's teasing pastoral dream of hedgerows that are barely hedgerows, as if to imagine boundaries and conventions that would somehow be barely boundaries and conventions. Here in Blake's poem the church, the palace, the charter, the forgings of the mind, have blighted and marked not only the faces and voices, but the very river and the new-born infant's tear. With "every" and "every" and "every" again, the poem insists upon the universality of the city, enveloping every quality and variety of life. Its institutions not only envelop, they also universally mark and blacken. These social forces are not imaginary or chimerical, but quite real: the violent disarray of revolution will turn one of these poets reactionary; the other will stand trial on charges of sedition.

But just as the undertow in Wordsworth's account of pastoral peace is a certain measure of disquiet, Blake's poem generates—at least from the perspective of all our subsequent art about cities—an odd excitement and even glamor: midnight traffic; birth, marriage and death compressed in place and time; youthful harlots; violence; the streets by the river; the caverns of palace walls and blackening churches, funneling the population, diverse yet linked by the mysteriously animating charter or heart of the city. In this selective and distorted account of Blake's poem, I am appealing to what we might call the Romance of the city as a live atmosphere: a quality of feeling based on the urban flowing together of squalor and allure, hemmed-in darkness and sudden, outsize vaultings into space. The process of romantic art, in the rest of the poems I will read to you, is to infuse the cursed city of Blake's "London" with some of the emotional force Wordsworth finds in the orchards, the cliffs, the smoke rising from the woods into the quiet sky.

*   *   *

That is, in its fully developed form the Romance of the city takes something from the teasing, fragile pastoral calm in the opening lines of Wordsworth's poem, on one side, and from the revolutionary ardor and urban claustrophobia of Blake's poem, on the other. All of this takes place under the contrasting, yet reflective vault of the sky. Another Wordsworth poem illustrates that formulation:

COMPOSED UPON WESTMINSTER BRIDGE, SEPTEMBER 3, 1802

Earth has not anything to show more fair:
Dull would be he of soul who could pass by
A sight so touching in its majesty;
This City now doth, like a garment, wear
The beauty of the morning; silent, bare,
Ships, towers, domes, theaters, and temples lie
Open unto the fields, and to the sky;
All bright and glittering in the smokeless air.
Never did sun more beautifully steep
In his first splendor, valley, rock, or hill;
Ne'er saw I, never felt, a calm so deep!
The river glideth at his own sweet will:
Dear God! the very houses are asleep;
And all that mighty heart is lying still.

This poem presents the Romance of the city as a fresh discovery. The seemingly banal terms "fair," "touching," "beauty," "beautifully" come to life partly because they are so artfully deployed in relation to words that emphasize the city's rare stillness and its immensity: touching in its majesty, and the majesty evoked partly by the wonderful catalogue of "ships, towers, domes, theaters, and temples." The city's beauty under the sun and quiet and clear air is touching exactly because it is rare and temporary: the ships will sail in and out, the towers and domes will be crowded and busy, the theaters and temples will raise a deafening babble of noises and voices, as before. As before, the sun will be blocked, the air will be smokey. Because all of this is true, and because the city is beautiful in sleep, and open to the sky, Wordsworth can perceive with a shock of awe that the city is alive: it is a heart.

* * *

That heart, still at this moment seen from the bridge on a particular morning, but nevertheless a brimming pump, is a romantic discovery that penetrates our books and movies. It is the brooding space of Dickens, cruel and magnetic, and in the spirit of Dickens it is also the alluring city of *film noir,* the lonely New York or San

Francisco or London of literary and cinematic detectives, Sherlock Holmes and Philip Marlowe, the animated, wounded Vienna of Carol Reed's *The Third Man*. This city, a pump of cries and silences, is the poetic city we inherit from the nineteenth century. It stirs in the nightmare of Blake's "London," almost against Blake's will, and lives quite clearly in the briefly ideal moment of Wordsworth's "Composed upon Westminster Bridge." Here is that city and its dark romance in what seems to me quite pure form, a sonnet of Charles Baudelaire:

RECUEILLEMENT

Sois sage, ô ma Douleur, et tiens-tois plus tranquille.
Tu réclamais le Soir; il descend; le voici:
Une atmosphère obscure enveloppe la ville,
Aux uns portant la paix, aux autres le souci.

Pendant que des mortels la multitude vile,
Sous le fouet du Plaisir, ce bourreau sans merci,
Va cueillir des remords dans la fête servile,
Ma douleur, donne-moi la main; viens par ici,

Loin d'eux. Vois se pencher les défuntes Années,
Sur les balcons du ciel, en robes surannées;
Surgir de fond des eaux le Regret souriant;

Le Soleil moribond s'endormir sous une arche,
Et, comme un long linceul traînant à l'Orient,
Entends, ma chère, entends la douce Nuit qui marche.

In English (my translation):

Hush, and behave yourself, O my Sorrow: be calm.
You cried for night to fall, and now here it is:
The deepening air of dusk envelops the town,
Bringing night's peace to some, to others, night's unease.

Now, while the herd of mortals, many and mean,
Under that torturer Pleasure's merciless whip
Go culling their flunkey's treat, remorse, again,
Come give me your hand, my Sorrow, we won't stop

Anywhere near them. Look: the spent years lean
From balconies of cloud in their dated dresses;
Surging from the dark water, Regret smiles, and rises;

Under an archway, the dying sun beds down;
And, like a long shroud trailing from the east—listen,
My dear one, listen how softly the night comes on.

Why is the city more beautiful if Baudelaire imagines for us that the clouds are balconies from which past years lean coquettishly and mockingly and sadly, like dead ladies, or like whores in last year's dresses? To see the fading sun as an ailing derelict going to sleep under an arch, or conversely to see the derelict as the sun, is to see the city as a living thing, a resolutely pumping heart wedded to the natural drama of the sky. If the moon can be seen to come up like a revenant suicide rising from the water where she drowned, with a pale smile, then the city as a heart has been made visible. Here it is not "lying still" as Wordsworth sees it from Westminster Bridge, but full of the dynamic, repellent movement, woe, sighs, curses, and blood marked by Blake. In Baudelaire's sonnet something like Wordsworth's open, clear perspective yields a vision into the tortured, animated streets of Blake's poem: a kind of Wordsworth sky over Blake's streets, to stretch the point a little. The clouds, the sun, the moon are so interpenetrated with the life of the city that the sky is like a calm mirror of the great heart, the pump that blackens, is chartered, is bloody or blighted. Baudelaire, unlike the earlier English romantics, explicitly recognizes the rather terrible sexual sweetness and spiritual excitement that mirror displays. The Romance he reads in the sky says that the city is flawed and squalid, but also sublime and alive, even in the midst of his own withdrawal from life.

* * *

Here is an ecstatic, Christian transformation of that Romance, mightily packed with imagery of the modern commercial city and of the Industrial Revolution:

GOD'S GRANDEUR

The world is charged with the grandeur of God.
    It will flame out, like shining from shook foil;
    It gathers to a greatness, like the ooze of oil
Crushed. Why do men then now not reck his rod?

Generations have trod, have trod, have trod;
    And all is seared with trade; bleared, smeared with toil;
    And wears man's smudge and shares man's smell: the soil
Is bare now, nor can foot feel, being shod.

And for all this, nature is never spent;
    There lives the dearest freshness deep down things;
And though the last light off the black West went
    Oh, morning, at the brown brink eastward springs—
Because the Holy Ghost over the bent
    World broods with warm breast and with ah! bright wings.

I've tried to look at Baudelaire's sonnet as an eroticized sublimated skyscape, transforming the oppressed, bloodied, prostituted, and chartered night of Blake's "London." In this sonnet, Gerard Manley Hopkins creates a sky that implicitly goes further, and transforms earthly energies suggestive of industrialism and air pollution: soil stripped bare; jets of flame; rippling and shining sheet metal; crushed oil; the smells and stains of labor; the searing emanations of trade. The images of redemption and energy are not outside this terrifying life, but in it, and of the industrial earth, "charged" like a responsibility and like built-up electrical energy. Baudelaire's sunset embodies a sublime vision of whores and dying bums. The sunrise of Hopkins—with "brown brink" suggesting a cloud of industrial smoke—presents the streaks and colors of the sun, seen through the air full of coalsmoke, as an image of the Holy Ghost. Even the searing and blearing, the scorched soil and overtrodden earth, are charged with sublime energy. The exclamation "ah!" wonders at that energy in a way like the startled "Dear God!" of Wordsworth on Westminster Bridge. Sudden evidence that the city is a heart, or that there is a freshness deep in things, even in factories and in the bleared, smeared vistas of trade, generates wonder.

* * *

The next poem, Hart Crane's "To Brooklyn Bridge," returns to the setting of the Wordsworth poem, and the spatial meanings of the city bridge. A bridge is a conduit, a ganglion of the city, at right angles to the natural ganglion of the river to which it is mated. Structurally, the bridge is an elevation toward the sky, but unlike such architectural features as Wordsworth's towers, it is an elevation that descends as well as rising, thus enacting the gesture of a skyward reach and falling back. And the bridge provides perspective: it is not only an elevation, but an elevation along a clear space; a central process of the city, it provides a view as if from outside of both the city and of the elsewhere interrupted or occluded city sky. Physically, just as the bridge both reaches out and upward, and returns to earth, it both concentrates the city traffic to an artery, and steps away from the city into open space and air. In short, it is the city's gesture toward, and away from, the quiet of the sky.

Crane's poem is in a way the climax of this guided tour because it includes, combines, and extends everything I have tried to point out thus far. The poem's embracing inclusiveness is part of its point, and within the poem Hart Crane clearly intends the bridge to be, among other things, an image of such inclusiveness:

TO BROOKLYN BRIDGE

How many dawns, chill from his rippling rest
The seagulls wings shall dip and pivot him,
Shedding white rings of tumult, building high
Over the chained bay waters Liberty—

Then, with inviolate curve, forsake our eyes
As apparitional as sails that cross
Some page of figures to be filed away;
—Till elevators drop us from our day . . .

I think of cinemas, panoramic sleights
With multitudes bent toward some flashing scene
Never disclosed, but hastened to again,
Foretold to other eyes on the same screen;

And Thee, across the harbor, silver paced
As though the sun took step of thee, yet left
Some motion ever unspent in thy stride,—
Implicitly thy freedom staying thee!

Out of some subway scuttle, cell or loft
A bedlamite speeds to thy parapets,
Tilting there momently, shrill shirt ballooning,
A jest falls from the speechless caravan.

Down Wall, from girder into street noon leaks,
A rip-tooth of the sky's acetylene;
All afternoon the cloud-flown derricks turn . . .
Thy cables breathe the North Atlantic still.

And obscure as that heaven of the Jews,
Thy guerdon . . . Accolade thou dost bestow
Of anonymity time cannot raise:
Vibrant reprieve and pardon thou dost show.

O harp and altar, of the fury fused,
(How could mere toil align thy choiring strings!)
Terrific threshold of the prophet's pledge,
Prayer of pariah, and the lover's cry,—

Again the traffic lights that skim thy swift
Unfractioned idiom, immaculate sigh of stars,
Bending thy path—condense eternity:
And we have seen night lifted in thine arms.

Under thy shadow by the piers I waited;
Only in darkness is thy shadow clear.
The City's fiery parcels all undone,
Already snow submerges an iron year . . .

O Sleepless as the river under thee,
Vaulting the sea, the prairies' dreaming sod,
Unto us lowliest sometimes sweep, descend
And of the curveship lend a myth to God.

I have implied that Blake's "London" and Wordsworth's "Composed upon Westminster Bridge, September 3, 1802" represent components of a kind, elements that are both present in poems like Baudelaire's "Recueillement," an example of what I take to be the full-blown romantic perception of the city. Without making too much of the idea of components or ingredients, one can find brought together in Crane's poem many elements in the others I have read to you: for example, something of the transforming energy by which Hopkins finds grandeur in the seemingly shabby or soiled vistas of trade and toil.

Crane takes for his subject the overwhelming, terrible abundance and volume of the city, its unanticipated excesses and splendor, anchored and paced by the Brooklyn Bridge. The idea behind the phrases "inviolate curve," and "as though the sun took step of thee, yet left / Some motion ever unspent in your stride" is hyperbole, the curve that extends outward forever (unlike the recurring cycle of the sun across the sky). Crane's enraptured, deeply unparsable syntax, as in the dissolved rhetorical question of the opening line, pursues that symmetrical but unclosing curve.

Here, more violently and ecstatically than the cliffs near Tintern Abbey, the bridge connects the landscape with the quiet of the sky—not only visually, but because it seems equally of the landscape and of the sky, the string of carlights an "immaculate sigh of stars" that seems able to "condense eternity." Like the sky, with its unfractioned idiom, the bridge "vaults" the population under it. And like the city with its cloud-flown derricks, the bridge cannot be the artifact of "mere toil": the city and the bridge, like the "cinematic sleights," go beyond the appetites and capacities of work: a fury, something more irresistible, appetitive, and uncontrolled, unleashes such symmetries and confusions.

Because Blake and Crane both are visionaries, and because extreme opposites meet, much in this hymn of celebration reminds us of the dirge of indictment:

> How the Chimney-sweeper's cry
> Every blackning Church appalls,
> And the hapless Soldier's sigh,
> Runs in blood down Palace walls.

The anonymous and the helpless of the city, those subjected to the power and conceptual order that framed the city and the bridge, take an all but central place in Crane's poem. The bedlamite leaps from the bridge with an "accolade . . . of anonymity," a spatial swallowing-up that evades the enumerations and notations of time itself. As interesting as "speechless caravan" is the spatial sequence "Out of some subway scuttle, cell, or loft"—the closed private spaces, above ground or underground, of the city. The spatial and architectural locating of the bedlamite places his suicide socially, as well as visually. A capitalized word that appears in Blake's lines as well comes right after the suicide, with its memorable "shrill shirt ballooning":

> Down Wall, from girder into street noon leaks,
> A rip-tooth of the sky's acetylene;
> All afternoon the cloud-flown derricks turn . . .
> Thy cables breathe the North Atlantic still

Wall is a street, down which the sun leaks at apogee, and though the street is named for a wall around the city, it evokes, as in Blake, the tall, seemingly impenetrable stone walls that protect and embody power. Coming after that tilting and falling white shirt, the scale of these images is tremendously eloquent: the sky's acetylene, the turning derricks like feeding mythological beasts, the animated bridge breathing the wind off the North Atlantic, all in motion, all chained and at liberty.

* * *

I will read you one more poem, Elizabeth Bishop's "Night City." The sky, which was an unattainable calm in the opening of the Tintern Abbey ode, a barely-implied midnight absence in Blake, a kind of proscenium from Westminster Bridge, a theater of gorgeous symbols in Baudelaire, blighted but divinely and rhetorically transformed in the Hopkins poem, is actually entered in Crane's poem "To Brooklyn Bridge." This progression is partly a technological matter: smokestacks, taller and taller buildings, the sweep of the suspension bridge supplanting masonry and iron strutwork, the cloud-flown derricks and the Manhattan buildings called, with a dated jaunty optimism, skyscrapers. The bridge, so to speak, reaches harder and higher.

In Bishop's poem, the bridging technology leaves the ground altogether, though again it also descends and returns. The airplane, like the bridge, epitomizes the city and rises out of it, provides perspective on the city, and brings us—both imaginatively and practically—to a vision of the city's heart, lungs, and bowels:

NIGHT CITY

[from the plane]

No foot could endure it,
shoes are too thin.
Broken glass, broken bottles,
heaps of them burn.

Over those fires
no one could walk:
those flaring acids
and variegated bloods.

The city burns tears.
A gathered lake
of aquamarine
begins to smoke.

The city burns guilt.
—For guilt-disposal
the central heat
must be this intense.

Diaphanous lymph,
bright turgid blood,
spatter outward
in clots of gold

to where run, molten,
in the dark environs
green and luminous
silicate rivers.

A pool of bitumen
one tycoon
wept by himself,
a blackened moon.

Another cried
a skyscraper up.
Look! Incandescent,
its wires drip.

The conflagration
fights for air
in a dread vacuum.
The sky is dead.

(Still, there are creatures,
careful ones, overhead.
They set down their feet, they walk
green, red; green, red.)

Especially coming after the poems by Hopkins and Crane, but also
in itself, "Night City" is an affecting, sober, and clear-eyed post-
lude to ecstasy. It is like Bishop to get this spectacle in a poem, and
to bring out the spectacle's emotional and historical vibrations. Re-
fineries, furnaces, chemical plants, and disposal sites, silica rivers,
incinerators, and pools of bitumen are first imagined as a literal ter-
rain, a place one might stand. They are after all, in their infernal
way, beautiful. But no foot could stand where heaps of broken
bottles not merely melt, but burn. Shoes are too thin.

Yet this too is, in Wordsworth's phrase a mighty heart, a place somehow organic and in its uncanny way vital. Variegated blood, lymph, tears, these caustic fluids and smoking lakes or moons are part of a great body, sublime in the sense of overwhelming, however repellent. In a minor, bitterly ironic key, the poem echoes the Elizabethan grandeur of Crane's "harp and altar, of the fury fused," though the emotion behind this creation seems less like fury, and more like a monstrous grief or melancholy, the obscure weeping of a capitalist Polyphemus:

> A pool of bitumen
> one tycoon
> wept by himself,
> a blackened moon.
>
> Another cried
> a skyscraper up.
> Look! Incandescent,
> its wires drip.

The word "incandescent," in American speech, ordinarily means either the kind of light bulb that is not fluorescent, or that someone is straining to be poetic. But here, in the skyscraper wires that are so hot they glow, and that nevertheless drip, the word "incandescent," like "tycoon" and "skyscraper," helps create the air of a decayed, perhaps obsolescent, but tremendously powerful virulence and creativity. The opposites burning and wetting comprise another image of inclusiveness, like the chained bay water's liberty. Terrifying that in the next stanza, the stubborn conflagration itself struggles for air in a dread vacuum. Over this bright, horrible, grotesquely gorgeous landscape of trade and toil, no Holy Spirit spreads its bright wings.

—Terrifying too, in a smaller way, to think of ending this reading with the dry, quiet, but awesome line, "The sky is dead." That is not the quiet which it pleased Wordsworth to feel connected by cliffs to the landscape. But Bishop does not end her poem with that apocalyptic sentence, but with an added parenthesis:

> (Still, there are creatures,
> careful ones, overhead.

They set down their feet, they walk
green, red; green, red.)

The airplanes, like the "mighty heart," are charged with life, and a
kind of life that makes them able to descend onto the seemingly impossible brimstone landscape below them.

If the sky is dead, still we are alive. As Bishop's subtitle indicates,
we inhabit our creatures—airplanes, buildings, bridges. All of these
poems, I suppose, suggest the ways that our creatures, including
cities, also inhabit us. The careful artifacts to which we trust ourselves bear their cautious and cautioning code of affirmation and
negation, green, red; green red. The planes bear this fundamental
binary convention—go, stop; yes, no; safe, bloody—as a way to
navigate down through the quiet of the sky, which we may or may
not have established as the quiet of the dead, bearing us living into
the living city.

The wistfulness that dwells on hedgerows that are hardly hedgerows, and that imagines the inhabited woods as "houseless," under-
lies the yearning for haven in "Night City," and even survives in the
poem's final gesture, which is to imagine in the buglike airplanes an
artifact—shoes are too thin, so merely to be shod is not enough—
that will let us walk our city. On the one hand, poetry from the
romantics on has learned to see what we have made as beautiful, and
even alive; on the other hand, poetry has also seen in that strange,
unnatural fabricated beauty all the tears and fury of us who made it.

Wordsworth and the Options for Contemporary American Poetry

❧

Charles Altieri

Wordsworth exerts very little direct influence on contemporary American poetry—a condition that tells us less about Wordsworth than it does about contemporaneity. If we seek strong historical influences or even Bloomian rivalries relevant to most contemporary poets, we will find ourselves unable to go further back than the beginnings of the twentieth century. But this does not exhaust the question of Wordsworth's significance for these poets. He becomes extremely important as soon as we turn attention to more general structural and ideological issues. For it is arguable that there is no better exemplar for the basic models of lyrical intensity and even of ideal lyric emotional economies that pervade contemporary poetry. At one pole Wordsworth's resistance to eighteenth–century high culture defines the basic imperatives for our own quest for immanence within common life, and at the other his confronting the limits of his own model for such immanence makes clear the terms of a similar struggle facing some of the most interesting younger contemporaries. Frustrated by the indulgent lyricism of what might be called the scenic mode in contemporary poetry, these writers devote themselves to the Wordsworthian project of testing the powers of personal eloquence to mediate between the margins of cultural life, where transforming insights take place, and the social theater, where such values must be applied.[1]

The stakes in getting clear about this Wordsworthian presence were made strikingly evident by a recent quarrel between two of the best commentators on the contemporary scene. On the one hand Marjorie Perloff saw his continuing relevance as a sign of the reactionary tendencies dominating the mainstream in recent American poetry. For any survey of standard journals and prizes finds everywhere an "instant Wordsworth designed for quick packaging" ("Contemporary / Postmodern: The 'New' Poetry?" 4). Richard Hugo's "In Your Young Dream" provides her a telling example:[2]

> You are travelling to play basketball. Your team's
> a good one, boys you knew when you were young.
> A game's in Wyoming, a small town, a gym
> in a grammar school. You go in to practice.
> No nets on the hoops. You say to the coach,
> A small man, mean face. "We need nets on the rims."
> He sneers as if you want luxury. You explain
> how this way you can't see the shots go in.
> You and another player, vaguely seen, go out
> to buy nets. A neon sign on a local tavern
> gives directions to the next town, a town
> a woman you loved lives in. You go to your room
> to phone her, to tell her you're here just
> one town away to play ball. She's already
> waiting in your room surrounded by children.
> She says "I'll come watch you play ball."
> Though young in the dream you know you are old.
> You are troubled. You know you need nets on the rims.

Despite its down-to-earth contemporary diction, this poem has almost nothing to do with the present. Projecting "dream content but no dream work," the plot of such poems follows the most conventional of narrative epiphany structures. And, more important, the overall fantasy of poetic authority based on "willingness to *express* troubled emotion and a sense of what is vulgarly called alienation" simply fails to address the "postmodern condition" in which

almost a century of thinking about dreams makes us especially conscious of far more fluid shifting boundaries between person, dream,
and language. For Perloff a truly postmodern lyric would instead
emphasize "stark particulars that refuse to cohere in a consistent referential scheme at the same time that they tempt the reader to un-
scramble their associations and find the missing links."

Jonathan Holden took the opposite position. For him it is precisely the uncritical insistence on modernist experiment in Perloff's
postmodernism that blinds her to the real revolution taking place as
poets return to Wordsworthian principles:

> The vast majority of such poems are in the first person singular, fea-
> turing the poet as protagonist, as, in the phrase of Wordsworth, a
> man speaking to men. The vast majority of poems conform to the
> criteria Wordsworth sets forth in the "Preface" to *Lyrical Ballads:* they
> 'choose incidents and situations from common life,' 'relate or de-
> scribe them' in open-form verse 'in a selection of language really used
> by men,' and 'throw over them a certain coloring of imagination
> whereby ordinary things' are 'presented to the mind in an unusual
> aspect.' In most of these poems the 'feeling therein developed gives
> importance to the action and the situation, and not the action and the
> situation to the feeling,' and they attempt to imitate a 'spontaneous
> overflow of powerful feelings.' (*Rhetoric of the Contemporary Lyric*
> 112–113)

This Wordsworthian version of lyric rhetoric can free poetry and
criticism from the narrow confines of Perloff's essentially epistemo-
logical criteria. If poets adapt it as their emblem for poetic practice,
they can begin the difficult process of demonstrating the limits of
modernist impersonality, and thus can resist the myth of the alienated artist that eventually transformed poetry into a mandarin
experimentalist laboratory. While most of this work lacks Wordsworth's depth, it at least inaugurates the tasks of adapting modernist
technique to the processes of constituting significant personal roles,
and therefore it creates the possibility of recovering for poetry the
reading public lost by modernist elitism.

Both positions have their problems: Perloff relies on a narrow and
abstract standard for contemporaneity, and Holden is not fair to
modernism and (perhaps because of that) is forced to praise a body

of rather slight poetry while relying on rhetorical categories that do not acknowledge the range of imaginative forces that poetry can wield. Yet Holden's perspective, especially as modified in his recent *Style and Authenticity in Postmodern Poetry,* seems to me better attuned to the best recent American poetry.[3] For the L=A=N=G=U =A=G=E poetry that Perloff praises strikes me as for the most part perversely intent on pursuing precisely the narrow modernism that Holden constructs. As a result this appropriation of the avant garde puts strong pressure on other poets equally disillusioned with the dominant scenic mode to seek as their alternative the possible contemporary resources in traditional lyric concern for personal voice, whether it takes the form of Pinsky's discursive reflections, the ecstatic intensities of a Jory Graham, the experiments in negotiating multiple selves that one finds in Ashbery and in Crase, or the direct personalizing energies of a Rich, a Lauterbach, or a Hass.

However, the cast these critics give the issues will not get us to the core of the problems that these poets face or the value of the work that they have produced. For, like most of the contemporary poets who do invoke Wordsworth, they concentrate only on the prose doctrine of the Preface to *Lyrical Ballads.* And so long as we stay with Wordsworth's prose we will have nothing better than common sense models of the person and its community, models which seem to me of little use for the necessary task of constructing a post-Freudian and post-poststructural lyric subject. Therefore I shall try to demonstrate his relevance to the contemporary scene by turning instead to his best early poetry. Here we find an imaginative theater enabling us to spell out both the historical tensions creating our contemporary disputes and the emotional logic on which plausible ideals of poetic personality can still be proposed. Moreover, Wordsworth's particular emphasis on what might be called a testimonial eloquence helps make it clear how this new personalism can build on and transform fundamental modernist efforts to make poetry a vehicle for sustaining modes of ethos. Where modernism tried to subsume the empirical subject under the constructive and transpersonal energies made literal by the work's formal relations (most obviously in painters like Mondrian), the contemporaries return to a lyric eloquence that can test the modes of engagement in the real made available by socially situated personal voices.[4]

For a concise rendering of what Wordsworth seeks in lyrical eloquence I have chosen to dwell on "Nutting." He offers no other single lyric as complexly engaged in mediating between a numinous source and an exemplary ethical model of lyrical self-presentation. (There is, in other words, no other Wordsworthian lyric so painfully aware of what is involved in confronting the aftermath of dreams of cultural revolution.) For here idealization must be won against the prevailing models of lyric sensibility afforded by England's sentimentalized versions of Enlightenment principles. And that must be accomplished by a motley hero effectually banished into the world of low mimetic situations and filiations. Exiled from the domain of high art and the interpretive languages which that art has come to sustain, Wordsworth cannot be satisfied with ironic inversions of that tradition. For such strategies will not help the hero come to terms with the imaginative energies alienating him from his heritage. Wordsworth must locate spiritual resources that sustain a very different hierarchy of psychic functions; he must stretch available conditions of representation so that they concentrate attention on a force which cannot be made to appear except in the process of poetic self-reflection; and he must locate through that reflection a mode of sublimity capable of restoring the ego's sense of connectedness with the natural sources of its energies. Rather than pursue the reflective pathos of "The Castaway" or the exalted contemplative scope of the voice in "Elegy on a Country-Churchyard," this poem demands our working against generalized sentiments and Horatian ideals for poetry in order to focus on very close readings of what the compulsion to narrate reveals about the mind's relation to its scenic context.

Given its setting, the poem should be able to rely on pastoral conventions. But within the speaker's narrative these conventions prove a seductive and dangerous form for representing experience. Traditional pastoral expectations seem to leave the mind a frustrating excess that finds its most ready outlet in adolescent violence:

> I heard the murmur and the murmuring sound,
> In that sweet mood when pleasure loves to pay
> Tribute to ease; and, of its joy secure,
> The heart luxuriàtes with indifferent things,
> Wasting Its kindliness on stocks and stones,

And on the vacant air. Then up I rose
And dragged to earth both branch and bough . . .
And with the green and mossy bower,
Deformed and Sullied, patiently gave up
Their quiet being: and unless I now
Confound my present feelings with the past;
Ere from the mutilated bower I turned
Exulting, rich beyond the wealth of Kings,
I felt a sense of pain when I beheld
The silent trees and saw the intruding sky.—
Then, dearest maiden, move along these shades
In gentleness of heart; with gentle hand
Touch—for there is a spirit in the woods.

Apparently the easy humanism of romance pastoral which the boy invokes cannot sufficiently handle difference, cannot handle the very sense of personal intensity that it elicits. Therefore as the heart luxuriates, the mind all too readily slips from its sweet mood to a sense that its objects become indifferent and its kindliness wasted. Pastoral rhetoric leaves the mind no way to express its increasing sense of its distinctive powers except by setting itself violently against a nature that becomes merely its object.

Yet this play on different and indifference soon reveals another power, another greater difference which becomes intelligible only by the poem's power to fuse psychological narrative with the pastoral setting. Here, then, we find a different version of constitutive subjective energies. Cast out of those conventional attitudes initially producing a coherent emotional scenario, the mind's momentary sense of power dissipates and the hero must learn how to turn himself into an object and acknowledge a fuller self-sufficiency encountered (or created) outside itself. Bower yields to silent trees and intruding sky, leaving the ephebe torn on the dualities of "Kindliness" on which the Enlightenment tradition would founder. From the humanist perspective "kindliness" refers to the appreciation of a distinctively human potential in the encounter. But this makes nature a little less than kin, reduced to hoping for the subject's kindnesses and hence also a fit victim for his tirades. Yet violence produces another kindliness, linking him to precisely that capacity for disorder in nature which probably made the effort to cover over the differences seem necessary in the first place. From this perspective, consciousness seems to share not nature's depth but the superficiality of its appearances, as if both domains distanced and distorted some deeper possibility of lawfulness.

The logic is pure Augustine: the secular dream of being more than nature reduces one to being less than one's own nature can be, so the awareness of this acculturated blindness demands new ways of redefining spirit. For Wordsworth, the new means is confessional narrative and the new goal a state of sublimity earned by the narrative's handling of lack and contradiction. In this more dialectical sense of landscape, poetry cannot be content with describing nature or reflecting on the general truths that nature might illustrate. Rather poetry must become self-reflexive enough to provoke errors, then test the capacities of the composing voice to spell out new lines of relation between a mind in excess of nature and a force of nature that reveals its powers only through the collapse of kindliness. Once the sky can become an intruding presence, the youth must learn how narrative enables him to take responsibility for both his difference from nature and the divisions from himself which generated so unreasoned and ostensibly spontaneous a destructive act. The result is a new, non-Burkean form of the sublime which gives moral force to the state of self-consciousness it calls forth. The rude shock of what one is not—not one with the appearance of nature and not one with the rhetoric that gives man superiority over a yielding nature—forces memory and poetry to the constructive work of the concluding lines. There is a spirit in these woods, but its meaning and force are reserved for those who can learn to read it as the poem does—through a series of negations which clear the way for this particular poetic naming to resist a history of false associations. Then it requires the dialectic of narrative memory to show why there must be a spirit and why it must remain on the margins of human experience, beyond the control of an interpretive violence which most ephebes in the culture never outgrow.

Wordsworth's great achievement here is to have his sublime romance and to moralize it too, while making the conjunction testimony to the powers of poetry. One could cast these Wordsworthian moments in the frame of Freudian instruction scenes, stressing the way the poem's resolution is overdetermined: this spirit in the woods becomes a surrogate father punishing the son for raping his sister-mother and thus composing (or imposing) nature as a super-ego figure. Yet Freudian language will not suffice because this over-determination is quite deliberate. The scene instructs because of its overt properties as scene, as a mode of presentation that can undo the received model of interpretive authority and make the specific process of unfolding which the poem enacts necessary to define what spirit can be. Rather than limit Spirit to something we find in the unconscious, we are invited to envision it as the active force to which narrative can testify once it comes to understand how the mind is capable of modes of attention and memory more sensitive and more capacious than the models of man the poem seeks to displace.

By so defining spirit Wordsworth simultaneously invents the logic of romantic poetry in English and defines the central problem producing the debate with which we began. Poetry in pursuit of that spirit must set itself against the mainstream culture, and at the same time it must turn to the artifact's dense internal relations (which we now glibly dismiss as efforts at autonomy) in order to attribute powers to that marginal presence. But how then can poets envision their language as giving access to that spirit without displacing it into another version of fashion masking as sensibility? The roman-tic tradition provides two possible answers—the poetry can provide a mode of attention exemplifying stances that lead beyond language to a sense of subliminal forces, or the poetry can be staged as itself the testimony to powers within language which provide the re-sources necessary to mediate that sublimity back into social life. Each answer, however, brings with it a serious problem. In the first case there is the danger of confining poetry to the domain of alien-ated spirit idealizing a consuming loneliness as the only access to the deepest spiritual forces in nature. In the alternative there arise con-stant temptations to mistake one's own self-congratulatory elo-quence for the influexes of spirit and to domesticate spirit once again within overgeneralized cultural forms. At one pole there lies inarticulate authenticity, at the other the egotistical sublime.

We have arrived at the options confronting contemporary Ameri-can poetry. But our terms are still too tied to the concrete language of "Nutting" to allow sufficient generalization, so I need to take a few moments to put that poem within the more abstract context provided by the overall project of Wordsworth's early poetry.

Wordsworth had to reject many of the poetic conventions he inherited because they could not handle what he felt was the need to adapt traditional lyrical ideals to the models of subjectivity and of cultural authority released by the empiricist spirit. Accommodating that spirit (without quite surrendering to its culturally dominant forms) required developing a model of the resources, the commitments, and the contradictions basic to poetic activity which could overturn the interwoven ideals of judgment, of nobility, and of eloquence that had taken form under the aegis of both Christian humanism and Enlightenment rationalism. These frameworks cast the noble self as one whose judgment and will managed to subordinate individual interests and passions to some more general categorical frameworks. Selves inherit traditions and through them develop powers of assessment enabling them to align themselves with those ideas and images which define a life worthy of respect. Under those dispensations the role of judgment and imagination is to subordinate the particular to the generalized model, at least in those domains where there are clear public ideals. But Wordsworth was obsessed by the problem of what authorizes those ideals. For him idealization had to remain connected to formative events and influences in particular lives, so that the idealizing would in effect be inseparable from a condition of remembering, and the qualities of the remembering could then be subject to public scrutiny against the backdrop of a common world. The result is what might be called a scenic logic which redefines the dynamics of judgment and thus requires shifting from the poetic ideal of Miltonic public eloquence to a version of eloquence that could take responsibility for its origins in an essentially domestic imaginative theater.

In this Wordsworthian scenic model for the formation of selves, the central terms for value derive from persons' capacities to define their own distinctive relationship to the sources of their most intense powers. Because the formation of selves thus involves the dialectical force of all that the intruding sky symbolizes, this scenic logic has affinities with idealist thought (as M. H. Abrams's *Natural Supernaturalism* magisterially demonstrates). But in order to accommodate his own empiricist values, Wordsworth develops models of reflection and of judgment that do not lead to Kant's and Hegel's synthetic rational processes, and that thereby do not require any specific teleological or transcendental claims. Judgment becomes

what Schlegel called a form of "spiritual sensuality" that must locate its generalizing principles within the scene that it composes.
No longer confined by abstract ideas or social norms of taste,
Wordsworthian judgment depends on a concrete history of negotiations with an environment. The self is scenic, then, because its investments derive from the scenes that it has been attached to and the
traces which those leave in his memory. Scenes are not mere instances passively awaiting the forming influence of the mind. Instead they serve as metonyms for behavioral complexes that spread
out over time and into a range of repeated habits and related social
practices. Because the self neither creates meanings nor can trust
dominant cultural generalizations, its deepest powers and most intimate loyalties are shaped by the history of the adjustments it makes
to those environmental forces. And because these adjustments involve the measure of time—of repeated connections to nature and
other people as well a history of rewards and instructive failures—
the energies they engage can be much more comprehensive and
more immediately compelling and flexible than anything generalized principles can afford. The expansive life of scenic consciousness both elicits and rewards a temperament gradually developing
patterns of attention and care binding it to its surrounding community. Were this model to take hold, society would have to replace
traditional ideals of a generalizable poetic truth by an ideal of repre-
sentativeness based simply on the capacity of a work to exemplify
certain powers that then help an audience adapt itself to similar
numinous forces. Because the spirit in the woods can become the
spirit defined by the field of energies the poem's narrative act composes, the narrated recognition scene becomes available for the entire society. There can be a spirit in a personal narrative's self-critical
activity that can engage the spirit in the woods and can make its
contribution to the community the exemplary modes of reflection
that it affords for such engagements. Ultimately that engagement
even makes it possible to transform the rape of feminine nature into
the making visible of imaginative resources that the poet can hope
to share with his maiden interlocutor.[5]

Once a poet accepts this scenic model for the self, Miltonic eloquence (or, for the contemporaries, Yeatsian eloquence) can no
longer suffice. Such versions of expressive nobility derive too directly from modes of judgment which subsume the formative

influence of scenic details under more general images and principles, and they thus risk losing touch with the sources in natural life and personal history which give the poetry its imaginative scope. If there is to be lyric eloquence, it must now take the form of a counter-eloquence earning its connection to spirit by its resisting the culture's idealized versions of itself. Wordsworthian domestic eloquence then is not the realizing of roles but the testing of energies which become available through specific attitudes toward negotiating personal memories as one tries to align oneself to contemporary events. In this new dispensation the sign of public authority is the capacity to focus in cadence and metaphoric scope a sense of the powers that stem from a particular personal path for adapting oneself to the flux of events.

If I am correct, we can see the arguments between Perloff and Holden as efforts to come to terms with contemporary poetry's return to this scenic logic, and hence to the temptations of absorbing the self into the otherness of nature or making the activity of speaking a vehicle for the egotistical sublime. Where Wordsworth could set himself against eighteenth-century versions of eloquence, the contemporaries set themselves against the constructivist sense of formal energies that for modernism provided the best index of the powers which poetry could mobilize. Ideally this counter-eloquence should be able to elaborate each of the two options marked by "Nutting." But both critics, Holden a bit belatedly, see that for contemporary poetry the first option holds little promise because we find it all too easy to adapt the gestures of imaginative empathy with a spirit in the "dark" woods, so that we end up leaving the spirit there. Consumed by their own sensitivity and caught in the conventions of a scenic lyricism that also pervaded a good deal of Victorian poetry, poets committed to such gestures tend to slide over what Robert Hass calls the terrifyingly pure arbitrariness of facts, and have no dramatic means to test their moments of numinous vision by projecting the identities made possible by such imaginative investments. Instead, such work typically assumes a flat recording voice with few individualizing traits, has as its only vehicles for inviting identifications from its readers a commitment to quotidian situations and a somewhat reductive sense of a common human nature, relies on a language that earns its resistance to the old eloquence by a studied and somewhat embarrassing simplicity, and makes those trees and intruding sky the vehicle for identifications with a nature whose sublimity comes only as a call to the deepest loneliness that the psyche can muster.

The question then is whether the other dimension of Wordsworth's legacy holds out more promise. For Perloff, and for the experimental poets she champions, personal eloquence is even more suspect because it relies on notions of a unifying ego and necessarily repeats outmoded fictions of lyrical sensitivity. I share those suspicions. But so do poets like Robert Hass, Adrienne Rich, and John Ashbery. Yet they turn increasingly to experiments in personal voice, so I think it is now necessary to adapt the hypothesis that while any cult of personal eloquence obviously risks narcissistic self-absorption, the values involved are so important that the chance must be taken. For without such exemplary tests of personal powers we run the danger of a greatly diminished poetry—purity of ideological critique risks banality of imaginative assertion. More important, it is by no means clear that our fashionable distrust of the unitary ego requires our dismissing either the efforts to create unity for certain segments of one's life or the project of making personal voices a significant means of exploring more flexible ways of staging first-person investments. In fact the efforts of the L=A=N =G=U=A=G=E poets to deny those investments seem to me to provide very strong evidence for their importance. For one must ask what that poetry can put in the place of first-person eloquence. It seems to me that their models of agency require them to replace the lyrical subject by providing a mode of political power through their constructive activity. But without first-person terms they cannot attribute any positive or particular value to the poem's specific configuration except a purely formal one. Then, unhappy with formalism, they claim also that the very unmaking of the conventions of language will enable the reader to try other ways of composing worlds and testing values. Their poems however can do no more than open that space; they cannot project and test their own visions of personal powers, and thus they cannot adapt or compete with the exemplary performances of possible states of subjectivity which the greatest lyrical poets leave as a legacy and a challenge.[6]

Given this situation, it is perhaps no wonder that poets are returning to the eloquent Wordsworth whom Coleridge tried to tease out from the populist ideologue. In Holden's recent criticism, for example, the man speaking to other men becomes instead a figure allowing Holden to mark the limitations of Hugo's "Lacanian" effort to have language "substitute for the poet's vaguely intimated, original merger of his identity with some nurturing other" (159): "In the Wordsworth passage, on the other hand, the figure of the poet is not paralyzed, not choked with the backlogged grief of some latent psychological crisis. He is free to move about in the foreground of his own experience, unafraid of time, absolved by the landscape and by his vision of it—a vision which, in its fullest development, is not static but dynamic, not psychological but religious" (160). To stop here, however, is not to appreciate the degree to which the best of the poets I have been mentioning develop their ideals of eloquence through lenses shaped by modernist constructivism.[7] At stake is not merely the possibility of imitating versions of the self no longer bound by regressive impulses or of saving us from psychology by religion. What matters is the exemplary role the speaking voice can play because it conceives the poem as constructing a site within which the very terms for identity and the possible links between psychology and transcendental forces can be mapped. Wordsworthian eloquence then becomes the capacity of the speaking or narrating to so stage its linguistic powers that they define and test related personal traits which can serve in poetry the same function that appeals to ethos play in Ciceronian models of rhetorical performance.

Let me suggest three generalizations which should clarify the force of this Wordsworthian example. First, contemporary poetry pursuing this eloquence is intensely personal without being highly dramatic or inviting us to identify with a history of emotional trauma. The personal is inseparable from the process of attempting to make one's own way of engaging the scenes within one's work take on the spirit that otherwise is banished to the woods. The language of the poem and the attitudes it sustains must establish the capaciousness and depth made available by one's commitment to certain paths of thinking, as if the poet's relation to time were the only plausible test of the ways in which the spirit's influx could assume significant force within social life. Second, this emphasis on compositional forces as aspects of personal expression both continues and transforms the modernist desire to make poetry not merely a reflection of social attitudes about the psyche but also itself a vehicle for proposing and testing possible understandings of the dynamics of human agency. That is why it is foolish to go to these poems hoping they will illustrate some psychology or epistemology which one takes from other contemporary discourses. The challenge facing the poet is to make us feel the inadequacy of such frames, so that we then understand that close reading is not an end in itself but a tracking of powers and modes of relating to the world beyond the self which literally comes into being because of the poem's expressive structures. What the mind can be depends on the specific powers of adaption that poems explore. Thus while it is now very difficult to repeat New Critical nostrums about poetry providing distinctive knowledge about the world, it remains feasible to talk about poems as establishing significant knowledge about who we can become as speakers and readers for that world. Finally, as we focus attention on these ways of composing the investments that reside in scenic images, we also make it possible to recover a Longinian sense of the sublime—one based not on nature but on the mysteries presented by what Wallace Stevens calls "A nature that is created in what it says" (*Collected Poems* 490). In this mode the nature that terrifies is a piece with the one that eventually imposes liveable orders because the poem's act of speaking stages those conditions as the very possibility of knowing how and why we are constantly at odds with what we desire.

Having set forth my case, I now want to illustrate it by concentrating on three contemporary poems that should make clear the options available within these Wordsworthian frameworks and support my own preference for the poetry that sets the powers for personal eloquence against the desire to find authenticity in lonely silences. As our example of the possibilities and limitations of the first, immanentist Wordsworthian model, I have chosen William Stafford's "With Kit, Age 7, At the Beach"—in part because the Wordsworthian echoes are so obvious, and in part because it does a better job than Hugo's poem of demonstrating the force of Wordsworth's scenic logic on both the poetry of common life pursued by Hugo and Simpson and on the deep image poetry that dominated the seventies:

> We would climb the highest dune,
> from there to gaze and come down:

the ocean was performing;
we contributed our climb.

Waves leapfrogged and came
straight out of the storm.
What should our gaze mean?
Kit waited for me to decide.

Standing on such a hill,
what would you tell your child?
That was an absolute vista.
Those waves raced far and cold.

"How could you swim, Daddy,
In such a storm?"
"As far as was needed," I said,
And as I talked I swam.

This, too, is a poem in which a casual sense of nature suddenly shifts
into a much deeper and bleaker sense of idenification that is the
price and reward for self-consciousness. But Stafford's version of
self-consciousness does not give the spirit much room to breathe—
as if the situation of "Elegiac Stanzas" could be resolved by "Anecdote for Fathers" or "We are Seven." Stafford is careful to contrast
the rather simple humanizing of the questions in the second stanza
with the sudden absorption in the image enacted by the realization
of the last line. However, in my view, the contrast he develops between the quotidian and the deeper sense of desperate effort does
not sufficiently elaborate the life of spirit that the mode invokes.
Part of my resistance stems from the cloying gesture toward other
parents. For here the poem accepts a purely rhetorical mode of existence that its concluding gesture works against, but only to find the
swimming still subsumed in the talking. Yet the talking itself has no
freedom or scope because the lyric intensity must be focused in that
physical act which carries all the fear and devotion. Consequently
the poem's scenic qualities pull against any expansive forces in the
reflective mind leading beyond the image and the bodily state which
it elicits. In order to invoke a deep sense of elemental spiritual
forces, the mode of expression must be reduced to straightforward

syntax, and the play of mind must fuse with the darker dimensions of natural scene. We understand how the father's relation to his child keeps the swimming poised between natural force and filial love, yet there is little that our understanding can do but posture in this gesture of the desperate swimmer (which in fact lacks the power of Cowper's "Castaway"). The resources of syntax yield to direct narrative indicatives; language submits to image, and spirit finds itself identifying with a purely physical and rather conventional expressive emblem. We are a long way even from the intricate temporality and pervading sense of self-contradiction that characterize "Nutting"'s willingness to put the poet in a less than flattering light.

There are two basic ways that contemporary poets have tried to expand this scenic focus on a lonely sublimity forcing the mind into the pure concentration of essentially physical states where it can share what is immanent to nature. The more radical model, typified by John Ashbery's work, has very little to do with Wordsworth, except perhaps to use him as its foil. For the emphasis there is on reversing the logic of Wordsworthian immanence: rather than focus on the relations between the discreteness of numinous scenes and the person's efforts to forge an expressive ethos from and through them, nature is reduced to already constructed allegorical figures. Now nature must be seen as simply a construct of eloquence. But then eloquence grows intriguingly problematic. At one pole it must define a position in relation to all the other constructs that now are on a single plane, with no numinous objects. And at the other the inability to "represent" nature teases us with the sense that underlying the eloquence there may be unutterably simple needs and desires that emerge only when one treats the rhetorical constructs as implicit signs of latent dramas. Rather than adapt the mind to nature, one must learn to read an underlying spirit in our rhetorical adaptions of nature. But because his mode tends to be as frustrating in its irreducibly intricate intelligence as instant Wordsworth is in its programmatic reductiveness, poets anxious for an art with more overtly public resonance have tried more direct parallels to Wordsworthian eloquence. While there is little hope of recuperating the sense of symbolic density that Wordsworthian rhetoric wrings from such analogies, poets like Rich, Hass, and Richard Kenney seek a mode of expressing human groundedness and purposive endurance through time which can in its own right project a desirable psychic basis for our social lives.[8]

For my example of Ashberyean strategies I have chosen a poem by Ann Lauterbach in which I think a remarkable talent nonetheless creates what will seem problems for those, like Hass and Kenney, seeking a more assertive public register. This is the first stanza of her "Still," a text whose irresistably Wordsworthian title introduces the volume *Before Recollection:*

> The sleeping urgencies are perhaps ruined now
> In the soul's haphazard sanctuary.
> Ignored like a household
> Dormant in the landscape, a backwoods dump
> Where the last care has worn through its last
> Memory. We might think of this as a blessing
> As we thrash in the nocturnal waste:
> Rubble of doors, fat layers of fiber
> Drooping under eaves, weeds
> Leaning in lassitude after heavy rain
> Has surged from a whitened sky.
> Thunder blooms unevenly in unknowable places
> Breaking distance into startling new chambers
> We cannot enter; potentially, a revelation.

In order to capture the psychic depths where these sleeping urgencies lie, Lauterbach uses nature strictly as self-conscious metaphor: nature rhetoricized becomes the vehicle for giving a physical texture to those aspects of mental life that are otherwise condemned to the abstract and ineffable. So we find ourselves in the traditional aubade situation. But the physical dawn quickly gives way to the more abstract feel of the dawning of certain aspects of the world in the moment of stillness that precedes full conscious waking. Poised between the nocturnal waste that is dreaming and the backwoods dump of a deeper sense of need where even memory seems to have worn through its cares, the mind so rendered can represent to itself what waking really entails—waking offers the opening of new chambers ironically blocked by the very conditions of self-consciousness that they elicit.

There are few contemporary poems that construct so intimate

and yet so thoroughly abstract a state of mind. Were this Ashbery's poem, those qualities would sound alarms forcing him to dissipate the scene by modulating it into other voices and other metaphoric chains. The one thing the mind cannot do is be seduced by its own eloquence because then it loses sight of the forces that compose the metaphors and elicit the mind's unsatisfiable interest in its own processes. More important, the person then risks losing the sense of his or her own limits, and so cannot stay back and side with those who share the turning of emotional seasons. But Lauterbach has different, more dramatic ambitions. She is less interested in what can emerge within these processes of constant transformation than in the blend of pathos and self-possession that poetry can bring to this sense of irrecoverable loss. Perhaps it will take the entire volume to locate and then to extend what here appear only as things kept in storage even though their urgencies have been ruined:

> *Deep Midnight,* a song on the Chinese zither.
> This must be long after the storm, long
> After the revolution. It seems some things
> Were kept in storage after all: cool air
> Quietly throbbing, a few candles, chance songs
> "Soul to soul" on the radio. Chance is a variant
> Of change, the weather changing, chancy
> But destined. Our trust is that we, too, are
> Forms attached to content, content to meanings
> Aroused. It is our custom to bring things about.

The tonal shift is stunning. This is a much deeper calm than that of the moment of waking. For rather than concentrate on complex momentary balances, the mind now views itself from a peaceful and lucid distance, the dream of revelation having yielded to an equally physical rendering of how reflexive judgment might afford the self a way to dispose itself towards the general phenomenon of change. The dynamics of loss and anticipation give way to a set of forces intended to replace the imagistic mode by a combination of dense puns and projected generalizations—first about the aspects of the psychic landscape that endure, then about the capacity of powers of reflection on such scenes (and the linguistic registers that give them form) to provide a mode of personal identity that endures through change and extends into communal identifications. Because Lauterbach can now use the weather metaphor to gather all the elements of the mental landscape, she earns the right to posit a destiny informing change in the same way that the weather integrates the semantics of change and chance to suggest a more comprehensive force informing both. And then she has what becomes a more abstract metaphoric ground on which to derive from the idea of weather a model for a self capacious enough to unify the levels of form, content, and the momentary revelation of aroused meaning. We can see ourselves bringing "things about" both by engendering change and by making poems which, as things, provide a form for that aboutness in exactly the same way that all the weather has composed a form for the psyche's own movements.

But who is this "we"? And what powers can it actually wield? However much we are attached to "meanings aroused," the most the poem can make of them is this rather arch and ironic bringing of "things about." Once the speaking voice is this abstracted, eloquence becomes primarily a matter either of formal complexity or of this kind of inordinately precise naming. "Our trust" is itself akin to those "sleeping urgencies" since the poet can do little but maintain a complex tonal distance from the assertion. Lauterbach's greatest strength then becomes this poem's greatest weakness. For in so carefully bringing things about, the speaking voice renounces everything to this effort to establish the full tonal complexity capable of naming the poem's relation to the flux and the repressions that set it in motion. By absorbing all scenes into images and tones carefully defining the problem of bringing the urgencies to life, the poet simply does not allow herself a synthetic intelligence that can get beyond such balances. The voice itself collapses into a highly self-conscious thing.

These problems are clearest in the poem's concluding sentence. Lauterbach turns to the arch "it is our custom" in order to place in one practical context the full interchange between formal frames and shifting particulars that reflection claims to have earned. "Custom" links change and chance, the passing of time and the effort to locate meanings which at best only partially arouse the sleeping urgencies. How then can she conclude in good faith, except by asking the bringing of "things" about to carry such complex reservations and distances that the poem itself can aspire to no more immediate breathing human passion? So having taken her cue from Ashbery, Lauterbach ends up running a risk that he manages to avoid, perhaps because he remains fluid enough never to have to confront his own making as a thing or his own thinking as the work of a collective, transpersonal "we." While there is no personal revelation in his poetry, there is a sense of individual voice working through its needs for its particular form of eloquence because the metamorphic processes remain tied to specific formations and refuse the temptation to negate the personal into the general. There are, in other words, some modes of eloquence which cannot cogently seek their own reflective stillness. Lauterbach heroically tries to produce that stillness, only to diminish the sense of productive force that she wants to ground and to exalt.

For Robert Hass's "Songs to Survive the Summer," things are all too much about. It is necessary then to envision poetry as the articulating of modes of personal attention which can define a stance for adapting them within some comprehensive attitude. That project begins with the poet irreducibly caught up in those Wordsworthian particulars which demand forging a responding self:

> These are the dog days,
> unvaried
> except by accident,
>
> mist rising from soaked lawns,
> gone world, everything
> rises and dissolves in air,
>
> whatever it is would
> clear the air
> dissolves in air and the knot
>
> of days unties
> invisibly like a shoelace.
> The gray-eyed child
>
> Who said to my child: "Let's play
> in my yard. It's OK,
> my mother's dead."

The opening seems to share Stafford's and Hugo's insistently scenic concreteness as well as their concern with the paternal roles that now seem the only guise of authority which the poet can assume. But this is concreteness with a Wordsworthian difference, concreteness which will set a stage requiring sixteen more songs before the air will sufficiently clear. First, one notices that the play of *a* sounds builds an evocative resonance for the relationship between "unvaried" and "accident." Accident keeps its practical connotations, especially in conjunction with the disturbing casualness by which death intrudes upon the scene. But at the same time, the term carries a range of philosophical associations suggesting that the necessary relief depends upon the poet's capacity to handle all the implications of these casual differences—one must learn to treat the accidents as productive differences within a world otherwise consumed by repetition. Then we realize that this same play between accident, difference, and repetition shapes the casual yet intricate syntax governing the single sentence that composes the first eleven lines. As this scene unfolds in language, the effect is to invite our positing for it an imaginative site not quite parallel to the one we grant most contemporary landscape poetry. Clearly the scene is to be taken as a description: there is none of Lauterbach's foregrounded metaphorical displacement of nature into psyche, and there is none of Wordsworth's or Robert Bly's hopes for some principle of value latent within the landscape. Yet the description is suffused by what can only be called half-metaphors which almost have Ashbery's dizzying scope without calling attention to an authorial playfulness as their ground. Instead, the metaphoric dimension gives the speaking voice a strange complexity. The overall tone is insistently flat and distanced, yet there is a surprising delicacy and intimacy to the scene, as if there were a Cézanne-like pressure hovering within the atmospheric effects.

I am tempted to say that this play of accidental details ultimately allies the poet to the child's finding new permissions in the death of his mother. For this "everything" seems profoundly Wordsworthian, seems the poem's emblem for a power that can modulate between sensitive detail and the abstract, even portentous search for "whatever it is would clear the air." Through that abstracting gesture the actual physical description so engages time (the "knot of days") that the only way to resolve the feelings elicited is to turn from nature to culture. And this is beautifully reinforced by the quick shift to the conceit of the untied shoelace, which we resolve by realizing that this casual detail perfectly captures within the familiar cultural order the blend of the casual and the mysterious pervading the natural scene. So we are led back to a responding mind free in the world of facts to register its own complexities without displacing them into either the old eloquence or the theatrics of the deep image. It is then no surprise that the child is handled with consummate economy: its strange relation to death gathers the intricate tensions between accidents, overall weather, and the compromises we make in order to find our release from such forces. Yet, as in Hass's master Chekov, such taut and intense shaping intelligence does not impose any stateable "meaning." Poetry too is a matter of atmospheres in which we tie and untie knots.

I cannot summarize here the ways in which Hass elaborates this conjunctive style in order to compose a set of recurring details, events, memories, and desires which modulate between the ecstasy of glimpsing another world and the constant pressure of care and fear characterizing this one. We must turn immediately to the last song in *Praise,* where, in adapting all these recurrent details and shifting tones, he makes Wordsworthian domestic eloquence a compelling imaginative resource for composing contemporary selves:

> That is what I have
> to give you, child, stories,
> songs, loquat seeds,
>
> curiously shaped; they
> are the frailest stay against
> our fears. Death
>
> is the sweetness, in the bitter
> and the sour, death
> in the salt, your tears,
>
> this summer ripe and overripe.
> It is a taste in the mouth,
> child. We are the song

death takes its own time
singing. It calls us
as I call you child

to calm myself. It is every
thing touched casually,
lovers, the images

of saviors, books, the coin
I carried in my pocket
till it shone, it is

all things lustered
by the steady thoughtlessness
of human use.

Here Stafford's swimmer is transformed into a fully Wordsworth-ian talker. The simple directness comprises Hass's version of anti-eloquence. There is no melodramatic self-staging, and there is the not entirely successful effort to avoid grand statement so that the poet's sentiments will be contoured to the "steady thoughtlessness of human use." Yet there remains a remarkably expansive sense of scope and cadence, primarily in the swelling appositions and in the playing of long, elaborately structured sentences against the simple sentences on death constituting the central moment of the passage. Where Lauterbach locates her "we" in the movement from form to content to aroused meanings, Hass's "we" is composed within the physical registers organized by our awareness of participating in death's song. But because that song takes its own time, there need be no desperation and no bitterness. Instead, that song, now one with the poet's songs, winds its way back out through another chain of appositions to generate, and to sanction, a moment in which one hears again the Wordsworthian "all," this time bound not to nature but to the cultural order which gives a form to that nature by the one miracle we can perhaps still trust—"the steady thoughtlessness of human use."

In one sense this closing line relies on the oldest of poetic devices. All the details exist to make this particular rhetorical generalization a resonant principle for reinforcing identifications with a communal life. However, it is precisely the traditional dimension of such sentiments that make them seem like Derrida's "used and usorious coin," contaminated by whatever cultural currency they have managed for themselves. In order to make poetry of that thoughtlessness, in order to share what Hass calls "Wordsworth's discovery of his own inwardness and the problem of what it can mean, what form it can take in the world" (*Pleasures* 41), Hass faces a problem of testimony perhaps more daunting than any facing modernist abstraction as it tried to compose art exemplifying those powers that would enable it to cast itself as redefining our images for the psyche. Now the challenge is not to restore the old heroes but to make precisely those domestic attachments which such heroes must reject the basis for poetry's idealizations.

Hass addresses this need for a new poetic eloquence in three basic ways. First he elaborates the casual particulars into an intricate and suggestive field of relations—in part by the allusiveness to figures like Rilke, in part by his mastery of Wordsworthian apposition which moves fluidly between the material particulars (books, coins, tastes) and the sense of the longing and the fear that composes them into a single "all" linking physical and emotional atmospheres. The effect is of a voice able to modulate its tones and sympathies while neither losing sight of the sufferings that call it to speech nor covertly revelling in them. Second, the imaginative and syntactic fluidity among and upon concrete particulars enables the poem to move easily between scenic details and a discursiveness that seems to issue from them. Thus the poet is allowed the full play of mind—this spirit need not align itself with the woods. In fact this poem ultimately serves culture, not nature. As one goes through the details summer tosses up, and as one refuses the temptation for single intense lyric responses like those of the best modernist poets, one in effect aligns oneself with the level of caring and even the distinctive modes of thinking attachment that are sustained by the "steady thoughtlessness of human use." But now one does so in a manner that can thoughtfully embrace its ground in the spirit which those resources make available. Because discursive speech can suffuse our specific emotional attachments, we can celebrate the power to make selves of scenes and to make of those selves exemplary figures that others are invited to adapt for their own human uses.

It is more difficult to describe the third aspect of the model of

eloquence which Hass develops, largely because that comprises
what is most distinctive and suggestive about his best recent work
(like his "The Apple Trees at Olema"). Wordsworth is a quintessentially western poet, in the sense that his eloquent self is essentially
synthetic. Its way of adapting itself to the energies made available
by its responsiveness to nature is to elaborate a human form containing those energies within an interpretive symbolic structure.
Hass does not quite break from this, but his sense of self is considerably modified by his interest in Buddhist philosophy and Japanese
poetry. The self which gathers and proposes meaning also becomes
a force within nature that one sets at an imaginative distance so that
one can understand its relation to what encompasses it. His prose
on Buson's poetry sets the agenda:

> It is the turn of phrase that gives the poem its deepest, most amaz-
> ing effect. It is why the poem does not record sickness, yearning, un-
> satisfied hunger. Nor is it exactly objective or detached. It sits just in
> between, not detached but not attached either. Intense sadness and
> calm; non attached the Buddhists would say. (*Pleasures* 278)

> In Japanese the poem does not even end with that stutter of won-
> der, . . . The tone is quite level. Buson is not surprised by the fullness
> and emptiness of things." (308)

Admiring such a vision is not the same thing as achieving it, as Hass
clearly knows. However, such passages attune us to what is happening in the lovely movements of self-referring terms in the poem's
conclusion. "I"s frame the discourse. But between them we find
death opening into the set of physical analogues which sustain the
claim that "We are the song / death takes is own time / singing,"
and we find the details it touches leading back through the personal
"I" to the generalized sense of sharing the luster of human use. In
addition we must recall the easy movement of the "I" throughout
the poem as it enters a range of identifications. This personal note is
not something we find in Gary Snyder's quest for a discipline enabling him to align himself with an all-encompassing order because
for Snyder that discipline requires the suppression of self. Correspondingly, Hass's poetry cannot share Snyder's understanding of

eloquence as a celebration of the clarity that comes when one steps outside of certain lyrical needs and desires—a counter-eloquence with religious depth. For Hass such desires are too constrained, both as religion and as poetry. His mode of personal speech seeks to include the full complexity of American personal relations and intellectual traditions within an overall perspective exemplified in Buddhist art. The self must continue to occupy center stage, but the stage itself must be understood in this highly generalized context of shared human desires and practices. By framing that stage in lyric poetry, Hass then recasts "Nutting"'s demonstration of the power of readerly models to shape psychological ones—for the fluid movements both gathering and dispersing selves becomes poetry's evidence of the powers that one gains from this distanced responsiveness to the fullness and the emptiness of things. There is probably no other way to sing death's song so that it elicits our living out the fullness latent within our social affections.

Hass's art is not without an increasingly bitter sense of loneliness and frustration, which paradoxically he does not quite want to give up, in the same way that Wordsworth did not want to give up the spirit in the woods. But the greater this pressure and the more he commits himself to the fact that a poetry about contemporary American life must include rather than overcome such bitterness, the more he makes the entire philosophical and poetic project of recuperating the eloquence possible within the "thoughtlessness of human use" our most plausible stay against confusion or, more important, against the desire to escape into irony or into the profitable pleasures of alienation.

Notes

1. I define the scenic mode and discuss its uses and limits in my *Self and Sensibility in Contemporary American Poetry*. In this essay I hope to extend that book by demonstrating that the claim it makes there for a necessary self-consciousness in poetry need not require fundamentally ironic self-reflexive strategies. Self-consciousness is simply a public taking responsibility for the

rhetorical principles that the poetry relies on in proposing its claims on our emotional lives.

2. To be fair to Perloff's opponent Jonathan Holden, I must note that in his defense of a Wordsworthian style he admits that this Hugo poem is not very good. I will therefore use below a different poem, William Stafford's "With Kit, Age 7, At the Beach," which he does treat favorably, and I will discuss the changes of Holden's own position as evidence for the cultural transformations that Wordsworth helps us define.

3. In his new book Holden remains loyal to Hugo and to the idea that the dominant mode in American poetry is a "low mimetic mode . . . whose tradition leads from Whitman and Wordsworth" and whose focus is on the forming of personal ethos out of vernacular situations (5). The difference lies in the fact that he has apparently been reading his Wordsworth, so that he now has a much richer sense than in his earlier book of how that ethos is formed. Yet I still think his model of constructed personality is a bit narrow. For Holden ethos is a matter of what we attribute to the rhetorical intention which the poem fosters: "A good poem is the test of the capacity of its author. Just as in the plot of a realistic story, novel, or movie, the choices which the protagonist makes eventually give us a clear sense of that person's character . . .—so does a poem, through the action of its author matching choices of language to choices of value, choices between what or what not to notice and bring to attention, give us a clear indication of the author's ethos and total alertness" (176). However, poems are not simply matters of dramatic choice—this confines us to his low mimetic mode. For me, as for Wordsworth, the important issue of ethos in a poem is its eloquence, that is its capacity to make the making of the poem an expression and a testing of exemplary powers which it can plausibly be argued illustrate what a certain mode of attention makes available as language. This view still emphasizes the character of the poet, but puts more emphasis on what the poetry affords that character and thus allows us to treat the poems less as definers of character (as in novels) than as the presentation of exemplary powers giving readers possible stances towards what is potential for making in the kind of scenes that the poetry engages.

4. For a rare but very suggestive example of a contemporary writing actually using Wordsworth's poetry in a critical and exploratory capacity, see Robert Hass's essay on James Wright in his *Twentieth Century Pleasures* (especially pp. 38–45). And for my own critiques of the Wordsworthian vein in contemporary poetry, which I now see are too limited in their modernist fealties, see my essay "What Modernism Has to Teach the Contemporary Poet," and *Self and Sensibility in Contemporary American Poetry*. I still believe that poetry in the twentieth century must take responsibility for its own rhetoric in ways best illustrated by the testimonial, self-referring strategies of modernism. But that is not the only way to transform defensive self-consciousness into the exemplifying of powers made available by certain imaginative stances. The ideal of a Wordsworthian eloquence tries to make the presence of personal voice carry essentially the same force as the formal energies are asked to carry

in Modernism because in both cases the example of heightened consciousness is tested for how it makes it possible to extend the poem into the world.

5. Jonathan Arac's *Critical Genealogies,* 34–39, proposes a very different reading of the role that the maiden plays in the poem, so different that we disagree completely on both the poem and on the possible roles poetic eloquence can play.

6. I do not intend this as an attack on all language poetry, some of which (like Charles Bernstein's and Douglas Messerli's) has considerable personal pressure put on the material. But I do find disturbing its need for a political rhetoric that can attribute no positive powers to the particular way that the poetic imagination constructs its materials. For my arguments in this vein see my "Without Consequences is No Politics: A Response to Jerome McGann."

7. For the best measure of the difference that has emerged in Holden's sense of Wordsworth, and for the best evidence of how easy it is to end up in instant Wordsworth even when one adapts the rhetoric of personal eloquence, we need only consider what happens in the description Holden's earlier book gives of a Wordsworthian poetics. After praising the importance of a poetry that can be "personal and confessional—the rhetoric of 'a man speaking to men'," Holden goes on to make the distinctive mark of a postmodern poetry its tendency to "borrow the form from a nonliterary source instead of relying on the standard literary conventions as a basis for form" (118–119). The result is that the personal must then take "a more peripheral position in the poem" (40), so that at best we get the coy dreamer of Hugo's poem rather than the Wordsworthian self directly confronting its own need to establish its authority through the way that it composes its own enabling scenes. Later Holden admits a wider range of rhetorics, but he still concentrates on the mimetic situation and so cannot fully accept a model of eloquence that requires relating the authorial performance to the represented situation.

8. Although I did not at that time have either Wordsworth or the concept of eloquence in mind, I think that my discussions in *Self and Sensibility* sustain what I will say here. Richard Kenney also makes an interesting test case because his first book, *The Evolution of the Flightless Bird,* pursues a more traditional literary model of eloquence with an absoluteness of verbal and syntactic energy that outdoes even Merrill, especially since for Kenney the verbal structures literally compose the world, with almost no event sustaining them. Then his second book, *Orrery,* makes an apparently radical shift to the narrative of a year's events focused largely on family, land, and the most common of sentiments. But there remains the glorious intricacy of the orrery as instrument for measuring time, an intricacy matched by Kenney's verse movement and elaborate structural contexts that allow the simplest emotions a firm grounding in an admirable adult intelligence. For other variants on eloquence I think of Robert Pinsky's virtually Augustan concern for pointed speech at one pole and, at the other, the recent work of Bill Knott which brings into English Mallarme's gorgeously lucid syntax grafted on to the slipperiest semantic and dramatic gestures.

Works Cited

Altieri, Charles. *Self and Sensibility in Contemporary American Poetry*. New York: Cambridge University Press, 1984.

———. "What Modernism Has to Teach the Contemporary Poet." In Hank Lazer, ed. *What Are Poets For*. Montgomery: University of Alabama Press, 1987, 31–65.

———. "Without Consequences is No Politics: A Response to Jerome McGann." In Robert von Hallberg, ed. *Politics and Poetic Value*. Chicago: University of Chicago Press, 301–308.

Arac, Jonathan. *Critical Genealogies*. New York: Columbia University Press, 1987.

Hass, Robert. *Praise*. New York: Ecco Press, 1979.

———. *Twentieth Century Pleasures*. New York: Ecco Press, 1984.

Holden, Jonathan. *The Rhetoric of The Contemporary Lyric*. Bloomington: Indiana University Press, 1980.

———. *Style and Authenticity in Postmodern Poetry*. Columbia: University of Missouri Press, 1986.

Hugo, Richard. *31 Letters and 13 Dreams*. New York: Norton, 1977.

Johnston, Kenneth R. "The Triumphs of Failure: Wordsworth's *Lyrical Ballads* of 1798." In Johnston and Gene W. Ruoff, eds. *The Age of William Wordsworth: Critical Essays on the Romantic Tradition*. New Brunswick: Rutgers University Press, 1987, 133–159.

Kenney, Richard. *The Evolution of the Flightless Bird*. New Haven: Yale University Press, 1984.

———. *Orrery*. New York: Atheneum, 1985.

Lauterbach, Ann. *Before Recollection*. Princeton University Press, 1987.

Perloff, Marjorie. "Contemporary / Postmodern: The "New" Poetry." Lecture delivered at the 1978 MLA Convention.

Simpson, Louis. "The Originality of Wordsworth." In his *The Character of the Poet*. Ann Arbor: University of Michigan Press, 1986.

Stafford, William. *Stories That Could Be True*. New York: Harper and Row, 1966.

Stevens, Wallace. *Collected Poems*. New York: Knopf, 1954.

Wordsworth, William. *Selected Poems and Prefaces,* ed. Jack Stillinger. Boston: Houghton Mifflin, 1965.

Culture

Narrative and De-Narrativized Art

୬

Karl Kroeber

The most characteristic feature of earlier twentieth-century painting may fairly if inexactly be called its "abstractness." Modern paintings are distinguished by having no subjects, by referring to nothing other than themselves. Only in our century, admirers of high modern art claim, did painting fully realize its true nature by thus becoming self-sufficient. But every cultural success comes at a price, even if it takes time for the cost to appear. Disposable plastics seemed cheap and convenient until we admitted the expense of saving an environment polluted by our casual discardings. So it is not to devalue but rather to define the real worth (yield over cost) of modern art that I undertake to describe the price of its self-sufficiency, its eliminating of referential subject-matter.[1]

Description tends to be skewed, however, by traditional critical terms such as "subject," "abstraction," and "reference." I propose, therefore, that we consider early twentieth-century subjectless paintings referring to nothing other than themselves as anti-narrative.

I want to shift our terminology, because at the beginning of the nineteenth century, in the romantic era, the rising popularity and prestige of landscape painting was bringing toward culmination the first major movement to de-narrativize graphic art, a movement finally rejected by the greatest romantic painters, who chose the opposite path: to narrative landscape. The romantic decision *for* narrative dramatically illuminates the significance of the modern decision *against* narrative, especially if one declines to trace out, as I must here, the intricate historical connections that inextricably affiliate epochs whose fundamental aesthetic directions, as Ezra Pound and T. S. Eliot asserted long ago, radically diverge.

Narrative is a mode of verbal discourse, an enormously important one.[2] Ninety-five percent of all the world's literature, at a conservative estimate, is narrative. Literature, of course, is a sequential art, like music. That has suggested to some critics that paintings and sculpture *ought not* to be narrative, since painting and sculpture are spatial arts, static not temporal. Verbal narrative is of action, of change; therefore, this line of thought concludes, narrative painting is a contradiction in terms.

Yet until the twentieth century most people assumed not only that paintings could and usually did "tell stories" but even that they *should* tell stories. Most narrative painting was accepted as being appropriately referential or illustrative: a picture was expected to refer the viewer to a pre-existent verbal narrative. A marvelous instance of graphic narrative as illustrative reference is a medieval mosaic of Jonah and the Whale from a pulpit in Ravello showing the lower half of a human body protruding from the monster's mouth in the panel to the left, and in the panel to the right the upper half of a human with hands joined in prayer emerging from the same monster's jaws. Could this vivid mosaic be narratively meaningful to someone unfamiliar with the Bible and the Christian tradition, someone who might not even recognize the position of Jonah's hands as indicating prayer? One is tempted to think that the figure being swallowed into and disgorged by the monster would be more or less correctly interpretable even to an observer totally ignorant of our traditions. Yet would such an observer know which way to read the action? Might he not read the pictures from right to left and from the monster's point of view—the story of a big one that almost got away?

The Ravello mosaic demonstrates that though a picture may on occasion be worth a thousand words, it is more likely that a picture without a verbal context will be incomprehensible, for there are few if any visual cues that are not intrinsically ambiguous. A painfully vivid example was provided by the widely published photograph of a family of one of the astronauts watching the Challenger shuttle, a picture identified in many newspapers as the family's reaction to the vehicle's explosion, though in fact it portrayed their response to the apparently successful launch. Such mistakes explain why some have questioned whether there are *any* examples of narratives located *in* a picture, narrative readable purely from images themselves.

Recent students of narrative, of whom I cite Wendy Steiner as a popular exemplar, take an easy way out of this problem of graphic narrative. They assert that in the visual arts there an be no narrative unless more than one temporal moment is represented by means of a repetition of one or more figures. Unless a figure, like Jonah or the whale, *re*appears, it is not possible for a viewer to recognize the change or difference that constitutes action necessary for narrative. Only through the recurrence of identical actors can narrative be visually represented. This line of argument inescapably links narrative to some kind of realistic representation and the depiction of human or creaturely forms, since the repetition of identical shapes merely produces design.[3]

A consequence of this view is the judgment that inherent within the Renaissance concern for mathematical perspective, representation from a single viewpoint and one moment of time were powerfully anti-narrative implications.[4] What the Renaissance celebrated as "realistic" representation, essentially the illusion of instantaneously-perceived, three-dimensional forms, discouraged painters from depicting change, for by definition change cannot appear in the portrayal of a single instant from a unique perspective. There is important truth in this observation, but what is most interesting about it is that—apparently illogically—Renaissance painters and their audiences seemed to have thought that narrative pictures could and should be painted. The weakness in the argument of formalists such as Steiner is its insistence that *only* sequences of representations, like what one has in comic strips, constitute the essence of pictorial narration, an undue minimizing of the role of *audience* in storytelling. A good storyteller, in whatever medium, appeals to imagination; much of the effect of story derives from what is omitted, and visual omissions may be as potent as verbal omissions. Narrative consists of someone telling somebody about something: story cannot not exist without *both* narrator *and* audience. Narrative is a social transaction that cannot be understood without recognition of the contributory force of all participants in the transaction.[5]

The inadequacy of a merely formal definition of graphic narrative lies in its confining attention to what is literally present *in* the artwork, in what may be called the formalists' graphocentrism.[6] The difficulties provoked by their assumptions appear in the circumstance that visual sequentiality is often not easy to construe. As even the Jonah and the whale mosaic proves, unless you know the story being illustrated, you may have no definitive grounds for deciding where to start reading a pictorial sequence.[7]

The significance of reference to pictorial story is illustrated by one of the earliest Mesopotamian narrative representations, the so-called Stele of the Vultures, which only recently has been given a satisfactory interpretation by an art historian who suggested we read it not, as had been customary, from the top down, but from the bottom up, and, furthermore, with awareness of the relation of depictions on one side to those on the other side of the stone (what is necessarily made invisible by perception of one face), as well as to where geographically, as a boundary marker, the entire stone was physically located. In other words, we can "read" the story of the Stele of the Vultures only when we restore it to its condition as—in this case with literal physicality—a social transaction.[8]

A large number, perhaps a substantial majority, of sequence pictures, moreover, do not present us with simple consecutive orderings. A favorite medieval system was that of the ploughed field, left to right, right to left, then left to right again, and so on—an ordering that assures collocations of out-of-sequence units, a phenomenon to which I'll return shortly. Sequencing may be so intricate or so difficult to perceive that even the most experienced and knowledgeable observer can follow it only with some effort. In cases such as Trajan's column, described as the most important visual narrative of antique art, one's *in*ability—literally—to follow the sequence is part of the intended effect. That isn't absurd if you assume the artists anticipated imaginative responses from their audiences, that they conceived their story as a transactive process.[9]

Indeed, if we accept the theory put forward by people like Steiner, Giotto's sequences of pictures in the Arena Chapel in Padua may be termed narrative, but not a single one of the frescoes there can properly be called narrative. Giotto seems the best test case because he is a recognized genius in narrative art. While the depth of his skill and his spiritual profundity reveal themselves only to careful study, almost everyone enjoys his pictures. So what we learn about narrative painting from Giotto should be significant to an understanding of all painted stories.[10]

In the Arena Chapel Giotto paints stories of Joachim and Anna, the Virgin Mary, and Christ, seeming to introduce minimal specialized or esoteric features, making use of quite conventional representational signals, and introducing few distractingly "original" details. Giotto depicts the familiar religious scenes the way you and I *think* we would depict them. This accessibility makes it specially noteworthy that few commentators on the pictures in Padua have felt that the chronological sequentiality of each register was essential to their narrativity. The narrowness of the chapel interferes with easy perception of horizontal progression, and the asymmetrical wall structure to which Giotto adapted his paintings (if he did not in fact help plan the chapel), discourages merely sequential readings. Yet commentators over the centuries have praised the narrativity of individual frescoes. To deny narrative impact to the marvelous *The Kiss of Judas,* for instance, would seem perverse. Giotto's individual frescoes, such as this, *are* illustrative: they refer to very well-known events—indeed, as I noted, Giotto seems attracted to what is familiar and employs unmistakable details for referencing his scenes: Peter cutting off the soldier's ear, for instance. But that *The Kiss of Judas* is illustrative does not preclude its being also pictorially narrative. To the contrary, the obvious referentiality of Giotto's fresco frees him to evoke in us an original rethinking of the famous episode. Giotto's presentation of *The Kiss of Judas* compels us freshly to reimagine the story of this most famous of betrayals. It is a dull viewer indeed who is not provoked to intense contemplation of this confrontation of Jesus and Judas in the instant following the false kiss—a vividly silent encounter which only an extraordinary telling in words could achieve without falsification.

This example brings to light the danger in formalists' assumption that all narratives are in essence alike. Actual narratives, like actual conversations, are infinitely diverse. Theorizing about universal principles of narrative tends to obscure the fact, for example, that particularized emotional representations such as Giotto's had never previously been achieved in graphic storytelling. His emotionally provocative narratives are totally different, for instance, from those characteristic of Romanesque sculpture, to name another graphic form devoted to storytelling. I cite Romanesque capitals because it is revealing how seldom the rows of columns in churches or cloisters are narratively sequential, though if narratologists like Steiner were correct, artists so dedicated to telling stories in stone (as the Romanesque sculptors manifestly were) would have taken advantage of the opportunity provided by columnar rows for the repetitions supposedly necessary to storytelling. These unsequenced medieval sculptures suggest a different critical approach: by making *use* of referentiality a graphic artist may realize images narratively in a manner peculiarly appropriate to a visual, not a verbal, medium.

Sequential depiction is undubitably one form of pictorial narrative, but it is by no means the only form. And it may be less likely than a single scene to realize the full, complex potentialities of truly pictorial narrative. Hogarth, for example, is not only rigorously unidirectional in his *Progresses* but also relies heavily on verbal elements to tell his stories, and there is justice in the charge against him that he is too literary a painter. The seeming paradox disappears as soon as we remember that all significant stories are familiar, that enjoyment of them depends very little on curiosity as to what will happen next.[11] Successful stories are, and are intended to be, reheard or reread or reseen, and a story is significant if it continues to satisfy audiences who already know it, and for whom, therefore, structures merely determinative of the ordering of events are relatively unimportant. Most of the best verbal narratives, furthermore, are distinguished by various interruptive devices that serve to bring together sequentially disjunctive features; the flashback, elaborately deployed even by Homer three thousand years ago, is the best known of these configurative techniques, some of which are as accessible to a pictorial storyteller.

Let me illustrate by returning to the Arena chapel, where we encounter more than one story, for there are three bands or registers containing the stories of Joachim and Anna, of the Virgin, of Christ. As a result, when one looks at any painting in a sequence one also apperceives above or below it, or both above and below it, pictures that seemingly have nothing directly to do with it or its place in its register. Nobody who spends much time in the chapel, however, will believe that these vertical conjunctions are merely accidental or arbitrary. Giotto has established formal and thematic linkages between the vertically contiguous paintings which visually enrich and refine the meaning of the linear sequences.

An obvious illustration is the rendering of Christ's baptism directly above the crucifixion, the vertical/horizontal play of relationships emphasized by the angels in the top fresco on the left holding Christ's clothes, while below, the Roman soldiers to the right prepare to gamble for Christ's robe. Another vertical pattern is provided by the placing of the *Marriage of Mary and Joseph* in the top register directly above the *Entry Into Jerusalem,* and below that, Christ's *Ascension.* In the top picture the unsuccessful wooers to the left are excluded, while in the middle, Christ is welcomed into the city, and, finally, in the bottom fresco, He ascends from earth toward the heavenly Jerusalem, heralding the possibility of redemption for all. This thematic relation is enriched by a formal pattern. The top picture is compositionally enclosed, the middle one opens its center, both to the sides and in depth, because we see the palm-frond cutters to the left and right in the background, and this opening of the center is dramatically completed in the bottom scene displaying the Ascension—particularly striking because this rising and opening movement contravenes the general character of the lowest register as compositionally the heaviest, as if the real effect of gravity were felt closest to ground level even in the pictures.[12]

One sees Giotto's skill at blending of compositional and thematic features through an interplay of vertical/horizontal relations in his placing of the impressive *Lazarus* over the beautiful *Noli me tangere* scene, appearing immediately to the right of the *Lamentation at the Cross.* The figure of Christ vertically "moves" from his upright position in the left of the upper Lazarus scene to the right in the lower *Resurrection,* these verticalities contrasting with the horizontal form of his figure in the *Lamentation* directly to the left of the *Resurrection.* We thus almost literally see Him die, rise, and move away from the touch of mortality, while the placing his risen figure directly beneath that of Lazarus dramatizes this definitive spiritual triumph over death only prefigured in the earlier miracle.

Obvious also is the positioning of the *Adoration of the Magi,* kings kneeling before the holy child, directly above Christ kneeling to wash the disciples' feet. But characteristic of Giotto's special human touch, it seems to me, is his vertical alignment of the camel-driver tending his animal, and so not looking at the wonderful child, directly above the disciple concentrating on retying his sandal: the wonder of Christ's presence is how it irradiates the most trivial and ordinary circumstances of common life, even as the difference between these mundane concentrations makes us imagine the past with its entourage of kings before Christ's birth in contrast to the future faring of humble disciples on foot to preach a new glory through Christ.

These few examples remind us that it is scarcely logical to argue that visual narrative must be purely sequential, because visual perception, unlike aural perception, is not merely temporal. In the Arena chapel sometimes it is easier for the eye of the spectator to move vertically than horizontally. Furthermore, it is a naive view even of *verbal* narrative that overemphasizes sequence. All significant stories conceal as well as reveal, doing so both through omissions and through a composition of elements complicating and obscuring direct logical progression. Giotto's vertical ordering achieves an effect analogous to that perhaps no more successfully attained, for example, by Homer when he interrupts telling of the nurse's dramatic recognition of the scar on Odysseus's leg with the story of how thirty years before the hero had been injured by a wild boar. What is crucial in both tellings is that the artist's deliberate cross-cutting depends on his confidence in his audience's familiarity with his material. That confidence is an expression of the teller's commitment to the socially transactive nature of narrational art, the commitment which is the basis of all effective storytelling.

Let me illustrate this principle with a work that will display romantic narrativized landscape. Turner's famous painting *Ulysses Deriding Polyphemus. The Odyssey,* which inspired Turner, has been endlessly retold since Homer's days, most patently through translations in dozens of languages. As this history of re-citings piles up, the heritage of retellings, even though "extraneous" to the original core of the poem, becomes increasingly difficult to ignore: a later reciter knows that neither he nor his audience can respond with the relative innocence in which the original was conceived and articulated. In retellings, the transactive nature of the story inevitably undergoes changes. In a fashion that would not be easy for a poet, Turner embodies something of that history of the retellings of *The*

1. *J.M.W. Turner,* Ulysses Deriding Polyphemus, *The National Gallery, London.*

Odyssey in his picture, as is suggested by its title, which uses the hero's name in its Latin form. That name, Ulysses, was a kind of curse for the Romans; Homer's wily protagonist, for instance, appears as the epitome of Greek untrustworthiness in Virgil's *Aeneid,* the greatest reworking of the Homeric epics. Analogously, the water nymphs disporting themselves around the ornate vessels, which are themselves extraordinary elaborations of the simple boats described in Homer's poem, suggest later mythologizings of the hero Homer represents as intensely mortal. Odysseus, after all, rejects the offer of Calypso to become an immortal. In the Homeric work he is what one must call an historical figure, not least in contrast to a mythical monster such as Polyphemus, who in Turner's scene is represented so as to call to mind the Cyclops's association with volcanic forces by post-Renaissance scientific interpreters of classic myths. Turner's canvas, therefore, dramatizes both the mythologizing and demythologizing bound into the history of Homer's epic in western culture.

Even these few details suffice, I hope, to illustrate that in retelling the Homeric episode Turner adds to dubieties and contradictions and self-concealings intrinsic to the original, which was, we must remember, itself a retelling of traditional material. The episode depicted by Turner is that in which Odysseus, who had falsely called himself "No Man" to trick the giant, now boasts of his true name and parentage. The vaunt almost destroys him and leads to the death of all his followers, because it enables the blinded Polyphemus to identify for his father Poseidon who should suffer the sea god's vengeance. This crossing of a brilliant stratagem of concealment with self-destructive revelation dramatizes the significance of Odysseus's name, which roughly means "trouble," in the sense in which a stranger in a saloon of the old west says, "Call me trouble." The near-anonymity of the hero in Turner's painting seems to add to these self-complicating ironies of the original. Odysseus in this picture might be almost any of the undistinguishable individuals swarming on the ships, so any man, not just a hero, means trouble, for himself and others: each of us risks becoming no man when we boast of our individual genius, when we proudly display our uniqueness, as this canvas flaunts its spectacularly original sunrise at sea.

What I call Turner's narrativizing of landscape here is impressive because no such uniquely brilliant sunrise is mentioned in Homer's *Odyssey,* in which the sun comes up formulaically—everyone remembers the rosy-fingered dawn. And by the early nineteenth century it would have been possible, both aesthetically and commercially, for Turner to represent only the sunrise at sea without narrative content. Yet not only is Turner's landscape narrativized, but the natural scene is engaged with story in a variety of imaginatively provocative ways, not least that it embodies an event by no means certain in its implications either for its protagonist or for the viewers of its representation. As Turner originally painted the picture, Helios, God of the Sun, the immediate cause of the death of all Odysseus's shipmates, was clearly visible within the rising orb lashing his divine horses. Yet the sunrise is also thoroughly "naturalistic," so that its brilliance suggests the continuing indifference of nature to the fate of men, the indifference against which every story, every work of art, asserts a defiant human culturality. As I've remarked elsewhere, the fading from the painting of the horses of the sun is wonderfully appropriate, for the Greek gods *have* faded (what remains for us is the history of them preserved in Homer's ancient tale whose freshness is recovered through obscuring retellings such as Turner's) which urges us to reimagine through perception of a history of reshapings of the story the specificities of how human experience may combine splendor and tragedy, human triumph as human trouble.[13] It is by thus multiplying imaginatively self-reflexive perspectives, even presenting illuminations that conceal by their very brightness, that Turner's picture makes its visual scene into a complex storytelling event, and in so doing revitalizes the ancient epic, "revitalizing" here means forcing us to look anew into the exhilarating and terrifying abysses and contradictory forces unfolded in that complex social transaction we denominate with such deceptive simplicity by the name of *The Odyssey*.

Because recent criticism has emphasized the importance of intertextuality, we should be alert to the degree to which stories derive from and are about other stories, something John Milton, for example, understood when he undertook the epic retelling of the story of Adam and Eve in *Paradise Lost*. What has not been emphasized sufficiently is the analogue to intertextuality in the situation of the graphic artist, whose reference, or illustration, is a form of *retelling*. A painting that is narrative in character is not inferior because dependent on verbal, non-visual "original" sources. Indeed, in one respect at least, illustrative pictorial narrative may claim superiority, as I've suggested, since spatial juxtapositions possible in pictorial representation are unachievable in verbal telling, wherein simultaneity is simply not feasible. As Thomas Carlyle complained, in verbal narrative it is impossible to represent the density resulting from the fact that no human action occurs in isolation: everything that happens is surrounded by other things happening at the same time—*that* a painter can represent better than a writer.

Carlyle brings us back to the romantics and their narrativizing of landscape, a phenomenon that enables us to consider the functions of story in social life—a topic too often ignored by contemporary literary narratologists and art historians alike, particularly those concerned with twentieth-century art. But surely the purposes served by narrative ought to be of interest if its elimination by modernism is to be claimed as an advance or liberation of graphic artistry, when narrative painting had been esteemed for so long by so many. At the least one must ask why for centuries does it seem to have been so difficult *not* to tell a story in painting? Response to this question is facilitated by consideration of John Constable. In his work one can discern the influence of the monumental international best-seller, James Thomson's *The Seasons,* a blank-verse poem of great length that is almost entirely descriptive in character, and which owes much to seventeenth-century landscape art. Constable, who was all his life an admirer of Thomson, began painting in what may broadly be termed this anti-narrative tradition, as is evident from the absence of figures from his early work (Bermingham 96); but in his maturest and finest work his landscapes are profoundly if unostentatiously narrativized.

Limits of space compel me to oversimplify my account of this development and its effects, which may perhaps most quickly be suggested by the familiar observation that the paintedness of Constable's canvases became more ostentatious as he matured. The later works are distinguished by Constable's "snow," a flecking of the surface of the picture with dashes of light pigment. This characteristic led a contemporary reviewer to remark that "It is evident that Mr. Constable's landscapes are like nature; it is still more evident that they are like paint."[14]

Such blatant paintedness accompanies a tendency toward increased, even though unobtrusive, narrativizing of his landscape subjects, developing with particular significance in the great six-foot canvases of the 1820s, attaining a climax in *The Leaping Horse,* but unobservable even in *The Hay Wain,* to which I will principally refer, since it is Constable's best-known work. Critics have emphasized how assiduously Constable labored over these canvases in his studio, "at some remove from nature" (Rosenthal, 192). Constable, of course, is not the only landscapist to rework in a studio his open-air sketches. But his profound and unwavering commitment to the ideal of naturalistic accuracy justifies Bermingham's description of this intense studio painting as productive of a *fictionalized* spontaneity of impression (Bermingham 128). Constable's success in his later work is his achievement of the *illusion* of transparently realistic representation; merely accurate rendering of empirical facts is no longer satisfying to him; as Rosenthal puts it, in the latter part of his life actual appearances lost their importance in his representations of natural phenomena (Rosenthal, 117). Yet, paradoxically, in the later works a lower vantage point and visual engagement with the messy detail of natural actuality immediately in front of the viewer tends to replace the high perspective and the simpler, less tangled fore-

2. *John Constable,* The Hay Wain, *The National Gallery, London.*

ground details of his earlier scenes (Rosenthal 158; Bermingham 119–123). A cause is Constable's increasing narrativizing of his landscapes, his forcing of the viewer to deal with complexities, obscurities, uncertainties, even contradictions in what are as much stories as scenes, depictions of events, not just appearances.

An aspect of this paradox is the indubitable justice of scholars' insistence on the intense personal significance to Constable of *The Hay Wain,* their demonstrations of how significantly the painting is enriched by our understanding of the picture's expressive quality. Yet all the evidence suggests that non-scholarly viewers are unaffected by the canvas's expressivity, being more impressed by it as a kind of "objective" representation. This attainment of the *effect* of impersonality, or objectivity, by a work which can be shown to be so intensely personal in so many ways in part derives, I suggest, from Constable's success in compelling naturalistic description to subserve a narrative function. For the ordinary viewer *The Hay Wain* is the portrayal of an *event* represented transactionally, luring the viewer's imagination into constructing what is happening, thereby deflecting attention from the depiction's special concern to the painter. The cart in the stream tells a small, simple, unexciting story, a tale, in Wordsworth's phrase, "unenriched with strange events" but for just that reason appealing to the viewer's imagination, urging the viewer, again to adapt Wordsworth's appropriate term, to *make* a story of the incident, to imagine the possible significance of the human interactivity implied.[15] Indeed, precisely because the narrative is so undramatic, no more than the wain taking a shortcut through the river to get back to the field where it will be filled again like the wain in the distance, we are encouraged—especially by the density and even opaqueness of detail in the foreground through which we must visually "advance" to the perception of more distant objects—to imagine all that may surround and be involved in these simple actions within an unspectacular setting. Because its provocation toward story urges us to recreate imaginatively the human meaning of unextraordinary activities, the painting, therefore, does not strike us as expressive, for it visually *defamiliarizes,* if I may be allowed to transfer a term from literary criticism.

The Hay Wain, to put the matter crassly, is addressed to an audience of non-haymakers. Constable's canvas compels our attention to aspects of life which in his day were beginning to be pushed to the background of general social awareness by the onset of industrialized civilization, even as the picture for Constable himself was "retrospective," painted away from the Stour and intended to gain him the respect of London connoisseurs. And *The Hay Wain* succeeds admirably in defamiliarizing, for it enables us to regard seriously, not merely sentimentally or nostalgically, what industrialized society teaches us to ignore. Haying, once generally familiar, has become an uncommon sight in our urbanized existence, both in the direct experiential sense and also in the sense that it has been made culturally invisible by the dominance of ideologies of technological progress indifferent to, if not disdainful of, agricultural processes. Where our food comes from, how hay is collected, and what it contributes to our supply of nutriment, few of us now know, or even care to know. We have taught ourselves to forget something basic to our survival, to which Constable's picture would force us to reattend.

Because *The Hay Wain* visually defamiliarizes in this fashion, recalling our imagination to an essential function of our society which we have grown accustomed to overlooking, the painting—in contrast to most of Constable's earliest work—can be said not to be an end in itself, not to strive to be transparent representation. The picture cannot even be regarded as a mere reaffirmation of the Georgic tradition of celebrating the benefits of rural labor, which critics like Rosenthal see as central to Constable's work in the decade preceding the 1820s. The landscape of *The Hay Wain* is made, quite literally, to signify in a new fashion, to mean beyond its representational accuracy and within the received traditions from which it derives, through being narrativized. As story, the painter's naturalistic style takes on a significance not merely personal or subjective, nor, on the other hand, circumscribed by traditional generic implications. Neither expressivity nor symbolic emphasis could remind us so effectively as such naturalistic storytelling of the importance of a simple yet essential function of our society that our society encourages us to ignore. The specificity of *The Hay Wain* is, therefore, essential to its effect, as is its provocatively unspectacular narrative. Who could possibly care about a haywagon—but what *is* this one doing in the middle of the river? By engaging us in imagining the story of so trivial an event, Constable, without subordinating realistic accuracy of observation to either personal or symbolic reference, signifies the value of activities we teach ourselves to disregard. Quietly, almost surreptitiously, then, *The Hay Wain* develops a moral position, through its story, since it encourages us to think of what we've dismissed as not worthy of thought.

A decade later than *The Hay Wain, Salisbury Cathedral from the Water Meadows* confirms the progressive narrativizing of Constable's landscapes. Weather and scene as story here become almost obtrusive. But this painting's narrative consists in more than the representation of the English church under threat. The thematic opposition between religious edifice and dangerously lowering cloud over the darkly looming trees above dank burial ground focuses a more oppressively self-reflexive conflict, the conflict generated by man's spiritual aspirations to transform the energy of natural processes. Man's creative spirit arising out of these processes strives to transform natural curvatures into mathematized straightnesses. Cultural accomplishment asserts humanness upon natural energies embodied in forces of vegetation, wind, water, all the eroding operations of nature that relentlessly wear away the products of our creativity. This painting signifies man's dependence upon the natural systems he utilizes to affirm his supranatural culture. The cathedral stands between the graveyard where a corpse has just been buried and a rainbow, mythological covenant of hope, but also between the murky wateriness of the meadows and rainstorming turbulence of the sky, terrestrial and celestial embodiments of evanescence. The deepest passion informing this canvas is the anguish of the depicting itself. The ultimate complexity of Constable's art, realizable only through narrative functioning thus self-reflexively, consists in his making us conscious of the implication of his having made out of nature so transnatural an artifact as this painting of Salisbury Cathedral. This picture's overt paintedness is profoundly functional, for it *is* the dramatic intersection of activities depicted and the depicting activity itself. This doubling-back of story on its own "telling" required Constable to move beyond the relative transparency and smoothness of his early work (Bermingham 145), away from that clarity toward the thickly conflicted style of chiaroscurist density distinguishing his late canvases.

Because he was less committed to storytelling than other great romantic landscape painters, Constable's increasing narrativizing of his fervently scientific naturalism is peculiarly revealing of central *functions* of story in graphic art. That Constable, finally, could not paint as "realistically" as he desired without organizing his scenes narratively illuminates the ideology of what he called his "natural painture," a politics of representation that high modern art was to reject. This is not simply a matter of Constable's resistance to reformist movements of his day, though of course his "conservatism" founded on nationalistic patriotism is not irrelevant. But more important is his implicit assertion of the central *function* of valuable painting. Because *Salisbury Cathedral* is not just a scene but also a story, it signifies ethically. One could just as easily reverse that phrasing, because, as even critics like Wendy Steiner recognize, narrative is intrinsically evaluative.[16] This does not mean that stories conclude in summarized formulaic judgments. It does mean that to be effective as narrative, a story must appeal in some way to its audience's judgmental powers, must to that audience seem to matter, to be worth hearing or seeing. A good story by definition is one worthy of telling, not provocative of the response, "So what?" A good story, we all agree, must be interesting, or exciting, or repulsive, or subversive, or amusing, or unusual. That all such adjectives contain ethical implications is by no means accidental, for it is its power to evoke evaluative response that constitutes the whole-ness and completeness, the total meaningfulness, of any story. And the failure to provoke such evaluative response may account for the limitedness or odd incompleteness we often feel in front of pure landscape paintings, however vast. Goethe observed this deficiency even in our perceptions of the natural world, noting that after a few minutes even the most spectacular sunset becomes boring. The thinness that is dissatisfying even in Constable's most skillful, de-scriptively naturalistic early work arises from this lack of ethical sig-nification. What Constable learned in the pursuit of his ideal of naturalistic art was that to eliminate narrative from painting, what-ever gains that exclusion may bring in immediacy and direct sensual effect, was to preclude evaluative response, thereby to diminish, not enhance, the significance of naturalistic representation.

De-narrativized twentieth-century painting, which deliberately opposes the direction of Constable's development, is not necessarily meaningless, but it is necessarily ethically enfeebled. If that judg-ment seems harsh, I can claim support for it from the greatest of all philosophers. Plato, after all, banned art from his ideal Republic. Art for Plato was inseparable from narrative, partly because for all the ancient Greeks the supreme exemplary artist was Homer, and the stories artists told, even Homer, Plato argued, inculcated bad morals. Narrative is capable of corrupting, Plato insisted, because it evokes evaluative responses, exactly what, in Plato's ideal Republic, was to be fully predetermined.[17]

As always, Plato centers our attention on an essential issue, in this instance, that the understanding of a story necessarily involves the understander in an ethical activity, in an act of evaluation. In an ideal society, a society, that is, in which all ethical problems have been definitively solved, there obviously should be no place for nar-rative art, because there could be no need to raise ethical issues: all evaluative acts would be preprogrammed. Plato is not only logical, but provides us with penetrating insight into the potency of nar-rative. Plato objects, to cite his primary concern, that stories always deal with change, or at least the possibility of change. For Plato, change is inherently bad because it is evidence of imperfection; that which is perfect, that which is good or true or beautiful, is by his definition unchanging.

Plato describes an ideal. But most of us live in imperfect societies, in which existence depends on making evaluative judgments in response to shifting circumstances. Imperfection and transformativeness are conditions that demand exactly the complexly evaluative understanding that good narrative evokes. Myth is narrative. And it is no accident that all genuine religions consist of mythology, because religions must efficaciously address consequences arising from changes and imperfections in human experience. The Bible, which is predominantly narrative in form, beautifully illustrates the potency of narrative as a mode of discourse that simultaneously articulates and expounds doctrines and principles, while evoking evaluative responses and so rendering those doctrines and principles open to questioning, refinement, subtilization, improvement. Story thus allows principles and doctrines to persist vitally, to continue to be effective amidst shifts in social and cultural circumstances. The story of Adam and Eve, to cite, again, an obvious instance, explains why the human condition isn't as good as we can imagine its being, yet in so explaining the story poses problems that enable us, indeed, almost compel us, to keep reinterpreting the story. Why did God allow the serpent into the Garden? Was not God malicious to put the tempting tree in Adam and Eve's way? And so on. Reinterpretation does not destroy the value of the story. To the contrary, it enables the story to serve as a continuing focus for the most probing moral questions we can devise, every retelling and rehearing being—and demanding from its audience—a reevaluation of the essential conditions of our existence.

One reason story can be so effective is plain enough. Ethical abstractions, the absolutes in which Plato likes to trade, for most of us are useless, because—alas—we lead harried, practical, unideal lives: lives constantly entangled with contingencies. Our problem, normally, is not *knowing* what is good or bad abstractly, but in figuring how to apply our beliefs about what is good and bad in specific social transactions. And that fact suggests why story for so long was central to the graphic arts as well as to the verbal ones. As E. H. Gombrich has observed, in a pictorial narrative "any distinction between the 'what' and the 'how' is impossible to maintain. The painting of the creation will not tell you, like the Holy Writ, only that 'in the beginning God created the heaven and earth.' Whether he wants to or not, the pictorial artist has to include unintended information about the way God proceeded and, indeed, what God and world 'looked like' on the day of creation."[18]

As narratives particularize and specify, they evoke ethical implications, which, as Plato recognized, inescapably bring into question even the moral doctrines that the stories seem most directly to enforce. Stories can thus arouse "unintended" ethical effects because the very act of narrating compels abstract principles into the dust, heat, and pollution of contingent experience. And throughout most of the history of western civilization it was in that engagement, rather than some fugitive and cloistered "aesthetic" appeal, that art justified itself. Romantic painters' narrativizing of landscape, therefore, reflects an intriguing conservatism that sought to retain—even in the midst of innovative practice—the utmost ethical significance under circumstances tempting them toward what we know as modern aestheticism.

We see, then, that the contrary choice of early twentieth-century painters, their denial of narrative, is important because it implicitly excludes the evaluative from the reception of graphic art. The gain for modern art in banishing story consists in increased intensity of the specific immediate experience of the viewer, often accompanied by enhanced spontaneity of effect, qualities linked to modernism's often-remarked abandonment of depth for increased attention to surface. All this, as Meyer Schapiro has observed, assures that "what makes painting and sculpture so interesting in our time is their high degree of non-communication."[19] The non-communication is "interesting" because deliberate, not a failure: communication can be disregarded once the transactive quality of narrative has been dismissed. What Schapiro does not draw attention to is the trivialization of ethical force that is inseparable from any rejection of narrative.[20] Dislike of that trivialization, as well as a desire to reassert in an appropriately new fashion transactive functions of art, was to contribute significantly, I believe, to the 1960s postmodernist reaction against high modernism—but that is another story.

Notes

1. My focus of contrast is between romantic and early twentieth-century art; the latter, in the larger work of which this essay forms a part, I distinguish sharply from postmodern art of the last twenty years. One of the best sources for analyses of the modern-postmodern distinction is *The Anti-Aesthetic:*

Essays on Postmodern Culture, ed. Hal Foster (Fort Townsend, Wash.: Bay Press, 1983).

2. Amongst the vast body of literature on narrative, the following are most germane to this essay: Barbara Herrenstein Smith, making good use of work by Robert A. Georges and Paul Ricoeur, in "Narrative Versions, Narrative Theories," *Critical Inquiry* 7:1 (1980), 213–236, most cogently articulates the social, transactive nature of storytelling. Ricoeur's contributions have culminated in his two-volume *Time and Narrative,* translated by Kathleen McLaughlin and David Pellauer (Chicago: University of Chicago Press, 1984, 1985), although one should not overlook several of his earlier essays, for instance "The Hermeneutical Function of Distanciation," in *Hermeneutics and the Human Sciences: Essays on Language, Action, and Interpretation,* ed. and trans. John B. Thompson (Cambridge: Cambridge University Press, 1982). Georges, "Toward an Understanding of Storytelling Events," *Journal of American Folklore* 82 (1969), 313–328, is a seminal article overlooked by most narratologists. Peter Brook, *Reading for the Plot* (New York: Knopf, 1984) is illuminating on the relevance of transference to narrative transactions, and Hayden White, *The Content of the Form: Narrative Discourse and Historical Representation* (Baltimore: The Johns Hopkins University Press, 1987), a reworking of several of his most important essays, has much of value on problems of narrative and excellent references. So far as I can discover, the only critic fully to recognize that to understand narrative one must recognize that it is told to be *re*-told is Walter Benjamin in his essay "The Storyteller: Reflections on the Works of Nikolai Leskov," available in the volume *Illuminations,* ed. Hannah Arendt, trans. Harry Zohn (New York: Schocken, 1969), 83–110, esp. 91–93.

3. Wendy Steiner, *Pictures of Romance: Form Against Context in Painting and Literature* (Chicago: University of Chicago Press, 1988). The source for most of Steiner's theoretical positions is Gerald Prince, although she cites only two of his essays, "Narrativity," in *Axia: Davis Symposium on Literary Evaluation,* ed. Karl Menges and Daniel Rancour-Laferriere (Stuttgart: Akademischer Verlag Hans-Dieter Heinz, 1981) and "Aspects of a Grammar of Narrative," *Poetics Today* 1:3, 45–52, and not his *Narratology: The Form and Function of Narrative* (Berlin: Mouton, 1982).

4. Steiner, 25–26, 41–42.

5. Especially illuminating on these matters is Barbara Herrenstein Smith, see note 2 above. It is the transactional nature of narrative, of course, which has opened the way for critics committed to reception theory and reader-response approaches to enrich criticism of narrative in the past few years, though this kind of work has so far little influenced art criticism.

6. My debt to Jacques Derrida is obvious. Probably his most important work on visual art appears in *The Truth in Painting,* trans. Geoff Bennington and Ian McLeod (Chicago: University of Chicago Press, 1987).

7. I here leave aside the more profound problem of whether or not a sequence exists, a central issue for the cave art at Lascaux and Altamira, to cite only the best-known instances.

8. See Irene J. Winter's fascinating essay "After the Battle is Over: *The Stele of the Vultures* and the Beginning of Historical Narrative in the Art of the An-

cient Near East," in *Pictorial Narrative in Antiquity and the Middle Ages,* ed. Herbert L. Kessler and Marianna Shreve Simpson (Washington: National Gallery of Art, 1985), 11–34.

9. Richard Brilliant, *Visual Narrative: Storytelling in Etruscan and Roman Art* (Ithaca: Cornell University Press, 1984), 90–123, extensively analyzes the column.

10. On the Arena Chapel frescoes one may consult the collection of essays, *Giotto: The Arena Chapel Frescoes,* ed. J. Stubblebine (New York: Norton 1969). Still the best study of the vertical relations of the frescoes is the essay of M. Alpatoff, "The Parallelism of Giotto's Paduan Frescoes," *The Art Bulletin* 29 (1947), 149–159, repr. in Stubblebine. There is an excellent essay by Hans Belting in *Pictorial Narrative in Antiquity and the Middle Ages:* "The New Role of Narrative in Public Painting of the Trecento: Historia and Allegory," 151–170. Bruce Cole's *Giotto and Florentine Painting 1280–1375* (New York: Harper and Row, 1976) is a popular and unpretentious work based on a thorough command of the scholarship and admirably lucid in its presentation of Giotto's achievements and the central problems posed by his art.

11. E. M. Forster, of course, is most famous for the simplistic definition of story as dependent merely on curiosity as to "what will happen next," in *Aspects of the Novel* (New York: Harcourt Brace, 1927). Forster's view is founded on a contemptuous identification of storytelling with primitivism, and his association of story with the "primitive" and culturally undeveloped (itself an expression of the modernist aesthetic bias) lingers in some of the work of recent narratologists.

12. These and other parallelisms are discussed by Alpatoff, while Howard M. Davis has analyzed "Gravity in the Paintings of Giotto" in an essay appearing in Stubblebine 127–165.

13. An extended discussion of this painting which locates its place in Turner's career and includes references to important earlier scholarship on it will be found in my *British Romantic Art* (Berkeley: University of California Press, 1986), 193–196.

14. Cited by Lawrence Gowing, *Turner: Imagination and Reality* (New York: The Museum of Modern Art, 1966), 10. My hasty sketch of Constable's career is especially indebted to the fine scholarly work of Michael Rosenthal, *Constable: The Painter and His Landscapes* (New Haven: Yale University Press, 1983) and of Ann Bermingham, *Landscape and Ideology: The English Rustic Tradition, 1740–1860* (Berkeley: University of California Press, 1986), both cited in my text by author's name and page number, as well as Bermingham's forthcoming essay, "Reading Constable," in which she justifies at length the "fictionality" of Constable's "six-footers." My commentary has also been influenced by the admirable work of both John Barrell and Ronald Paulson, nor can I omit mention of Graham Reynolds's *The Later Paintings and Drawings of John Constable,* 2 vols. (New Haven: Yale University Press, 1984), along with the now old but still valuable essay of Michael Kitson, "John Constable, 1810–1816: A Chronological Study," *Journal of the Warburg and Courtauld Institutes* 20 (1957), 345–357.

15. "Unenriched by strange events" is from Wordsworth's "Michael," and

the adjuration to the reader to "make" a story comes from his poem of "an incident" concerning "Simon Lee" in *Lyrical Ballads*. Chap. 2 of my *British Romantic Art* contains a detailed comparison of Wordsworth's and Constable's use of narrative.

16. See Steiner, 11, drawing on William Labov, *Language in the Inner City* (Philadelphia: University of Pennsylvania Press, 1972), who introduced "evaluation" into discussions of narrative form, though not himself recognizing its inseparability from the total form of story.

17. Central passages in *The Republic,* 2d ed., trans. Desmond Lee (Harmondsworth: Penguin, 1974) are to be found in Part 3, 129–157, and Part 10, 421–439.

18. E. H. Gombrich, *Art and illusion* (Princeton: Princeton University Press, 1960), 110.

19. Meyer Schapiro, *Modern Art: Nineteenth and Twentieth Centuries* (New York: George Braziller, 1982), 223. Schapiro is one of the most significant commentators on modernism precisely because his extensive knowledge of other periods and styles makes his defense of the modern both cogent and persuasive. It is worth nothing, however, that Oscar Wilde as early as 1890 identified Modernism as assuring that "the sphere of Art and the sphere of Ethics are absolutely distinct and separate," that separation making possible not merely a new style of art but also the formalistic criticism of which narratologists like Prince and Steiner are the inheritors, and against which various postmodern critical positions, such as those linked to reception and reader-response theory, have defined themselves, often through a denial of modernism's separation of the aesthetic from popular culture; excellent on this point is Andreas Huyssen, *After the Great Divide: Modernism, Mass culture, Postmodernism* (Bloomington: Indiana University Press, 1986). My quotation from Wilde is taken from his "The Critics as Artist" in *The Complete Works of Oscar Wilde,* 5 vols. (New York: Doubleday, 1923), 5:226.

20. Although a few critics have engaged with the problem of the relation of modernist aesthetics and ethics, one of the earliest significant essays being that of Eugene Goodheart, "The Failure of Criticism," *New Literary History* 7:2 (1976), 377–392, only Tobin Siebers has systematically explored the implications of the separation of art from ethics that Wilde foretold: see *The Ethics of Criticism* (Ithaca: Cornell University Press, 1988).

The Historical Novel Goes to Hollywood

Scott, Griffith, and Film Epic Today

James Chandler

If, as some scholars argue, there were many romanticisms, even in Britain, there are surely many modern cultures, even in America. I would like to call attention to a modern culture—Hollywood and its epoch-making ambitions—that otherwise might go overlooked in a symposium that takes romantic poetry as its starting point. My own starting point will be certain experiences in the everyday life of the community in which I grew up—a procedure, I realize, that itself has an identifiably romantic, even Wordworthian, pedigree.

The community was Asbury Park, a Jersey Shore resort that, in addition to its public beaches, boardwalk, ferris wheel, and two carousels, could boast seven movie theaters by the 1950s, remarkable for a town of seventeen thousand residents. Some of these theaters were designed in the fashion of the Hollywood movie palaces: very large, with plush seats, multiple balconies, and, at the St. James Theater, a high ceiling upon which hidden projectors cast the illusion of moving clouds in an evening sky. Normally, the movies changed once a week, but at the St. James the policy in the 1950s was to land the most lavish movie spectacular of the year—this was a period in which the expensive epic routinely won the Oscar for

Best Picture—and to run it through the summer with a promotional campaign to match the grand scale of its action. The first one I remember was Cecil B. DeMille's *The Ten Commandments* (1956), and this was followed by such spectaculars as *The Bridge on the River Kwai* (1958), *Ben Hur* (1959), *Spartacus* (1960), and *Lawrence of Arabia* (1962). When *The Bridge on the River Kwai* came to the St. James, the management constructed a replica of the bamboo structure named in the title to span the street in front of the theater: the bridge on Cookman Avenue.

People would dress a little better for the St. James extravaganzas than for ordinary movie occasions. They would pay higher admissions prices without strong complaint—they were seeing a movie of twice the ordinary length. They would break for intermissions with expensive refreshments, and sometimes purchase one-dollar souvenir program books with color stills. When for various reasons these productions declined in popularity—starting perhaps with the fiasco of the Taylor-Burton *Cleopatra* (1963)—the St. James discontinued its summer policy. A great emptiness yawned in the sentimental space created by the Hollywood epic. It had become, in retrospect, a kind of cultural paradigm.

At the period I am talking about, I had not yet seen *Gone with the Wind,* which was the most obvious forerunner to the film epics of the fifties. Selznick's Civil War movie had not yet come to television and was being released in theaters only every five years or so. That *Gone with the Wind* itself had had an epic prototype I had not imagined. I had never heard of *The Birth of a Nation* or of D. W. Griffith then, and I doubt that even avid moviegoers twice my age had heard of him. For both technological and institutional reasons, knowledge of the cinematic past then was hard to come by. I certainly did not know that DeMille had been Griffith's understudy, nor that he had been making Griffith-styled film epics since the 1920s. Nor did I know that *Birth of a Nation* had been the first American film to indulge such production extravangances (huge sets, cast of thousands, three-hour format) and to require such marketing strategies (advanced booking, expensive seats, long runs, lavish programs) as later impressed us moviegoers in Asbury Park.[1]

The national box office success of the Hollywood epic makes it clear that we in Asbury Park were not alone among Americans in being so impressed in the 1950s. Furthermore, subsequent bonanzas in the epic mode including the *Star Wars* saga, *Gandhi,* and, most recently, Bertolucci's *The Last Emperor*—not to mention such box-office disappointments as Bertolucci's previous epic, *1900,* and Goldcrest Studio's *Revolution*—all suggest that *Cleopatra* was not the end of the story begun by Griffith.[2] But in what sense does the story begin with Griffith? We take Griffith at face value when we call him by the title of his own autobiography: *The Man Who Invented Hollywood.* And we take the title of *Birth of a Nation* at face value when we think of its director as standing, like Wordsworth at the start of *The Prelude,* with the world of the modernized national epic all before him. But should we think of this emergence, to borrow a distinction from Foucault, so simply as an origin?

The first really strenuous effort to see a history of practice *behind* Griffith—without, however, denying him his due as an innovator—is the landmark 1944 essay by Sergei Eisenstein that is echoed in my subtitle. This essay—"Dickens, Griffith, and the Film Today"—is famous partly for its exposition of Griffith's parallel montage, the cinematic technique, much employed by Eisenstein himself, of cutting back and forth between different lines of action. The essay is also famous for Eisenstein's appreciative commentary on the achievement of D. W. Griffith, whom he regarded not only as a founder of Hollywood movies as we know them, but also as the innovator whose example enabled Soviet directors to surpass his own achievement. The burden of Eisenstein's essay, however, is to show that, just as Griffith's techniques had helped enormously to make Russian film what it had become by the 1940s, so Dickens, whom Eisenstein portrays as the representative Victorian novelist, had contributed enormously to what Griffith had been able to do with his films in the first place. "From Dickens," writes Eisenstein, "from the Victorian novel, stem the first shoots of American film esthetic, forever linked with the name of David Wark Griffith."[3]

Eisenstein prosecutes his case by suggesting that there are two major aspects of Griffith's film style and that they correspond to (or "reflect," as he puts it) the two faces of Griffith's America. The first face is the industrialized world of "speaking automobiles, streamlined trains, racing ticker tape, inexorable conveyor-belts" (198). The second face is the America that we identify with "an abundance of small-town and patriarchal elements in . . . life and manners, morals and philosophy, the ideological horizon and rules of behavior in the middle strata of American culture." The first, "Super-Dynamic America," is "the 'official,' sumptuous Griffith, the Griffith of tempestuous tempi, of dizzying action, of breathtaking chases;" the second, "Small-Town America," is the America of "the traditional, the patriarchal, the provincial" (198). Eisenstein associates each of these Americas with a technique that Griffith developed for the cinema—Small-Town America with the close-up and Super-Dynamic America with the parallel montage—and he argues that both techniques are derived from Dickens' practice in fiction.

I don't mean to contest either of these particular claims. There is evidence, which Eisenstein cites, that Griffith knew Dickens's work well; one of Griffith's earliest films, for example, was based on Dickens's *The Cricket and the Hearth*. And there is also the famous anecdote recorded by Linda Arvidson Griffith, which Eisenstein relates, about the filming of *Enoch Arden*. In planning this 1911 two-reeler, Griffith proposed repeated crosscutting between the seafaring husband shipwrecked on his island and the patient wife awaiting his return on the seashore near their home. Asked by an unnamed executive how he expected audiences to find such a series of images intelligible, Griffith is supposed to have replied: "Well, doesn't Dickens write that way?"[4] This seems to constitute ample warrant for Eisenstein's elaboration of how Griffith developed the practice of montage out of Dickens's conspicuous tendency to shift abruptly between his novels' subplots.

In the course of his argument, however, Eisenstein eventually locates his claims about the literary sources of particular film techniques within a larger horizon of argument, as Dickens comes to stand in for the entire literary tradition before film:

> Let Dickens and the whole ancestral array . . . be superfluous reminders that both Griffith and our cinema prove our origins to be not solely as of Edison and his fellow inventors, but as based on an enormous cultured past. . . . Let this past be a reproach to those thoughtless people who have displayed arrogance in reference to literature, which has contributed so much to this apparently unprecedented art and is, in the first and most important place: the art of viewing—not only the eye, but viewing—both meanings embraced in the term. (232–233).

This is an eloquent and powerful admonition, and perhaps not heeded as often as it ought to be. But for critics who may be disposed to look at the literary preconditions of the cinema, the emphasis that Eisenstein has placed on Dickens, both as a synecdoche for the literary tradition and as the source of certain film-narrative techniques, can be misleading in the way it obscures another literary genealogy for Griffith's filmmaking, especially in *Birth of a Nation*. In accepting too entirely Eisenstein's focus on Dickens and on Griffith's "Victorianism," on which so much has been written, we lose sight of connections, on which nothing has been written, between Griffith's seminal film epic and what might be called the *romantic* line in nineteenth-century fiction, the line that follows from Walter Scott.[5] The Dickens line also obscures Griffith's involvement in a program to rewrite history on film, and thus blocks the way to a consideration of Griffith in respect to a crucially understudied issue in current cultural studies: the use of film in the representation of history. In its way of "viewing" history, and indeed of "writing" it, *Birth of a Nation* marks the intersection of what Raymond Williams would call emergent and residual cultural formations. Given Griffith's explicitly apocalyptic conclusion, one might even be tempted to place the film at the interpenetration of two Yeatsian gyres, one spiraling outward toward its position of dominance in American modernity, the other winding down from its position of dominance in British romanticism.[6]

Walter Scott is an almost exact contemporary of the romantic poet whose work is celebrated in the exhibition that occasioned our look at the relationship of romanticism to modern culture. It would have seemed strange to most of their informed contemporaries that Wordsworth, and not Scott, would someday be chosen to epitomize the cultural history of the romantic period. Scott was the dominant poet of the period from the turn of the century until about 1813, when he turned down the poet laureateship. In the field of poetry, Scott's popularity gave way to Lord Byron's, but Scott retreated from poetry only to attack the literary marketplace under a different banner. His second conquest was unprecedented in its success. Keats wrote in 1819 that there had been "three literary kings in our Time—Scott—Byron—and then the scotch nove[ls]."[7] But this was actually a way of saying that there had been only one literary king, for "scotch novels" is a nickname for the extraordinary series of works that Scott published when, after declining the laureate-ship, he decided to complete a novel that he had begun in 1805 and that appeared in 1814 as *Waverley, Or 'Tis Sixty Years Since*. In the two decades until his death in 1834, Scott would produce more than two dozen more works of fiction in the series that came to be called the Waverley Novels.

Most of the best of these were completed by 1819, when Keats made his comment, and by which time Scott had already added to his list such novels as *Guy Mannering, The Antiquary, Rob Roy, The Heart of Mid-Lothian, Old Mortality, The Legend of Montrose, The Bride of Lammermoor,* and *Ivanhoe*. With these books, Scott changed the course of all kinds of writing about the past, left his mark on drama and opera as well, and eventually became, without question, the most widely influential of all British authors except for Shake-speare. Even Scott's most relentless adversary, Mark Twain, seemed to acknowledge this point, negatively, when he said that Scott "did measureless harm, more real and lasting harm, perhaps, than any other individual that ever wrote."[8] To speak only of fiction: if Scott had not lived, the literary oeuvres of Balzac and Hugo in France, Cooper and Hawthorne in America, Manzoni in Italy, and Tolstoy in Russia would all look substantially different. In England, specifi-cally, the same can be said for most of Thackeray, much of George Eliot, and, indeed, some of Dickens's own work, especially *A Tale of Two Cities*—although it is a matter of some moment to us here that, for Dickens, Scott's work figures as an object less of emulation than subversion.

What Scott's successors recognized in his fiction was a new liter-ary form, but different writers seized on different aspects of that form, and it is not monolithic even from Waverley novel to Waverley novel. What is distinctive about the novels as a group is certainly nothing so simple as the location of an action at an earlier period. There had already been ample precedent for that in the eighteenth-century's novel-of-the-past, chiefly in the Gothic tradition that peaks in the 1790s with the popular works of Ann Radcliffe and Monk Lewis. The difference is that, in the eighteenth-century cases, a past setting contributes only atmosphere and ornamentation. These works are informed by neither historical knowledge nor historical theory; they are marked by unsignaled anachronism at every level, and by no recognition of how a historically specific culture sets conditions upon the characters or the plots in question. There is no effort to establish historical relation between the past moment and the present because there is so little sense of what it is that makes a past moment different. The conditions for marking out a historically specific culture had not yet emerged with sufficient force to shape, or be shaped in, a new form of fiction.

The place where such conditions were developing during the late eighteenth century was the young Scott's Edinburgh, capital of what is now called the Scottish Enlightenment. Scott attended Edinburgh University in the 1780s, and there he was schooled in the principles of the so-called "philosophical history," as worked out by David Hume, Adam Smith, and some of their less well-known contemporaries, Adam Ferguson, William Robertson, and John Millar. One explanation of how philosophical history emerged in Scotland when it did posits a historical self-consciousness induced by the country's accelerated development through several economic stages in relatively little time after the Union with England in 1707. Scott himself offered such an account in the Postscript to *Waverley* in 1814, and when he turned to his first English historical novel with *Ivanhoe* (1819), he explained that his choice of period for an English novel had been guided both by the wish to find a stage of civilization in England's history equivalent in primitiveness to, say, early eighteenth-century Scotland and by the sense that, to do so, it was necessary to go all the way back to the English Middle Ages.

Another factor that contributed to Scott's sense of a historically specific culture, although this affected Scott's audience as powerfully as it did him, was the experience of the French Revolution and the Napoleonic Wars. The age defined by 1789 and 1815, the Pan-European dates of the Bastille and Waterloo, was the period that helped to define what the notion of an historical period *was* for nineteenth-century historiography. It can scarcely be an accident that the historical novel sweeps Britain and Europe in the half-decade after Napoleon's final defeat. This was, after all, a defeat that lent at least a temporary sense of closure to the Revolutionary period, and that allowed various nations to take stock of the cultural transformation that had been wrought during the previous quarter-century of tumult and change. In the century that followed, the historical novel helped more than one nation to invent a tradition about its own genesis.[9]

A more thoroughgoing account of the influences on Scott's

historicism would include other factors as well—for example, his early exposure to the developing German sense of history in such works as Goethe's *Götz von Berlichingen,* which Scott translated into English. But to speak of a developing awareness of historical change and cultural specificity is not yet to raise the question of a literary form in which this awareness might have been articulated. The new form, as it was developed by Scott and imitated by great nineteenth-century novelists in each of the western nation-states, can be sketched under several primary rubrics. First, under the heading of *subject matter,* Scott normally represented an earlier stage of society as divided against itself, with that past conflict itself typically defined as a struggle between older and newer centers of power, and usually leading to a social resolution, but often at great human cost. The second rubric is *documentation.* Scott was a serious antiquarian long before he took to fiction. He specifically offered his novels as a record of former manners and struggles, and he thus took pains to indicate, in footnotes and multiple prefaces, just what evidence had guided him in representing the past as he had. Third comes the term that Scott used to designate what it was that he was concerned to document in the past culture in question: *manners.* Manners (what the French social commentators called *moeurs*) are, for Scott, what a culture primarily consists in. His prefaces stress that the great challenge facing the historical novelist is to make past manners live for modern readers without either leaving them unintelligible for the sake of fidelity or creating anachronism for the sake of making them intelligible. Fourthly, as for *plot,* Scott's method here would set a local or domestic action, in which the intimate manners of the culture could be displayed, against the background of a larger historical development. This arrangement allows for much negotiation between the strictly factual and the more broadly typical historical representations in the novel—as well as between official or public or political history, on the one hand, and unofficial or private or popular history on the other. As Hugh Trevor-Roper has shown, Scott's accommodation of the political and military chronicle to the materials of domestic history changed the practice not only of novelists but also of nineteenth-century historians.[10]

The fifth and last rubric is *characterization,* for which Scott developed a number of related and influential practices. Virtually all of his novels are populated with actual historical personages whose

characteristics and actions he elaborated out of standard biographical materials. These are the kinds of characters whom Hegel called
"world historical individuals," and they correspond to the heroes
and protagonists of the classical epic form—Achilles and Odysseus,
for example, who stand not only as the leaders of their societies but
also as the epitomes of their respective unified cultures. However,
because Scott tends to project his incipient nation states not as culturally unitary, but rather as divided against themselves, these kinds
of figures are not the protagonists of the historical novel. As Georg
Lukács has shown in his great but problematic study of the historical novel, the world historical individuals become minor characters
in Scott's world, and the protagonist at center stage is a relatively
mediocre character who is caught between the two factions whose
conflict at once defines his character and produces the emergent nation for which he or she comes to stand.[11]

So in *Waverley,* for example, the historical Bonny Prince Charles
is a minor character who represents one side of the Scottish-English
conflict of the mid-eighteenth century. The title character, Edward
Waverley, on the other hand, is Scott's invention and is designed to
play the role of someone caught between sides, whose ordinary and
typical character formation is defined precisely by his having experienced two sides of the conflict. This much becomes clear early on
in the novel when it is explained that his Whig English father elects
to share Waverley's upbringing with a Tory uncle who is a sympathizer in the cause of Scottish rebellion. In *Ivanhoe,* to take one of
the other better-known examples, the historical Richard the Lion-
hearted and his brother (later King) John are minor characters who
represent aspects of a political conflict in the novel, whereas Ivanhoe
himself is the fictional personage whose character is formed out of
the conflicts that he finally tends to mediate. In respect to the Saxon-
Norman conflict, for example, Ivanhoe is a Saxon who is sympathetic with Richard's (i.e., not John's) wing of the Norman regime.
In the end, he helps to reconcile his recalcitrant Saxon father, Cedric, to the cause of his cultural father, Richard, and thus to prefigure
the social compromises that, on this account, lay ahead in English
social development.

Taken together, all the features of Scott's form provided a way of
representing large historical events and movements as *felt* in the

popular experience. This is the point emphasized by Lukács, and it was not lost on the nineteenth-century authors who followed Scott. If space permitted, a story well worth telling here would be that of the eclipse of the nineteenth-century historical romance in the shadow of modernism. A high modernist novel such as *To the Lighthouse* (1927), for example, turns the historical novel inside out—not showing domestic action within a framework of history but, so to speak, history within a framework of domestic action. The first and last of the book's three sections are separated by the interlude section—"Time Passes"—that deals with the period of the Great War. But here, as in David Jones, the war is represented only in parenthesis. Woolf knew Scott's fiction well—her commentary on it is as incisive as any we have—and in *To the Lighthouse* itself she seems to acknowledge the challenge her fiction poses to his tradition when she makes Mrs. Ramsay's extended reflections on her husband's reading of Scott the climactic passage of the book's long opening part. For Mrs. Ramsay is given to understand Mr. Ramsay as contemplating precisely the extinction of his own work in the mirror of the great Scottish author who, by 1927, is no longer read.

The story of Scott's extinction in high modernism is not immediately to the point here, however, since this movement was twice removed from the southern American culture in which Griffith, a Kentuckian, matured. Mark Twain reported on what he saw of this culture in the chapter he devoted to Scott's influence on the South in his 1883 *Life on the Mississippi:*

> If one take up a Northern or Southern literary periodical of forty or fifty years ago, he will find it filled with wordy, windy, flowery "eloquence," romanticism, sentimentality—all imitated from Sir Walter, and sufficiently badly done, too—innocent travesties of his style and methods, in fact. This sort of literature being the fashion in both sections of the country, there was opportunity for the fairest competition; and as a consequence, the South was able to show as many well-known literary names, proportioned to population, as the North could.
>
> But a change has come, and . . . the North has thrown out that old inflated style, whereas the Southern writer still clings to it. . . . There is as much literary talent in the South, now, as ever there was, of course; but its work can gain but slight currency under present conditions; the authors write for the past, not the present; they use obsolete forms and a dead language.[12]

Reports of Twain's exaggerations have been greatly exaggerated. In his analysis of Scott's influence, to which we will return, he stands on very solid ground.[13] In 1883, when Twain wrote this, young David Griffith was eight years old, and his father, Roarin' Jake Griffith, was still two years from his death. Friends of the Griffiths in this period report Saturday evening gatherings where, with young David hidden under a table to listen, his father, to whom he said *Birth of a Nation* was so powerfully indebted, would regale the company with tales of the war and readings from Shakespeare, Poe, and Scott, but not Dickens, who was after all, in the eyes of some observers, Scott's Yankee-supported rival.[14]

Nor did the Scott craze—what Twain called "the Sir Walter disease"—die out among Southern writers in the 1880s. The 1906 racist novel by Thomas L. Dixon (a South Carolinian) that caught Griffith's eye and eventually prompted him to undertake his epic film of 1914 is precisely one of the sort that Twain describes as still in the thrall of Scott's literary spell. That much is already indicated in its title, *The Clansman,* spelled in such a way as to emphasize the connection it envisioned between the Ku Klux Klan, whose aims the novel promotes, and the Highland clans that Scott had portrayed in "the scotch novels." The title character, Ben Cameron, comes from a Scottish family whose clan appears in *Waverley.* The archaic manor house on the family plantation is grandly referred to as Cameron Hall. When, late in the novel, young Cameron "summons the clans" for the Klansmen's ride to the rescue in defense of what is called their "Aryan Birthright," he does so under "The Fiery Cross of Old Scotland's Hills," a line used for one of Griffith's insert titles in the corresponding scene from the film. The summoning of the clans with the fiery cross is depicted in chapter eighteen of Scott's 1819 novel, *The Legend of Montrose,* and a long note to Scott's popular poem, *The Lady of the Lake,* discusses the passing of the cross as a logistical mechanism in rounding up dispersed clansmen and the symbol of the cross as an ideological occasion to show unquestioned loyalty to the chieftain.[15]

These are just the superficial indicators. The novel that Griffith chose for his epic venture is subtitled "A Historical Romance," and its subject matter embodies the paradigmatic traits of the form that Scott called by the same name. The subject matter of *The Clansman* is the prehistory of a nation divided against itself. It attempts to document its action by way of historically particularized debates on slavery. It emphasizes differences in "manners" both between the North and South and between nineteenth- and twentieth-century America. It creates a domestic plot, centered around the Southern and Northern families, respectively, of the young lovers, Ben Cameron and Elsie Stoneman, and it sets this plot against the larger national events of the Reconstruction Era. While giving center stage to the fictional lovers, it makes its historical personages minor characters who represent polarized ideological positions in the national crisis.

Some of these points can be illustrated from the novel's opening sequence. The novel (unlike the film) begins in a Washington hospital with the meeting of Elsie Stoneman, daughter of Pennsylvania Senator Austin Stoneman (closely modeled on the abolitionist, Thaddeus Stevens, also a senator from Pennsylvania during the War and Reconstruction), and Ben Cameron, the wounded Confederate colonel who becomes the Klansman of the title. Elsie is the boundary-crossing character in the novel. She later goes to South Carolina with her abolitionist father, but remains there with Cameron in the end, plighting her troth with the Klansman on its last page. Their meeting in the hospital at the outset takes place on the day of Lee's surrender at Appomattox, which is announced by newsboys outside the hospital windows. This interleaving of domestic-fictional and public historical events is conspicuously insisted upon throughout the opening sequence. It culminates with the evening scene, five days after the surrender, when Elsie and Ben go to Ford's Theater for a production of *Our American Cousin* which the President has announced in advance he will attend. The centerpiece of this opening sequence is a Scottesque episode, between surrender and assassination, in which Cameron's mother, having come from South Carolina to see her wounded son, is accompanied by Elsie to Lincoln's office to sue for a pardon from "the Great Heart." Elsie succeeds where Mrs. Cameron fails, but only after a series of debates between Lincoln and her father (the Stevens character) about larger policy questions of amnesty toward the postwar South.

This sequence depicts Lincoln not only as a Southern sympathizer but actually as a Southerner himself. At their White House interview, Mrs. Cameron and Lincoln hold the following exchange:

> "I must tell you, Mr. President," she said, "how surprised and how pleased I am to find you are a Southern man."

"Why didn't you know that my parents were Virginians, and that I was born in Kentucky?"

"Very few people in the South know it. I am ashamed to say I did not."

"Then, how did you know I am a Southerner?"

"By your looks, your manner of speech, your easy, kindly ways, your tenderness and humour, your firmness in the right as you see it, and, above all, the way you rose and bowed to a woman in an old, faded black dress, whom you knew to be an enemy." [16]

Dixon offers relatively little in the way of set-piece descriptions of "manners," but this shows that the subject has some importance in the novel, even if the concept of manners is beginning to undergo a shift toward its prevalent modern American associations with etiquette. "Easy, kindly ways" should have been enough without the particularization ("above all") of the "way [he] rose and bowed to a woman."

Coming to Dixon's opening sequence from Scott, one will also be quickly reminded of the role of pardons in the thematic structure of the Waverley novels. Pardons provide institutional agency for the work of reconciling opposing sides in a society at war with itself: *Waverley, Ivanhoe,* and *The Bride of Lammermoor* all involve crucial acts of pardon. Indeed, Elsie's appeal to Lincoln probably owes a specific debt to *The Heart of Mid-Lothian,* where, in the context of Scottish insurrection, the fictional Jeannie Deans, having traveled from Edinburgh to London, sues for the pardon of her sister Elsie to the historical Duke of Argyll, with like success, and with similarly large political resonances. [17]

If Dixon's book suggests the continuing power of Scott in early twentieth-century southern literary culture, then Griffith's selection of this book may be said to indicate something about his own taste in historical fictions. If Griffith had simply undertaken an unambitiously faithful rendering of Dixon's narrative (i.e., an "adaptation"), not much more could be said of the matter. [18] But what Griffith did, in the event, was to recast much of Dixon's action and to reframe the entire plot. Further, in undertaking this transformation of Dixon he seems to have been guided by purposes and principles themselves indebted to Scott's example. In neither his relation to Dixon nor to Scott, however, is Griffith engaged in a project of adaptation. Griffith reimagines Dixon's project with suggestions from Scott but in so doing he develops his own kind of cinematic "writing," what Truffaut might have called an *écriture cinématique de l'histoire*.

In order to lend the air of documentary authority to his film narrative, as Scott once did for his fictions, Griffith provided still shots of newspaper pages, citations of Woodrow Wilson's *History of the American People,* and various historical statistics. Far more ingenious, however, was what he did with the composition of certain scenes. At a half-dozen points in the film we are given insert titles to announce that the setting for the ensuing scene replicates a Civil-War-period photograph or historical painting. The first such setting we are given is the interior of the Lincoln's office in which Elsie and Mrs. Cameron eventually sue for pardon (fig. 1). This interior is first shown in the scene of Lincoln's signing of the proclamation to draft seventy-five thousand Northerners to serve in the Union army: the insert title declares the scene a "historical facsimile" based on a Matthew Brady photograph of the event. The pains taken with the details of the assassination sequence are famous—Griffith researched

1. *Mrs. Cameron and Elsie Stoneman (Lillian Gish) petition Lincoln for pardon in the set designed as a "historical facsimile" of his office.*

the line in *Our American Cousin* on which Booth pulled the trig-
ger—and at the beginning of this sequence, too, we are informed
that the setting is based on a historical facsimile of Ford's Theater.[19]
These and other such moments in *Birth of a Nation* create an illusion
of what might be called "documentary space" for encounters of fictional characters with historical figures and circumstances. Griffith's deployment of textual sources and his replication of historical
settings combine to pioneer the cinematic equivalent of Roland
Barthes' "history effect": the "documentary effect."

An even more strenuous effort in Griffith's narrative transformation of *The Clansman* follows from his decision to add an hour's
worth of material of his own devising to introduce and contextual-
ize the event with which Dixon's novel begins. The meeting of Elsie
Stoneman (Lilian Gish) and Ben Cameron (Henry Walthall) in the
Washington hospital on Appomattox Day does not occur until one-
third of the way into Griffith's three-hour film. That first hour's
footage, then, is the obvious place to look for evidence of how
Griffith set about his task to rewrite not only Dixon but American
history as well. We can note, for instance, that whereas Dixon's
book starts with the end of the war, some of the most memorable
action in *Birth of a Nation* occurs in the battle scenes. In depicting
military struggles of the Civil War, Griffith managed to weave fictional elements into the military chronicle as Scott had done in novels like *Waverley* and *Old Mortality* and likewise Tolstoy, in the same
tradition, with the celebrated accounts of the Napoleonic Wars in
War and Peace. The camera locations on hilltops high above charg-
ing troops in the battles scenes, or over the serpentine progress of
Sherman's march to the sea, give the sense of both wide scope and
elevated historical perspective. Both the subject matter and the representational techniques in Griffith's pioneering battle footage lend
the Scott-like sense of epic scale to what, in Dixon, had been a more
modestly conceived historical representation. Like Scott's depictions of the Battle of Preston, the Porteous Riots, or the Siege of
Torquilstone, Griffith's military events unfold in a kind of "epic
space." On the one hand, then, Griffith's transformation of Dixon
showed his ambition to carry on Scott's project of updating the epic
form. In the Dedicatory Epistle to *Ivanhoe* (a copy of which Twain
said one could find on every Southern mantel piece in the 1880s),
Scott alludes to the creation of "the modern epopée," the task of

modernizing in prose the epic tradition he had received in verse.
Griffith further modernized, or better, *re*modernized, the prose epic
as it came to him by projecting it into film.[20]

In respect to the equally important *domestic* dimension of his project, on the other hand, Griffith also resorted to Scott's example to
produce a fuller representation than he found in Dixon of what
Scott, in the same Dedicatory Epistle, called "*la vie privée* of our
forefathers." In prefixing the hour of new material to Dixon's opening sequence, Griffith's twofold strategy was to preserve the sense
of the meeting of Elsie and Ben as a first encounter while simultaneously creating a prehistory for their relationship. His way of handling this balancing act, in a "script" that he apparently kept only in
his head as he shot the film, was to develop an expositional sequence
around a visit in late 1860 (dated by newspaper reference) of Elsie's
brothers from their eastern Pennsylvania home to the Cameron estate in Piedmont, South Carolina. The invitation for this visit,
extended from Ben Cameron to Phil Stoneman, obviously presup-
poses a still prior (but unexplained) friendship between them, perhaps as recent college friends; in Dixon's version, Cameron and
Stoneman meet for the first time on the battle field after Cameron's
ill-fated charge. Griffith takes the trouble to motivate and insert the
visit sequence because it enables him to offer a study in comparative
cultures or systems of manners before the outbreak of the war. This
intention is signaled forcefully at the moment when the younger
Stoneman brother descends from the carriage outside Cameron
Hall and faces the younger Cameron brother for the first time:
"Chums—the younger sons," reads the insert title, "North and
South." They immediately begin to twit each other about their
manners and attire: "Where did you get that hat?" (fig. 2). Their
friendship, with its Chaplinesquee sparring and horseplay, becomes
a comic leitmotif through the visit, but is given tragic symbolic authority later in the film when, wearing the more uniform costumes
of Union and Confederate soldiers, they meet on the battlefield and
die in a mutual embrace (fig. 3).

The narrative device of the visit is supported by the use of parallel
cutting that juxtaposes images of domesticity in the North and
South. It is made clear even before the visit, for example, that unlike the scene at Cameron Hall, the image of the domicile in the
North is dispersed among three different locations. The domestic

2. *"Where did you get that hat?" asks the youngest Cameron son of his visitor from the North.*

3. *Death-embrace of the younger Cameron and Stoneman.*

action of the Stoneman family, who are motherless, occurs partly in a Washington apartment where Elsie lives with her aunt, partly in a Pennsylvania house that offers the support of neither parents nor neighbors, and partly in the Washington office of Senator Stoneman, where Lydia, the mulatto housekeeper, is supposed to have usurped the role and vastly augmented the power of the absent mother.[21] The juxtaposition of each of these domestic settings with the self-consciously full and "organic" culture of the Southern manor, both before and after the visit, suggests invidious conclusions about fragmentation, perversion, and isolation in the North. One is particularly struck by a series of mirror shots involving the Pennsylvania household of the Stonemans and the Southern culture of Cameron Hall. In the former, the house stands on the left, its curtained doorway facing right, onto a walkway where the three young Stonemans appear alone and consistently parentless in the foreground and where the background is empty except for two laborers, one black and one white, whose work seems unpurposeful and who remain marginal in the life and attention of the Stoneman trio. In the corresponding shots of Cameron Hall, by contrast, the household appears on the *right* of the screen, its porched entranced way facing *left,* on to a street where a community—of which the Camerons old and young are very much a part, including contented-looking black slaves—carries out its affairs in ritualized harmony (fig. 4). To sustain this sort of contrast through the outbreak of the war, Griffith offers parallel scenes of farewell to departing soldiers. The Stoneman brothers exit right from the house to the empty walkway and then through a hedge, in a strangely barren farewell scene, played only with Elsie, who puts up a brave face in front of her brothers (fig. 5) and then collapses, distraught, into the arms of an unidentifiable older woman—her aunt, perhaps, or a servant—who emerges suddenly from the doorway in the background. In the mirror scene in front of Cameron Hall, the Cameron brothers exit left, to the crowded village street, with the support of assembled family and friends.

The juxtapositions are so routinely invidious that it is almost misleading to say that two cultures are being compared here.[22] And indeed the visit of the Stoneman brothers to Cameron Hall serves chiefly to introduce Southern culture. It occasions a survey of the system of manners that animates and organizes the domestic South-

4. *Henry Walthall as Ben Cameron, later the Little Colonel, in the opening sequence introducing Cameron Hall and its "integrated" community.*

5. *Lillian Gish seeing her brothers off to war in front of the "Pennsylvania" set designed to mirror the "Piedmont" set for Cameron Hall.*

ern "household" (here with the ancient resonances of "economy"), and it therefore enables Griffith to provide a form of attention to manners that is more patient and elaborate than the kind of shortcut Dixon takes, for example, in the dialogue he writes for Lincoln and Mrs. Cameron. Griffith stages scenes first on the porch of Cameron Hall, then in the large foyer, and then in the interior sitting room. Then, with the visitors, we move "over the plantation to the cotton fields" on an excursion in which the young whites loaf and court, and slaves work the fields as part of a "natural" setting. Finally, the young whites visit "in the slave quarters," where, despite the slaves' twelve-hour work day that the insert title acknowledges, there is supposed to be energy at mid-day for music and dancing: performed, in this case, for the entertainment of the white masters.

I mean to stress that, in its exposition of a culture through the manners and customs of a "household" ("economy"), Griffith's film is far more like the model of Scott's fiction, as outlined above, than it is like its immediate source in Dixon's novel. Indeed, the visit to the household across the cultural boundary of the incipient nation is a narrative strategy powerfully realized by Scott in the beginning of *Waverley* and *Ivanhoe,* and for something like the same purpose: to create a sense of "*la vie privée*" of the forefathers. The strategy is to suggest a deep cultural division within an emerging society and to bring strangers from one side of the cultural division to the other, as guests whose introduction to the objects and habits of the house serve to introduce the reader to those things. The action of Scott's first novel begins with Waverley's crossing of the Scottish border to visit the Baron Bradwardine at his estate, Tully-Veolan, and we follow his journey into the Highlands for another such visit, this time to the castle of Fergus Mac-Ivor. *Ivanhoe* begins with the visit by a hostile Norman pair, Prior Aymer and the Knight Templar, Brian de Bois-Guilbert, to Rotherwood Hall, household of Cedric the Saxon, father of Ivanhoe. In reimagining Dixon with help from Scott, Griffith is not finally "adapting" either author, but is rather developing his own kind of historical writing, an ambition Woodrow Wilson seemed to recognize when he praised the movie after its White House screening as "like writing history with lightning."[23]

One of the uses to which Griffith puts the image of the organically unified Southern household, once he has established it, is to make it the site where historical action leaves its mark on everyday

life. The porch, foyer, and interior sitting room of Cameron Hall
are the sites that compose what we might call the "domestic space"
on which Griffith will inscribe the events of the 1860s, thus bringing them home to the businesses and bosoms of his characters. As
the film moves forward from the early 1860 visitation sequence to
depict the outbreak of the war, various political struggles, and the
famous battle sequences—all still part of his own preface to Dixon's
action—he sees to it that these developments are signally registered
in Cameron Hall. This effect is achieved in several ways. The most
obvious and direct of these is the use of verbal message, either
through a messenger or by means of specific documents that usually
appear as still shots and are then allowed to occasion responses from
the family—what an insert title calls "read[ing] war's sad page"
(fig. 6). This practice is established early in the film, during the
Stoneman visit, when Dr. Cameron, "the kindly master of Cameron Hall," is shown reading a newspaper article of late 1860 that
predicts: "If the North Carries the Election, The South will Secede."
    The second way is by depicting the economic effects of the war

6. *Mae Marsh as the Little Sister, reading a letter from her brother in her last good
   dress, a Scottish plaid. News tends to be received on the porch and in the foyer,
   and contemplated in the interior sitting room.*

7. *Cameron Hall yields up some of the last of its furnishings to the Confederate cause.*

on the house and its furnishings. The most frequently recurring shot of the interior of the house is that of the grand foyer with the divided stairway ascending both to the upper right and upper left in the background. This space is steadily stripped of its original trappings and appointments as the war progresses. The actual carrying off of furniture and goods is explicitly depicted (fig. 7), and much is made, as again later in *Gone With the Wind,* of the women's efforts to provide makeshift replacements for the wardrobes they no longer have. The Cameron household is even used to suggest what might have become of the South if Lincoln had lived to implement his policy of postwar leniency toward the South. In the few days between Appomattox and Assassination, Griffith brings Ben Cameron home from Washington to Piedmont and shows the Cameron family already reconstructing their own household: not only by the physical labor of rehabilitation but also by advertising for boarders with a sign hung on the porch.

These first two techniques, showing both the information relay and the impact of the war on the domestic economy, prepare for a third: the use of parallel montage in the mode of sheer tour de force.

8. *Instance of "telepathic montage" in which the Camerons are shown praying for*
their son as if at the very moment of his greatest danger.

For Griffith suggests a kind of mental telepathic communication between characters at the Hall and actors in the great events elsewhere.
The most obvious example of this sort of telepathic montage occurs
during the battle scene when the Little Colonel is shot and wounded;
in the course of the charge that the Little Colonel leads against the
enemy, Griffith cuts intermittently to the parents and sisters back at
Cameron Hall, where they assume a posture of family prayer in the
interior sitting room (fig. 8).

Finally, the impingement of the war upon the family is also just
dramatized. For instance, when the Cameron sons are seen off to
war, the parents and sisters (in a shot that prepares for the later telepathic montage), are shown retreating to the interior setting room
to assume intensely self-absorbed postures of contemplation in
front of a camera so "candid" that it offers a badly obstructed view
of Mrs. Cameron (fig. 9). Contrasted with the pensiveness and sub-
tlety of this dramatization of the war's effect on the family is the
long sequence that shows the raid on Cameron Hall by a company
of renegade Union troops. In the course of this raid, the Cameron
daughters retreat room by room from the invasion of the black

9. *Camerons fall back to interior sitting room after departure of the two sons to the
front.*

Union troops until they reach the innermost sanctuary of the house.
Here they remain, while black soldiers plunder the house, until they
and the rest of the family are rescued by a company of Confederate
soldiers who happen to hear the commotion. The same black Union
troops reappear, as it were, in the siege of the small cabin that shel-
ters a group of Northern and Southern whites, represented as the
future of the nation, and the same Confederates reappear to rescue
them in the costume of the Ku Klux Klan. The difference between
the two raids will prove important. At this point I will only add that
the episode of the raid on the manor house may—like the woman's
plea to the great man for pardon of another, the succoring of the
fallen enemy, and the visit to the household of the cultural other—
derive specifically from an episode in Scott's fiction: in this case, the
raid on Tully-Veolan by the Highland renegades during Waverley's
first visit there. The term "raid" itself is a Highland corruption of
"road," as in "taking to the road" to plunder goods, and the very
availability of the word to Griffith may even have been a function of
Scott's influence in popularizing it.[24]

That there are crucial aspects of Griffith's mode of representing history which have little to do with Scott, or which may indeed run counter to salient tendencies in the Waverley novels, is a point too obvious to belabor. Miriam Hansen's important discussion of Griffith in "Myths of Origin in Early American Cinema" argues two claims, for example, that delimit the implication of what I have been trying to establish here. The first is that Griffith was committed to a view of his medium as a potentially transparent mode, a "universal language" or "moving picture Esperanto" that could overcome the Babel of the pre-Hollywood word. Though Scott's fiction has enjoyed global appreciation, his own stress seems to fall on the *un*transparency of his medium, and his frequent resort to writing dialogue in dialect seems a mark of his commitment to the power of the local. Secondly, Hansen shows that Griffith's historiographical ambitions for film participated in a wider contemporary discourse, which preexisted *Birth of a Nation,* about the capacity of the "new art" to effect "the unlimited reproduction of actual events on the screen."[25] With such limitations understood, however, I would like to consider, in closing, some possible implications of the argument I have been pursuing. What follows from the substitution of Scott's name for Dickens's in Eisenstein's formula?

In the first place, only by seeing how elements of Scott's fiction inhere independently in Dixon's novel and in Griffith's film can we begin to notice how Griffith's Scott differs from Dixon's. In Dixon's novel, the work of the clan produces a reincarnation of the splendor of the Old South, which had been implied but not been previously represented in the narrative. Griffith, by contrast, begins *Birth of a Nation* with a long exposition of antebellum Southern culture. Although this first hour of the film appears to express an elegiac longing for the Old South, especially in juxtaposition with the North, Griffith is actually providing us with a way of seeing that the feudal aspects of the antebellum Southern culture must change. Griffith's insert titles in the opening visit explicitly introduce us to "the manners of the old school" and "a quaintly way of life that is to be no more." The recurrence of the camera and the narrative to the image of the house in which these qualities are invested permits the viewer to track their destruction. In *Waverley,* Scott had used a similar technique in his set-piece descriptions of Tully-Veolan before, during, and after the '45 Rebellion. When Margaret Mitchell and David O. Selznick combine, in effect, to revise *Birth of a Nation* as *Gone with the Wind,* they do not move beyond the indulgence of elegiac regret for the destruction of Tara, symbol of what the Old South is supposed to have been.[26] But as the prospective orientation of Griffith's very title means to suggest, the steady stripping away of the trappings of Southern splendor is finally to be viewed as a potentially salutary process, as is the analogous divestiture of the feudal in *Waverley.* The Confederacy's delusion of grandeur is identified in some of the film's significant details. When Cameron returns to Piedmont just days after Appomattox, his "little sister" (Mae Marsh) prepares for his homecoming by ornamenting the best of her ragged dresses with a cotton trim that she has marked here and there with short lines of black soot: "'Southern ermine' from raw cotton for the grand occasion," the insert title explains (fig. 10). The second half of the movie concerns the rise of Silas Lynch, the black man whom Austin Stoneman attempts to make his puppet ruler in reconstructed South Carolina. Once in power, he is identified in an

10. *The Little Colonel examines the Little Sister's "southern ermine" in the famous homecoming sequence.*

insert title as "the social lion of the new aristocracy," a man who seeks to be "king" of a new "empire" of which his co-conspirator, Lydia—Stoneman's mulatto housekeeper—seeks to be "queen." (Lynch himself seeks Elsie Stoneman for that role.) Black rule thus makes its appearance in Griffith's Reconstruction as the residue of all that was backward or self-deceived in antebellum white society.

The local culture of antebellum southern society was vital enough, on Griffith's representation, but he insists that its forms of life remained local. It could not, within the prewar social framework, overcome its own class structure nor make the necessary passage from national units (households, clans, states) to united nation. An early insert title for the scene of Lincoln's signing of the conscription act, opines that the "power of the sovereign states, established when Lord Cornwallis surrendered to the individual colonies in 1781, is threatened by the new administration." This comment seems defensive about states' rights in behalf of the Confederate position, but this is a viewpoint that the film will move beyond. Its representation of the war and the reconstruction advocates the unity of the racial nation at the expense of the autonomy of the state. This view, which Griffith offers as the longer perspective on current events, must be extended to the global situation, where his idea of the nation can be seen to transcend America itself. Only such an extension of the view can explain the film's ostentatious pacifism in the context of World War I, which Griffith seems to have regarded as benighted fratricide between political states that shared a common national—i.e., Aryan—birthright.

The debilitated Southern culture—both no longer and not yet a nation—whose feudal trappings are stripped away in the divestiture of Cameron Hall is reinvested with power, the film suggests, in the shabby log cabin to which Dr. Cameron, his only surviving daughter, and Phil Stoneman (her lover) take refuge. The resonances of this cabin in the Lincoln hagiography are called up by the bearded Union soldier who offers the group sanctuary—perhaps (as perhaps too with the Lincoln-look-alike Union guard in the Washington hospital scene) one of the thirty-odd actors who auditioned for the Lincoln part but lost out to the multi-talented Joseph Henabery. There are also resonances of Griffith's autobiography which opens with his account of how the "pretentious" antebellum Kentucky "mansion" of his family was destroyed by "guerillas, disguised as

Union raiders." So "the second house that father built was quite small. And it was here that I was born."[27] It is in this cabin that, in the film's self-mythology, the promise of a new nation is threatened and redeemed by timely rescue ride of the Ku Klux Klan. This ending is Griffith's and not Dixon's, and it corresponds to his change of title from *The Clansman* to *The Birth of a Nation*. No more than Dixon, can Griffith be excused from the charge of undisguised white supremacism. But Dixon's novel ends, as a late chapter title puts it, with "The Reign of the Clan," while Griffith's ends with the reign of "Liberty and Union"—the union to be born of the concluding double marriage of Stoneman sister and brother from Pennsylvania with Cameron brother and sister from South Carolina.

The shorthand way of putting the difference between Griffith's Scott and Dixon's is to say, roughly, that Dixon's Scott is more like the one that Twain puts down and Griffith's is more like the one that Lukács raises up. For where Lukác's Scott produced a form that is generally in line with an advancing social consciousness, Twain's Scott stood squarely in the way of such advances. Twain's account of Scott's relation to the French Revolution is directly relevant:

> . . . the Revolution broke the chains of the ancien regime and of the Church, and made a nation of abject slaves a nation of freemen; and Bonaparte instituted the setting of merit above birth, and also so completely stripped the divinity from royalty that, . . . they are only men since, . . . and answerable for their acts like common clay. . . .
>
> Then comes Sir Walter Scott with his enchantments, and by his single might checks this wave of progress, and even turns it back; sets the world in love with dreams and phantoms; with decayed and swinish forms of religion; with decayed and degraded systems of government; with the sillinesses and emptinesses, sham grandeurs, sham gauds, and sham chivalries of a brainless and worthless long-vanished society. . . . Most of the world has now outlived a good part of these harms, though by no means all of them; but in our South they flourished pretty forcefully still. . . . There, the genuine and wholesome civilization of the nineteenth century is curiously confused and commingled with the Walter Scott Middle-Age sham civilization, and so you have practical common sense, progressive ideas, and progressive works, mixed up with the duel, inflated speech, and the jejune romanticism of an absurd past that is dead, and out of charity ought to be buried. But for the Sir Walter disease, the character of the South-

erner—or Southron, according to Sir Walter's starchier way of phrasing it—would be wholly modern, in place of modern and medieval
mixed, and the South would be fully a generation further advanced
than it is. (12:376–377)

Most modern Scott scholars, even without the help of Lukács's
book, would call Twain's account an oversimplification. Twain saw
Scott's sympathy for feudal antiquity as unqualified and unbounded,
and he wrote *A Connecticut Yankee in King Arthur's Court* to de-
bunk such sentimentalization. Modern defenders of Scott would argue that the representation of chivalric culture in *Ivanhoe* is scarcely
the idealization that Twain sees there, and the same could be said
for the archaic Highland culture typified by Fergus MacIvor in
Waverley.

How to find and construe the evidence for Twain's view is best
indicated, paradoxically, in his most outlandish claim in Chapter 46
of *Life on the Mississippi:* "Sir Walter had so large a hand in making
Southern character, as it existed before the war, that he is in great
measure responsible for the war" (377). Even Twain himself acknowledges that this must seem a wild proposition. The way to
read it, if also to qualify it, is to recognize that the Scott who made
the Southern character what it was—i.e., among other things, a
character reckless enough to go to war against the North—is the
Scott that the South imagined when it read him: the Scott of the
idealized past and the romantic lost cause, the Scott of mythicized
Celtic aura and rigid class stratification. To back up Twain's breezy
and sarcastic overview of Scott's influence one can consult a more
patient analysis of the issue in a book like Rollin Osterweis's *Romanticism and Nationalism in the Old South*. Osterweis shows that the
sales of Scott's books in the South were massive. He mentions pil-
grimages of Southerners to Scott's medievalized house at Abbotsford
and argues that at least two Southern state houses were influenced
by Scott's taste in architecture. He cites much evidence of the kind
briefly alluded to by Twain that Scott's diction was much adopted in
Southern writing and conversation.[28] Grace Landrum's earlier research on the adoption of Scott's names had already turned up a host
of "Walter Scotts, Rowenas, Ellen Douglases, Flora MacIvors . . .
on family trees" and had discovered that one Richard Ivanhoe Cocke
had been commencement orator at William and Mary in the 1830s.[29]

Twain's extravagant claim about Scott gains particular credibility, I think, when one considers the degree to which, as the author who brings together the crusading medievalism of *Ivanhoe* with the celebration of the Highland clans in the Scottish novels, Scott articulated precisely that cultural conjunction in which the Ku Klux Klan conceived its own group identity. Scott's peculiar conjunction is discernable in the very name of the organization. It is obvious that the latter part of the name derives from the social unit of the Scottish Highlands, and we have already noted that, for example, the Klan's celebrated symbol of the burning cross derives from a Highland custom that was publicized and popularized by Scott in both fiction and poetry. It is less widely recognized, perhaps, that the first part of the organization's name, from the Greek for circle, *kuklos,* has medievalized origins in such antebellum organizations as The Knights of the Golden Circle. This K.G.C., as it was known, was already campaigning in the 1850s for a Southern empire to include what would become the Confederate states as well as most of Texas and Central America in a "slaveocracy," with themselves, as a sort of round table, at its center of power. This earlier organization, in turn, rode the wave of a Scott-inspired medieval revival of earlier decades, a revival that included renewed duelling and mock-medieval tournaments. When the Confederacy was formed, it identified itself powerfully with an archaic chivalric code obviously associated with Scott. As if to confirm this association, Confederate military men composed Scottesque and Scottish-sounding ballads about how "Like heroes and princes they lived for a time."

> Chivalrous, chivalrous people are!
> In C.S.A.! In C.S.A.!
> Aye, in chivalrous C.S.A.![30]

It would clearly be a mistake to go all the way with Twain's assumption that one writer, no matter how powerful his influence, can be called the cause of such large cultural tendencies. But the really disturbing point about those Klansman on parade in their Crusader costumes at the end of *Birth of a Nation* is that their resemblance to the knights at Scott's Ashby-de-la-Zouche is not just a function of Griffith's or Dixon's knowledge of *Ivanhoe*—not just an issue at the level of treatment, so to speak—but goes back to white supremacist groups before the war who emulated what they thought they read in Scott to constitute themselves a Southern knighthood.

There is certainly a residue of this Southern Scott in *Birth of a Nation*. Griffith did, after all, shoot much of Dixon's story as it was. He said that *Birth of a Nation* owed more to his father than to himself, and his autobiography opens with a raft of idealized stories of Roarin' Jake:

> Suffering from a festering shoulder wound, he was about to lead a charge at the Battle of Corinth in Tennessee when he received a Minié ball through his hip. Unable to mount a horse, he turned the charge over to a subordinate. But when he saw his troops preparing to go into the fray without him, the fires of battle flamed high in the Old War Horse. Commandeering a horse and buggy, he rushed to the front of the long curved line of sabers sweeping down the field, leading the charge in person. This was a moving picture indeed . . . a hatless middle-aged man, his long beard flying in the wind; around him the roar of battle; behind him his charging troops . . . while he, in a careening buggy, rockets into the jaws of death, his great voice calling down the wrath of God and Lee upon the enemy. (25)

The implication is clearly that they don't make men like that anymore, except in movies. But Griffith protests in the same pages that he "hold[s] no nostalgic grief for the past" and embraces "Edison, Ford, and Marconi." The protest, too, must be taken seriously. Dixon looks back to a time of looking backward, but it is characteristic of Griffith's peculiar nostalgia that he looks back to a time of looking forward. Much more like Scott than Dixon in this respect, Griffith's work is at once modernizing and archaic. This was one of the truths about Griffith captured in Eisenstein's analysis of the two faces of Griffith's America, and it is uncannily close in kind to the truth that Virginia Woolf captured about Scott in "Gas at Abbotsford," the essay that begins from the puzzle that Scott built himself a medieval mansion in the 1810s, but at the same time made it the first private residence in Britain to be fitted for the use of gas.[31]

Finally, I hope that attention to ways of reproducing the historical novel in the cinema may prove helpful in discriminating among various examples of the modern film epic. It may help to tell those epics which are great-man styled historical biographies—Abel Gance's *Napoleon*, and later *Spartacus, Lawrence of Arabia,* and *Gandhi*—from those which tend to employ some version of the mediocre fictional hero caught in the middle of a conflict—as with the Al Pacino character, a disinterested trapper drawn into the struggle for American War of Independence, in *Revolution*. The lavish film epic that swept the Oscars (fifties style) in 1988 was *The Last Emperor,* an interesting case to consider in these terms. At first it appears to be the glamorous film biography of a great man who changed history. This would have been a strong departure from the Bertolucci of *1900,* in which the depiction of Italian political struggles at the turn of the century is handled more along the lines suggested in Lukács's analysis of Scott. But the imperial splendor of *The Last Emperor* is jarring not only in the context of Bertolucci's prior work, but also in the face of the film's apparent endorsement of the 1947 revolution in China. The film ultimately enacts the undoing of the typical course of the great-man-centered film epic. For instead of presenting the great man's rise to greatness through his education toward certain monumental traits of character, *The Last Emperor* circumscribes the young emperor's education into the powers and pleasures of emperorship in the Eternal City within the context of his socialist re-education into the responsibilities of ordinary life. The film gives us a complex culture in which the would-be great man is remade for the purpose of popular citizenship.

I have offered these last suggestions only to indicate possibilities of application. Fully recognizing the residual forms of nineteenth-century historical fiction in twentieth-century historical cinema will involve a far more complicated analysis than I have produced here, but it is a task that needs to be carried out. Most "modern cultures" find themselves depending more and more on the film medium in establishing the antiquity against which they define themselves. We tend to rely on distinctions far too simple between, on the one hand, documentary films and, on the other, history films that have, as we say, gone Hollywood.[32] The French once developed a term for license-taking in historical representation that is a very close equivalent to what we mean when we speak of history gone Hollywood: they called it *histoire Walter Scottée*. I have tried to suggest that the connection between these two terms is more than happenstance or casual analogy. They are both aimed invidiously at forms that claim to represent the past in a way that rivals the work of antiquarians and professional historians.

Since both the historical novel and the Hollywood history are clearly epic forms, they aspire, as epics have always done, to shape the culture they represent. The "reconstruction" with which *Birth of a Nation* is ultimately concerned is the reconstruction of America in 1915; in the end, Griffith imagines *himself* to be riding to the nation's rescue.[33] When, breaking off from the Biograph Company, Griffith started his own operation for the purpose of making *Birth of a Nation,* he called the new entity "The Epoch Producing Corporation." Given his ambitions, the pun in the title has to be intended, and such ambition demands our most vigorous critical attention. Developing the connection between the romantic historical novel and modern film epic ought to be illuminating for both forms of epoch production. Without such illumination, our modern cultures will appear to us, in the darkened seats, with the inexorability of circling clouds in an evening sky.

Notes

1. See, for example, Tino Balio's account in *The American Film Industry,* ed. Tino Balio, rev. ed. (Madison: University of Wisconsin Press, 1985), 112–113.

2. The marketing of these recent epics tends to rely less on the notion of an upscale product, I believe, and thus to break with the line that leads from *Birth of a Nation* through, say, *Lawrence of Arabia.* Though I don't address them here, it seems to me that both the rise and fall of that marketing strategy have implications for the problem skillfully posed by Miriam Hansen when she sets Lewis Jacobs's "democratic acculturation" thesis about Hollywood against the Horkheimer-Adorno "culture industry" thesis—see "Universal Language and Democratic Culture: Myths of Origin in Early American Cinema," in *Myth and Enlightenment in American Literature,* ed. Dieter Meindle and Friedrich Horlacher (Erlangen: Universität Erlangen-Nürnberg, 1985), 321–351.

3. Sergei Eisenstein, "Dickens, Griffith, and the Film Today," in *Film Form,* trans. Jay Leyda (London: D. Dobson, 1951), 232–233.

4. Eisenstein, 200–201. See also Griffith's acknowledgement—"I borrowed the 'cutback' from Charles Dickens"—in "What I Demand of Movie Stars," collected in *Focus on D. W. Griffith,* ed. Harry M. Geduld (Englewood Cliffs, N.J.: Prentice Hall, 1971), 52.

5. But see Philip Rosen's brief but suggestive remarks on Scott, Lukács, and classical cinema in "Securing the Historical: Historiography and the Classical Cinema," in *Cinema Histories, Cinema Practices,* ed. Patrician Mellancamp

and Philip Rosen, AFI Monograph Series, vol. 4 (Frederick, Maryland: University Publications of America, 1984), 26–28.

6. For more on Dickens and Griffith, see Richard Schickel, *D. W. Griffith* (New York: Simon and Schuster, 1984), 112–113. On Griffith's "Victorianism," see Lary May, *Screening Out the Past* (Chicago: University of Chicago Press, 1983) pp. 94–97. I have found no discussions of Griffith's relationship to Scott and Scott's historical novel.

7. *The Letters of John Keats,* ed. Hyder E. Rollins, 2 vols. (Cambridge: Harvard University Press, 1958), 2:16.

8. Samuel Clemens, *The Writings of Mark Twain,* 37 vols. (New York: G. Wells, 1923), 12:377.

9. On the imagination of nationalism, see Benedict Anderson, *Imagined Communities* (London: Verso, 1983); on nationalist constructions of heritage, see *The Invention of Tradition,* ed. E. J. Hobsbawm and Terence Ranger (London: New York: Cambridge University Press, 1983); on the role of Scott in both projects see Tom Nairn, *The Break-up of Britain* (London: NLB, 1977), 148–169.

10. Sir Hugh Trevor-Roper, "Sir Walter Scott and History," *The Listener* (19 August 1971), 225ff.

11. Georg Lukács, *The Historical Novel,* trans. Hannah and Stanley Mitchell (London: verso, 1962), 19–47.

12. Clemens, 12:376–377.

13. George Dekker's recent *American Historical Romance* (1987), which reached my hands only after delivering the lecture version of this essay, is the first really full study of Scott's literary influence in America. Dekker devotes a long chapter precisely to the question of Scott's literary influence in the South; see 272–333.

14. Mentioned in two of the biographies, apparently on the authority of the Oglesby papers at the Museum of Modern Art in New York: Martin Williams, *Griffith: First Artist of the Movies* (New York and Oxford: Oxford University Press, 1980), 7, and Robert Henderon, *D. W. Griffith: His Life and Work* (New York: Oxford University Press, 1972), 28. Henderson also mentions readings from Goldsmith. Neither biographer makes anything of Griffith's early and powerful exposure to Scott in this way and in the context of his father's reputation as a Confederate-veteran raconteur of the war.

15. Dixon's novel has one major Dickensian moment, taken from *A Tale of Two Cities:* Phil Stoneman, Elsie's brother, sneaks into the prison where Cameron is being held, near the end of the novel, and changes places with him, very much à la Sydney Carton and Charles Darnay. But the framework of the novel remains mainly unDickensian.

16. Thomas Dixon, *The Clansman: An Historical Romance of the Ku Klux Klan* (Ridgewood, N.J.: The Gregg Press, 1967), 31.

17. In the hospital chapter, a Union eyewitness reports to Elsie how it was that Ben Cameron fell in battle and came to be placed in a Northern hospital. It is a scene that Griffith shoots in great detail. Having led one charge against a

regiment of Union troops commanded by Phil Stoneman, young Cameron, the Little Colonel,

> " . . . sprang on the breastwork. . . . He was a handsome figure—tall, slender, straight, a gorgeous yellow sash tasselled with gold around his waist, his sword flashing in the sun, his slouch hat cocked on one side and an eagle's feather in it.
>
> "We thought that he was going to lead another charge, but just as the battery was making ready to fire, he deliberately walked down the embankment in a hail of musketry and began to give water to our wounded men.
>
> "Every gun ceased firing, and we watched him. He walked back to the trench, his naked sword flashed suddenly above the eagle's feather, and his grizzled ragamuffins sprang forward and charged us like so many demons. . . , giving that hellish rebel yell at every jump." (8–9)

When Cameron falls during this charge, he is cared for by Phil Stoneman, as Cameron had cared for the Union troops. The whole episode echoes the charge in the central battle scene of *Waverley,* the Battle of Preston. Here the young Englishman, allied through circumstance with the Scots in the Civil War of 1745, helps to lead a charge with the Mac-Ivor clan, alongside the Cameron clan, against his own English countrymen:

> "Down with your plaid, Waverley," cried Fergus, throwing off his own: "we'll win silks for our tartans before the sun is above the sea."
>
> The clansmen on every side stript their plaids, [and] prepared their arms. . . . Waverley felt his heart at that moment throb as it would have burst from his bosom. . . . The sounds around him combined to exalt his enthusiasm; the pipes played on, and the clans rushed forward, each in his own dark column. As they advanced they mended their pace, and the muttering sounds of the men to each other began to swell into a wild cry. . . .
>
> "Forward, sons of Ivor," cried their Chief, "or the Camerons will draw first-blood"—They rushed on with a tremendous yell." (336)

In the course of the ensuing battle, Waverley saves one enemy (i.e., English) officer, and attempts to succor another one as well. When Griffith shoots the episode of the Little Colonel succoring a dying Union soldier, he seems to be following Scott's account even more closely than Dixon:

> Waverley could perceive that [this officer] had already received many wounds, his clothes and saddle being marked with blood. To save this good and brave man [who was actually his former commander], became the instant object of his most anxious exertions. . . . But [the dying warrior] felt that death was dealing closely with him, and resigning his purpose, and folding his hands in devotion, he gave up his soul to his Creator. (338)

It is true that the charge of the Scots Clansmen here leads to a victory rather than a defeat, but it is also true that overall, like the Confederate cause, theirs is a hopeless and romantic effort, doomed from the start. Further, just as

Cameron's helping the Union soldier is returned in kind by Stoneman, thus saving his life, so Waverley's aid to the first fallen Englishman, Colonel Talbot, leads to a later pardon of *his* life.

18. I do not here take up the question of Griffith's relation to the play version of *The Clansman* that achieved some popularity soon after the publication of the novel, though the connection between the play and the film is reinforced by the fact that the first New York run of the film took place at the Liberty Theater where, nine years earlier, the play had briefly run—see Schickel, *D. W. Griffith,* 267. Nor do I take up the important question of the relation of all of these works, Dixon's and Griffith's, to *Uncle Tom's Cabin* and its early nineteenth-century stagings; Leslie Fiedler offers a start on this issue in *The Inadvertent Epic: From Uncle Tom's Cabin to Roots* (New York: Simon and Schuster, 1979), 43–57.

19. Schickel comments that Griffith "stress[ed] to the point of exaggeration the amount of historical research that underlay the film," but he concedes that that amount was large"—*D. W. Griffith,* 237.

20. To "remodernize" in this context is to maintain the sense of the antique-modern distinction which is in fact elided in the movement called modernism, as I have tried to suggest in suggesting Woolf. If the "postmodern" is that which proceeds in the face of the antique-modern distinction (the synecdoche for antiquity in the films of the 1980s is often the 1950s), then Scott is the prototypical postmodern author and modernism in fiction, prepared for by Dickens's successful appropriation of Scott's readership, would be understood as the displacer of postmodernism, rather than the other way around.

21. For a full account of the role of the absent mother in *Birth* and indeed for a powerful account of various race and gender relations in the film, see Michael Rogin's tour-de-force essay "'The Sword Became a Flashing Vision': D. W. Griffith's *Birth of a Nation,*" *Representations* 9 (Winter 1985); 150–195.

22. The asymmetry of the mirroring can be seen in the detail of the pillars; the four grand ones in the colonial porch of Cameron Hall inadequately answered by the two small and squarish ones in the strangely curtained porch of the Stoneman house.

23. Quoted in Schickel, *D. W. Griffith,* 270.

24. See Ernest Weekley, "Walter Scott and the English Language," *The Atlantic Monthly* (November, 1931): 148:599. I thank Stuart Tave for the reference.

25. Miriam Hansen, "Universal Language and Democratic Culture," passim.

26. Fiedler does not comment at length on Selsnick and Griffith, but his discussion of Mitchell and Dixon is informative. He cites a letter from Mitchell to Dixon in which she says: "I was practically raised on your books and love them very much." *The Inadvertent Epic,* 59.

27. *The Man Who Invented Hollywood: The Autobiography of D. W. Griffith* (Louisville, Ky.: Touchstone, 1972), 19. Here I quote the passage in full, partly because the Prologue, from which it is taken, begins in a mode resonant of *Waverley's* preface:

A scant half-century ago Queen Victoria was firmly seated in the throne of Great Britain and the world slid along nicely at three miles an hour.

Down in Old Kentucky, near Louisville, was the house of my father, Colonel Jacob Wark Griffith, a Confederate cavalry officer. . . . Once there had been quite a pretentious place—more or less like the popular conception of Kentucky mansions—with poplar and osage orange groves leading up to its portals. Guerrillas, disguised as union raiders, burned the house down in the first year of the war. The second house that father built was quite small. And it was here that I was born. Here also was whelped the wolf pup of want and hunger that was to shadow me all my life.

28. Rollin G. Osterweis, *Romanticism and Nationalism in the Old South* (New Haven: Yale University Press, 1949), 41–53. I thank Neil Harris for the reference.

29. Grace Warren Landrum, "Sir Walter Scott and His Literary Rivals in the Old South," *American Literature* (November 1930) 2:256–276.

30. Osterweis, 46.

31. Virginia Woolf, "Sir Walter Scott," in *The Moment and Other Essays* (London: Hogarth Press, 1947), 50–59.

32. As this essay was going to press, the journal of the American Historical Association published an excellent forum, centering on just these kinds of issues, around an essay by historian and historical filmmaker (*Reds, The Good Fight*) Robert Rosenstone, "History in Images / History in Words: Reflections on the Possibilities of Really Putting History onto Film," *American Historical Review* (December 1988): 1173–1227. Rosenstone makes both of these points— that we are increasingly dependent upon film for our sense of the past and that the documentary / dramatic distinction is far more problematic than we tend to assume—and both are picked up by other contributors. See especially Hayden White's contribution to the forum: "Historiography and Historiophoty," 1193–1199.

33. I am indebted to Linda Williams's excellent discussion of this point in a public lecture series on Griffith at the Film Center of the Art Institute of Chicago in Autumn 1987. Her comments on and technical help with this essay have been invaluable to me. I also wish to acknowledge the technical help of Paul Buchbinder and Peter Ferry, the comments of Corey Creekmur, Arthur Knight and Robert Streeter, and the wisdom of the late Gerald Mast, who steered the essay into a much better course than I had once intended for it.

Why Women Didn't Like Romanticism

The Views of Jane Austen and Mary Shelley

✑

Anne K. Mellor

For many years scholars and critics have been speaking in one way or another of what we might call the romantic "spirit of the age." But the spirit we have been describing animated at best but a small portion of the people living in England at the time. Among those it did *not* animate were the leading women intellectuals and writers of the day. In order to understand their antipathy to the "spirit of the age," I must first offer a working definition of romanticism. I will not renumerate A. O. Lovejoy's multiple "romanticisms." Rather I wish to emphasize a few fundamental and shared beliefs of the major English romantic poets, beliefs which were profoundly disturbing to the women who encountered them.

When we try to define romanticism as a set of cultural ideas and values, we usually turn first to the beliefs that developed out of the eighteenth-century Enlightenment and that inspired both the American and the French Revolutions. Remembering Rousseau and Thomas Paine, we identify romanticism with the political doctrines of democracy and the rights of the common man, the assumption that every individual is born with an inalienable right to life, liberty, and the pursuit of happiness. This doctrine also assumes that human beings are born free of sin, whether we are seen as empty vessels which experience will fill, as noble savages, or as children of innocence trailing clouds of glory. Fundamental to romanticism, then, is a conviction in the value of the individual and a belief in an ethic of justice which treats every person equally under the law.

For the romantic poets, the assumption that the individual, rather than the state or society as a whole, was of fundamental significance meant that their poetry was concerned above all with describing the nature and growth of the individual. Wordsworth in *The Prelude; or, Growth of a Poet's Mind* implicitly claimed that his own autobiography, the development of his own mind and character, was of epic importance. And the stages of the growth of consciousness which all of Wordsworth's poetry traced was fundamentally an exploration of the nature of perception: how does the human mind come to know the external world? What is the relationship between the perceiving subject and the perceived object? For Wordsworth, as for Coleridge, Blake, and the later romantic poets who had been inspired by the philosophy of Immanuel Kant, the human mind actively shapes and transforms the sense-data it receives from nature into the "language of the sense." As Percy Shelley put it in "Mont Blanc":

> The everlasting universe of things
> Flows through the mind and rolls its rapid waves,
> Now dark—now glittering—now reflecting gloom—
> Now lending splendour, where from secret springs
> The source of human thought its tribute brings
> Of waters,—with a sound but half its own . . .

As the innocent child becomes a man, he comes to know the creative powers of his own mind, a mighty mind whose capacity to use language to transform, build up, and renew is as great as nature's own life-giving power. If the human mind creates the myths or meanings by which we live, then its powers can be compared to a god's. As William Blake repeatedly proclaimed, "All deities reside in the human breast," the "human form" is "divine," and "God becomes as we are, that we may be as he is." For the romantic poets, the creative powers of the human imagination are identical with the creative powers of the Infinite I AM; when inspired, the poet can imitate the works of God and create, as does the poet of Coleridge's "Kubla Khan," "a miracle of rare device." Without the transforming and myth-making work of the imagination, nature is but a vacancy, for as Coleridge insisted in "Dejection: An Ode," "we receive but what we give, / And in our life alone does Nature live."

If one celebrates the human imagination as divine and locates the source of all cultural meaning and value in the mythopoeic powers of the creative mind, then one must also celebrate those emotions that arouse and inspire the imagination, emotions above all of desire and love. As opposed to their Enlightenment forebears, the romantic poets insisted on the value of bodily sensations and emotions: in the moment of creation, not analytical reason but rather the uninhibited flow of powerful feeling is at work. The romantic poets therefore rebelled against the domination of reason, common sense, and rigorous logic, insisting like Wordsworth that "we murder to dissect." Or as Keats put it in *Lamia,*

> There was an awful rainbow once in heaven;
> We know her woof, her texture; she is given
> In the dull catalogue of common things.
> Philosophy will clip an Angel's wings,
> Conquer all mysteries by rule and line,
>
> . . . .
>
> Unweave a rainbow.

Turning against "cold" philosophy and abstract reason, the romantic poets insisted instead on the ultimate value of passionate love, that love which is embodied in Percy Shelley's *Prometheus Unbound* as Asia and which alone can overcome the evil of Jupiter and bring about the mystic marriage of man and nature, heaven and earth, that climaxes Shelley's epic poem.

Modern critics of romantic poetry, responding to these concepts, have offered various paradigms for organizing romantic thought. M. H. Abrams in his masterful *Natural Supernaturalism* argued that the greatest romantic poems traced what he called a "circuitous journey" from innocence to experience to a higher innocence, a quest that begins with the child's unconscious conviction of a primal oneness between himself and mother nature and his fall away from that communion into an experience of alienated self-consciousness and isolation. But this fall, like Milton's, proves finally fortunate, for it enables the poet to spiral upward to a higher state of consciousness, even a sublime transcendence, in which he consciously understands the ultimate harmony between the workings of nature and his own mind and consummates a marriage with nature through his "spousal verse." More attentive to the scepticism inherent in much romantic poetry, especially the writings of Byron and Keats, I suggested in my book on *English Romantic Irony* an alternative paradigm to Abrams's, the model of a poet's participation in an ongoing, chaotic life that is simultaneously creative and destructive. If nature is constantly in flux, as Byron, Shelley, and Keats believed, then all the structures designed by the human imagination, including the myths of the poets, are false, simply because they impose a static order upon a chaotic and constantly changing world. To represent such an abundant chaos, I argued, some romantic poets devised linguistic strategies which were simultaneously creative and de-creative— poems like *Don Juan* and "Ode on a Grecian Urn" which put forth symbols and ideals only to undercut them, as when Byron tells us that the snake is in the eyes of Juan's beloved and innocent Haidée, or Keats reminds us that the Urn's image of a love that can never change is but a "cold pastoral."

Commenting on both these paradigms of romanticism, Jerome McGann has subsequently called them "the romantic ideology," a description of romanticism as a creative *process*. McGann insists that we must critically detach ourselves from the values of romanticism when we interpret it and acknowledge the despair expressed in much romantic thought, the moments when Byron and Coleridge, Wordsworth and Keats, confronted the limitations of mortality and recognized the failure of their creative powers. McGann's emphasis on what Mario Praz first called "romantic agony" is entirely appropriate, but it is only half the story. I still believe that the English romanticism of which we have been speaking is best understood as an ongoing, enthusiastic engagement with the creative energy of both nature and the human mind, an engagement that acknowledges human limitations—as Byron said, man is "half dust, half deity"—but nonetheless continues in a dialectical, perhaps ever-to-be-frustrated, yearning for transcendence and enduring meaning.[1]

How did the women writers of the age respond to romanticism's celebration of the creative process and of passionate feeling? On both counts, they responded negatively, very negatively. But why? To answer that, I will take as representative Jane Austen and Mary Shelley, two of the best-known women writers of the day.

To understand Austen's and Shelley's hostility to the romantic imagination and to romantic love, we must think back to the book that perhaps more than any other influenced them both, Mary Wollstonecraft's *A Vindication of the Rights of Woman,* published in 1792. Wollstonecraft was Mary Shelley's mother and died giving birth to her; perhaps as an act of compensation, or simply in filial love, Mary Shelley throughout her youth obsessively read and re-read her mother's books. It is less well known that Jane Austen was also a committed disciple of Wollstonecraft's teaching. Austen frequently quotes *A Vindication* in her novels, even though she never dared to acknowledge openly her debt to Wollstonecraft, mainly because the publication of Godwin's loving but injudicious *Memoirs* of the life, opinions, love affairs, and suicide attempts of his dead wife had led the British press to denounce Wollstonecraft as a whore and an atheist. In Jane Austen's circle, no respectable woman could publically avow her agreement with Wollstonecraft's opinions. Even today, the extent of Jane Austen's debt to Wollstonecraft has only begun to be documented.[2]

In *A Vindication of the Rights of Woman,* Mary Wollstonecraft attacked her society's ideological definition of the female as innately emotional, intuitive, illogical, capable of moral sentiment but not of rational understanding. Pointing out that women are assumed to have souls and to be capable of sinning or becoming virtuous, Mary Wollstonecraft argued that if women are to be held ethically responsible for their actions, then it must follow that they are capable of ethical thinking. And if women are capable of thinking, they must have a rational faculty. And if they have a rational faculty which is capable of guiding and improving their character and actions, then that rational faculty should be developed and exercised to its greatest capacity. From this rigorously logical argument, Wollstonecraft launched a passionate plea for the education of women, for only if women were educated as fully as men would they be able to realize their innate capacities for moral virtue. Appealing to her male readers, Wollstonecraft further argued that more highly educated women will not only be more virtuous, but they will also be better mothers, more interesting wives and "companions," and more responsible citizens. In contrast, Wollstonecraft observed, her society's practice of teaching females only "accomplishments"—singing, dancing, needlework, a smattering of foreign languages—produced women who were obsessed with their personal appearance and fashion, who devoted all their energies to arousing a man's sexual appetites while duplicitously appearing "modest" and chaste in order to capture the husband upon whom their financial welfare depended, and who became "slaves" to their masters but petty tyrants to their children and servants. "Created to feel, not to think," the women of her time were kept in "a state of perpetual childhood" and necessarily became "cunning, mean and selfish."[3]

Inspired by Wollstonecraft's attempt to develop women's ability to think rationally, Jane Austen portrayed the heroines of her novels, not as the women of sensibility celebrated by the romantic poets and the prevailing ideological doctrine of the separate spheres which consigned women to the role of promoting the domestic affections. Instead her heroines are women of sense, women like Elinor Dashwood who refuse to succumb to erotic passion. Even those heroines who are seduced by Gothic romances and fairy tales of romantic love, like Catherine Morland in *Northanger Abbey,* are capable of recognizing the errors of their youthful delusions.

Indeed, all of Austen's novels are novels of female education, novels in which an intelligent but ignorant girl learns to perceive the world more correctly and to understand more fully the workings of human nature and society. Emma Woodhouse must recognize her own cruelty to Miss Bates, must understand how wrongly she has perceived both Jane Fairfax and Harriet Smith, before she can equal the intelligence and benevolence of a Mr. Knightley. Elizabeth Bennet must overcome both her proud confidence in her own ability to distinguish simple and intricate human characters and her prejudiced and inaccurate reading of Mr. Darcy, through a process of painful mortification, self-analysis, and learning, before she can recognize that Mr. Darcy is the man best suited to be her husband. Elizabeth Bennet's marriage to Fitzwilliam Darcy in *Pride and Prejudice* exemplifies Mary Wollstonecraft's ideal marriage, a marriage based on rational love, mutual understanding, and respect. It is a further sign of Elizabeth's intelligence that the overriding emotion she feels for Darcy, as Jane Austen repeatedly states, is "gratitude."

For in a society where every woman is in want of a husband with a good fortune, where marriage is, as Charlotte Lucas reminds us, "a woman's pleasantest preservative from want," a woman must above all be grateful to the man who rescues her from the financial deprivations of spinsterhood.

Jane Austen's conviction that women must above all be rational is perhaps clearest in *Mansfield Park,* where we are asked to endorse the cautious, chaste modesty of a Fanny Price rather than the energetic imagination of a Mary Crawford. Fanny is the voice of prudence in the novel, of good moral and intellectual sense, a voice that sustains the organic growth of the family within a clean, well-lighted home, a voice that is finally beyond price. In contrast, the women of *Mansfield Park* who are badly educated, like the Bertram sisters who can recite by rote but cannot recognize the insincerity of a Henry Crawford, or who rebel against the discipline of logic and morality, like Mary Crawford, whose wit and charm identify her as the romantic revolutionary in the novel, all end badly. Seduced by erotic desire, Maria Bertram Rushford must end her days in banishment from both the husband she abandoned and her family home at Mansfield Park, condemned to the foolish, selfish, and manipulative company of Aunt Norris. And Mary Crawford, despite her cleverness and capacity for genuine affection, cannot have the stable, enduring affection of an Edmund Bertram and must settle instead for the company of her restless, self-indulgent, and irresponsible brother.

Jane Austen's fierce commitment to hard, calculating good sense is most apparent in *Mansfield Park,* her least likeable novel. Its title was carefully chosen—Lord Mansfield's famous legal judgment in the case of Somerset versus Stewart in 1772 proclaimed that while the slave trade was appropriate for the colonies (we must remember that Sir Thomas Bertram owns a slave plantation in Antigua, which has been badly managed), nonetheless England "is a soil whose air is deemed too pure for slaves to breathe in."[4] But Jane Austen recognized that the English women of her day were little better than domestic slaves, bought and sold on the marriage market, and kept at home by fathers and husbands under "restraint."[5] The best that her countrywomen could attain was a generous master, one who must be cautiously and wisely chosen, one who would allow his wife, as Darcy allows Elizabeth, "to take liberties" with him.[6] In such a situation, women cannot follow the impulses and dictates of their feelings alone. For sexual desire and passionate love can too easily lead women into unhappy marriages, as we see when Lydia Bennet is punished for her "high animal spirits" and promiscuous desire by the indifferent contempt of Wickham. Or worse, it can lead women into the perpetual disgrace and ostracism endured by Maria Bertram and the two Elizas in *Sense and Sensibility.*

In direct opposition to the romantic poets' celebration of love, the leading woman writers of the day urged their female readers to foreswear passion—which too often left women seduced, abandoned, disgraced . . . and pregnant, with only the career of prostitution remaining to them—and to embrace instead reason, virtue, and caution. The overflow of passionate feeling in a female mind that has *not* thought long and deeply can be disastrous for the welfare of women. Whether we read Wollstonecraft or Austen, Susan Ferrier's *Marriage* or Hannah More's *Strictures on the Modern System of Female Education,* Eliza Haywood's *Miss Betsy Thoughtless,* or Mary Brunton's *Self-Control,* we hear a call, not for sensibility but for sense, not for erotic passion but for rational love, a love based on understanding, compatibility, equality, and mutual respect.

The second reason why women didn't like romanticism was voiced most powerfully by a woman who knew the romantic ideology as well as it could be known, by a woman who had lived it at home, first as the daughter of the radical philosopher William Godwin and then as the mistress and wife of the poet Percy Shelley. Mary Wollstonecraft Godwin Shelley articulated her profound disillusion with the central philosophical, poetic, and political tenets of romanticism in her mythic novel, *Frankenstein, or The Modern Prometheus,* written two years after her elopement at the age of sixteen with Percy Shelley. *Frankenstein* is a direct attack on the romantic celebration of the creative process. It is, first and foremost, the story of what happens when a man tries to have a baby without a woman. Victor Frankenstein, who shares Percy Shelley's first penname "Victor", his "sister" Elizabeth, his education and his favorite reading, also shares Percy Shelley's romantic desire to transcend mortality by participating directly in the divine creative energy of the universe. Frankenstein's goal, to discover "whence . . . did the principle of life proceed" (46), specifically echoes the goal of Percy Shelley's narrator in "Alastor" (whom Mary Shelley saw as his spokesman[7]), who addresses Mother Nature thus:

> I have made my bed
> In charnels and on coffins, where black death
> Keeps record of the trophies won from thee,
> Hoping to still these obstinate questionings
> Of thee and thine, by forcing some lone ghost,
> Thy messenger, to render up the tale
> Of what we are.

Percy Shelley's desire to participate continuously in the creative power of the universe and thus to become the equivalent of God is even more directly articulated in his "Ode to the West Wind." Here Shelley pleads with the Power that creates, preserves, and destroys the universe to lift him "as a wave, a leaf, a cloud" and make him its lyre or linguistic voice. "Be thou, Spirit fierce, / My spirit!" Shelley prays, and then moves to the triumphant rhetorical question that climaxes the poem:

> Drive my dead thoughts over the universe
> Like withered leaves to quicken a new birth!
> And, by the incantation of this verse,
>
> Scatter, as from an unextinguished hearth
> Ashes and sparks, my words among mankind!
> Be through my lips to unawakened earth
>
> The trumpet of a prophecy! O, Wind,
> If Winter comes, can Spring be far behind?

Shelley's words are "dead thoughts" because, once spoken, they become part of a static, fixed language-system which cannot represent the ever-changing flux of the universe of things which flows through the mind. As Shelley put it in *A Defence of Poetry:* "The mind in creation is as a fading coal which some invisible influence, like an inconstant wind, awakens to transitory brightness."[8] If the poem is at best a faded coal, mere ashes, then the most the poet can hope is that his words will arouse other minds to other creative actions, that his thoughts—dead in themselves—will nonetheless prophesy future revolutions and transformations.

But as Mary Shelley pointed out in *Frankenstein,* a romantic poetic ideology that celebrated the creative process over its created products, that dismissed the composed poem as but a "fading coal" of its originary inspiration, and that ironically insisted upon the inability of language to capture the infinite power, beauty, and goodness for which the poet yearned—such an ideology can be seen as profoundly immoral. For Victor Frankenstein, having stolen a "spark of being" from mother nature in order to animate the reconstructed corpse lying at his feet, looks with horror at his wretched composition and flees from the room. Victor Frankenstein thus abandons the child to whom he has given birth, and by failing to provide his creature with the mothering it requires, he creates—to use a modern idiom—a battered child who becomes a battering adult, a monster who subsequently murders his brother, his best friend, and his wife.

Mary Shelley clearly believed that a poet must take responsibility not only for the creative process but also for the created product. He must take responsibility for the predictable consequences of his poems and for the probable realizations of the utopian ideals he propounds. If Percy Shelley in *Prometheus Unbound* urges his readers "To defy Power, which seems omnipotent," and in the "Ode to the West Wind" invokes a political revolution that will bring down "black rain, and fire, and hail" upon the vaulted sepulchre of Europe, then he must also take responsibility for the deeds of those to whom the incantations of his verse become a clarion call to revolutionary political action. Mary Shelley was particularly sensitive to the suffering and cruelty that a romantic idealization of radical political change could cause. She had seen at first hand the devastations wrought in France by the fifteen years of war initiated by the French Revolution, the Terror, and the subsequent Napoleonic campaigns when she travelled through France on her elopement journey in 1814. She had then found the French village of Echemine "a wretched place . . . [which] had been once large and populous, but now the houses were roofless, and the ruins that lay scattered about, the gardens covered with the white dust of the torn cottages, the black burnt beams, and squalid looks of the inhabitants, present in every direction the melancholy aspect of devastation."[9] In her novel, she represented the havoc wrought by the French Revolution in the gigantic and misshapen body of Frankenstein's creature. As I have argued at length in my book on Mary Shelley, Frankenstein's creature—like the French Revolution—originated in the idealistic desire to liberate all men from the oppressions of tyranny and mortality.[10] But the Girondist Revolution, like the monster, failed to find the parental guidance, control, and nurturance it required to develop into a rational and benevolent state.

As a mother, Mary Shelley understood that all one's created progeny, however hideous, must be well cared for. One cannot simply ignore one's compositions because one has ceased to be inspired by them. Mary Shelley was profoundly disturbed by what she saw to be a powerful egotism at the core of the romantic ideology: an affirmation of the human imagination as divine defined the mission of the poet as not only the destroyer of "mind-forged manacles" and political tyranny but also as the savior of mankind, the "unacknowledged legislators of the world." She had seen at first hand how self-indulgent this self-image of the poet-savior could be. Her father had withdrawn from his children in order to pursue an increasingly unsuccessful writing career and had remorselessly scrounged money from every passing acquaintance in order to pay his growing debts; Coleridge had become a parasite on his admirers, unable to complete his Magnum Opus; Byron had callously compromised numerous women, including her stepsister Claire Clairmont; Leigh Hunt tormented his wife—and her best friend—Marianne Hunt with his obvious preference for her more intellectual sister Bessy Kent; and her own lover Percy Shelley had coldly abandoned his first wife and daughter in his quest for intellectual beauty and the perfect soulmate and might easily do the same again to Mary. Mary Shelley clearly perceived that the romantic ideology, grounded as it is on a never-ending, perhaps never-successful, effort to marry contraries, to unite the finite and the infinite, through the agency of the poetic imagination and its "spousal verse," too often entailed a sublime indifference to the children of that marriage.

In contrast to a revolutionary politics and a poetics grounded on the self-consuming artifact of romanticism, Mary Shelley posed an alternative ideology grounded on the trope of the family-politic and its gradual evolution and rational reform. Turning to Edmund

Burke, she invoked his concept of the organic development of both human minds and nation-states under benevolent parental guidance as her model of a successful human community. Her credo is based on what Carol Gilligan has taught us to call an "ethic of care," the moral principle that in whatever actions we undertake, we must insure that no one shall be hurt, an ethical vision that Gilligan has found most often articulated by women.[11] Mary Shelley voiced this belief in a passage in *Frankenstein* that functions both as moral touchstone and as a statement of her commitment to the preservation of the domestic affections and the family unit:

> A human being in perfection ought always to preserve a calm and peaceful mind, and never to allow passion or a transitory desire to disturb his tranquillity. I do not think that the pursuit of knowledge is an exception to this rule. If the study to which you apply yourself has a tendency to weaken your affections, and to destroy your taste for those simple pleasures in which no alloy can possibly mix, then that study is certainly unlawful, that is to say, not befitting the human mind. If this rule were always observed; if no man allowed any pursuit whatsoever to interfere with the tranquillity of his domestic affections, Greece had not been enslaved; Caesar would have spared his country; America would have been discovered more gradually; and the empires of Mexico and Peru had not been destroyed.[12]

If we take seriously the views of Mary Shelley and Jane Austen, in the future when we speak of romanticism, we will have to speak of at least *two* romanticisms, the men's and the women's. The male writers promoted an ideology that celebrated revolutionary change, the divinity of the poetic creative process, the development of the man of feeling, and the "acquisition of the philosophic mind." In opposition, the female writers heralded an equally revolutionary ideology, what Mary Wollstonecraft called "a REVOLUTION in female manners."[13] This feminist ideology celebrated the education of the rational woman and an ethic of care that required one to take full responsibility for the predictable consequences of one's thoughts and actions, for all the children of one's mind and body. The failure of the masculine romantic ideology to care for the created product as much as for the creative process, together with its implicit assumption that the ends can justify the means, can produce a romanticism that, as Mary Shelley showed, is truly *monstrous*. In his quest to participate in a divine creative energy, the English romantic poet—whether we think of Percy Shelley, Wordsworth, Coleridge, Blake, or Byron—acts out an egotistical desire for omnipotence and immortality that is the prototype of the modern scientist who seeks to penetrate nature in order to control and harness her powers to serve his own selfish interests. Mary Shelley's vision of Victor Frankenstein as the poet-scientist who creates a monster he can't control resonates ever more powerfully for us today, as we wrestle with the fallout of America's romantic desire to save the world for democracy, the nuclear age initiated by the Manhattan Project's creation of the atomic bomb, an age in which we are capable of destroying—not merely the enemy—but human civilization itself. As Frankenstein's abandoned and unloved monster tells him: "Remember that I have power; . . . I can make you so wretched that the light of day will be hateful to you. You are my creator, but I am your master;—obey!"[14]

The self-indulgent egotism of the romantic poets was painfully apparent to the women writers who knew them best. The valid insights these poets have given us have been many, especially into the philosophic debates we still continue concerning the relation of the perceiving mind to the object of perception, the role of feeling in shaping our mental processes, and the ways in which language determines human consciousness. But we must balance these insights with an understanding of the ways in which they encode a masculine-gendered and thus limited view of human experience. In dialogue with these powerful male romantic voices we must now hear other, female voices, voices that remind us that calm reason and the domestic affections may be necessary to preserve human society from a romantic idealism that might otherwise unleash, however unintentionally, a revolution with truly monstrous consequences.

Notes

1. See M. H. Abrams, *Natural Supernaturalism: Tradition and Revolution in Romantic Literature* (New York: W. W. Norton & Co., 1971); Anne K. Mellor, *English Romantic Irony* (Cambridge, Mass: Harvard University Press, 1980);

and Jerome J. McGann, *The Romantic Ideology—A Critical Investigation* (Chicago: University of Chicago Press, 1983). This view of romanticism was also promulgated in the exhibition on William Wordsworth and the Age of English Romanticism which appeared in New York, Bloomington, and Chicago in 1987–88; see the catalogue by Jonathan Wordsworth, Michael C. Jaye, and Robert Woof (New Brunswick: Rutgers University Press, 1987).

2. See Margaret Kirkham, *Jane Austen, Feminism and Fiction* (Totowa, N.J.: Barnes and Noble, 1983), 33–52; Claudia L. Johnson, *Jane Austen—Women, Politics, and the Novel* (Chicago: University of Chicago Press, 1988), xxii.

3. Mary Wollstonecraft, *A Vindication of the Rights of Woman*, ed. Carol H. Poston (New York: W. W. Norton, 1975), 167, 62, 9, 141.

4. "Somerset v. Stewart," *The English Reports* 98 (King's Bench Division 27) Lofft I (London: Stevens and Sons, Ltd; Edinburgh: William Green and Sons, 1909), 500.

5. Jane Austen, *Mansfield Park,* chap. 21: "She was less and less able to endure the restraint which her father imposed" (London: Penguin, 1966; repr. 1980), 216.

6. Jane Austen, *Pride and Prejudice*, 3:19: "by Elizabeth's instructions she began to comprehend that a woman may take liberties with her husband, which a brother will not always allow in a sister more than ten years younger than himself" (New York: Norton, 1966), 268.

7. That Mary Shelley regarded the narrator of "Alastor" as a spokesman for Percy Shelley is evident from her "Note on Alastor" in which she describes the poem as "the outpouring of his [Percy Shelley's] own emotions." See *The Complete Poetical Works of Percy Bysshe Shelley*, ed. Thomas Hutchinson (London: Oxford University Press, 1905; repr. 1960), 31.

8. Percy Shelley, "A Defence of Poetry," in *Shelley's Prose*, ed. David Lee Clark (Albuquerque: University of New Mexico Press, 1954), 294.

9. Mary Wollstonecraft Shelley, *History of A Six Weeks Tour through a part of France, Switzerland, Germany, and Holland, with Letters descriptive of a Sail round the Lake of Geneva, and of the Glaciers of Chamouni* (London: T. Hookham, Jr., and C. and J. Ollier, 1817), 22–23.

10. Anne K. Mellor, *Mary Shelley: Her Life, Her Fiction, Her Monsters* (New York and London: Methuen, 1988), chapter 4.

11. Carol Gilligan, *In A Different Voice—Psychological Theory and Women's Development* (Cambridge, Mass.: Harvard University Press, 1982), see esp. 173–174.

12. Mary Wollstonecraft Shelley, *Frankenstein, or The Modern Prometheus* (The 1818 Text), ed. James Rieger (Chicago: University of Chicago Press, 1974; repr. 1982), 51.

13. Wollstonecraft, *Vindication,* 192.

14. Shelley, *Frankenstein,* 165.

Romantic Lyric and the Problem of Belief

⁕

Gene W. Ruoff

The problem could be worse. At last report, Shelley has not been condemned to be reborn so that he can be rekilled for the milk-hearted progressivism of *The Revolt of Islam,* and the creeping evolutionism of Keats's *Hyperion* has escaped even the keen eye of the Texas Committee to Keep Textbooks Safe for Texans. That these fanciful instances hardly violate the recent spirit of public discourse about arts and letters, whether the issue at hand has been the fictive representation of the wives of Mohammed, the revision of the core curriculum at Stanford, the improper display of the American flag at the Art Institute of Chicago, or federal funding for art works deemed sexually or religiously offensive, suggests the temper of our times. It may point to one reason why the rift between the literary academy and the common reader is larger today than it has been in my academic lifetime, by the beginning of which questions of belief in literature had been largely shoved aside, however unresolved.

My title recalls an essay published just over thirty years ago by M. H. Abrams, "Belief and the Suspension of Disbelief," which appeared in *Literature and Belief,* the volume of proceedings of the English Institute meeting for 1957.[1] Reexamination of the topic seems timely, because we are experiencing in romantic studies clear signs that the cultural moment represented in the brilliant work of the past three decades, elaborating the expansive prophetic and spiritual mission of romantic writing, has passed. That work is emblematized for the academic reader in Abrams's learned and literate study, *Natural Supernaturalism* (1971), which has also attracted its share of lay readers. Its influence has been even more pervasive as it has been filtered through the great classroom text of which Abrams is general editor, *The Norton Anthology of English Literature,* now in its fifth edition. There Abrams himself has orchestrated the introduction of the romantics to several generations of college freshmen and sophomores. Even at its most persuasive, such work feels dated, an emanation from a kinder and gentler age of ecumenical readings and ecumenical hopes. That age was characterized in the larger intellectual sphere by the powerful syncretism of scholars like Joseph Campbell, Mircea Eliade, and Northrop Frye. In their various ways, and whatever their reservations about mythic criticism per se, many critics who flourished from the fifties through the seventies attempted to accommodate romantic texts to a sense of capacious spirituality, consistently undervaluing polemical dissonances in search of higher spiritual harmonies.

Our problem today may be not that these understandings have suddenly proved faulty, but that history has left their project behind. The age of ecumenicism, which had followed a solid Wordsworthian program in accentuating experiential and spiritual affinities while diminishing credal differences, is dead. Ecumenicism itself, which had seemed a turning point in the history of religions—perhaps an evolutionary growth—now appears to have been a narrowly based cultural detour given crucial energy by the memory of a war that had written in blood the frightening destructive potential of secular and sacred zealotry. The rush of enthusiasm inspired by Vatican II has become the faintest of memories, as any broadening of Roman doctrine lies wrecked on the shoals of the women's movement in developed countries and population explosion, famine, and radical politics in the third world. Holy wars rage in the Middle East. Our major growth industries in American religion are rigidly sectarian faiths, which know their truth and know it loudly. As dogmatic religion revives, humanism grows increasingly secular. The response of many younger critics to the spiritualized humanism of an older generation of scholars is a counter-humanist critique of all pieties, often conducted from post-Freudian or post-Marxist perspectives.

In looking again at the question of belief in poetry we do not have to reinvent the wheel. Gerald Graff's 1970 study, *Poetic Statement and Critical Dogma,* astutely reviewed the intellectual underpinnings

of a half-century of diverse critical theory and practice which, for all
its other powers and other benefits, had left us unable to deal not
only with questions of belief in poetry, but with the presence and
function of propositional or assertive language itself.[2] Graff's target
at that time was the broad spectrum of organicist criticism, running
from the practical neo-Coleridgeanism of I. A. Richards through
the mythopoeics of Frye and others, which he collectively dubbed
"mythotherapies." Graff had in mind a body of sweeping, widely
accepted, and lightly examined claims about the nature of literature
and literary experience: that a work's content is inseparable from its
form; that its meaning cannot be paraphrased, because poetry is itself a mode of knowledge; that its ideas, values, and beliefs are dramatic enactments, and consequently make no truth-claims; and that
a work of literature cannot be evaluated by criteria extrinsic to itself. Cleanth Brooks organized the 1957 English Institute program
on belief; his contribution was "Implications of an Organic Theory
of Poetry," an essay which remarks almost in passing that "critics of
quite various persuasions" have accepted poetry's "special kind of
unity" as "an empirical fact."[3]

Graff's book, which doubts throughout this "empirical fact,"
could hardly have been less timely. It called for a battle which was
never to be fought on its terms: the anti-organicist polemic which
took hold was to be conducted in the name of deconstruction, which
even more radically challenged questions of referentiality in poetry.
Deconstruction charges organicism with confusing the wish for the
deed in attributing representational as well as creative power to
literature. From its perspective, poetry constructs neither a tran-
scendent reality nor a self-sufficient fictive reality, but a pseudo-
reality that only patches over deep rifts in culture, society, and the
self. The proper mission of criticism, then, is not to demonstrate
and celebrate the higher unity poetry brings into being, but to un-
veil its illusions, to de-construct its constructions. More recently
the new historicism has extended this challenge, as it pursues the
socio-economic grounding, the material base, of what some of
its practitioners call "romantic ideology." As practiced by Jerome
McGann, Clifford Siskin, and others, this critique is as attentive to
the ways in which we have characteristically read romantic texts as
it is ot the texts themselves.[4] Because romantic ideology is always at
some remove from the conscious constructions of a text, questions of

belief, even of intention, are not instrumental to its investigations. If organicism found the sacred lurking behind the secular, and deconstruction the abyss papered over by the sacred, new historicism finds the political lurking behind everything. For all our methodological sophistication, so often befuddling to general and academic readers alike, we remain unable to face the specter of doctrine in poetry: our eyes go funny and we cease reading. I address here only one manifestation of this problem in romantic lyric and suggest a few of its consequences for our criticism, our teaching, and our loss of a public audience for poetry.

My example is Coleridge's "The Eolian Harp." In "Coleridge's 'A Light in Sound': Science, Metascience, and the Poetic Imagination" (1972), Abrams judged it a "flawed example" of the greater romantic lyric, the central poetic type he had so persuasively described several years earlier: "There are instances of stock diction and standard moral parallels. . . , and the concluding verse paragraph strikes the modern reader as a timid and ineptly managed retreat to religious orthodoxy from the bold speculation of the middle of the poem."[5] Still, the poem has been very important to postwar formulations of romantic aesthetics. According to Abrams in "Structure and Style in the Greater Romantic Lyric" (1965), its expanded version of 1796 "established, in epitome, the ordonnance, materials, and style of the greater [romantic] lyric," the form of poem that begins with a

> determinate speaker in a particularized . . . setting. . . . The speaker begins with a description of the landscape; an aspect or change of aspect in the landscape evokes a varied but integral process of memory, thought, anticipation, and feeling which remains closely involved with the outer scene. In the course of this meditation the lyric speaker achieves an insight, faces up to a tragic loss, comes to a moral decision, or resolves an emotional problem. Often the poem rounds upon itself to end where it began, at the outer scene, but with an altered mood and deepened understanding which is the result of the intervening meditation. (76–77)

No other single formulation of the practices of romantic lyric has been so influential as this, and none has proven so compatible with continuing lyric practice in this century.

In an earlier essay Abrams had described both the surface

properties and the spiritual and metaphysical groundings of "The Correspondent Breeze: A Romantic Metaphor" (1960), while all but avoiding "The Eolian Harp"—surely as seminal in its figural as in its formal aspects—in his numerous examples of the trope. The reason for this elision becomes clear in "Coleridge's 'A Light in Sound,'" which rounds off what we might call his "Eolian Harp" trilogy. The problem Abrams has with the poem is its foregrounding, through the retraction of its palinode, the problem of belief. This troubles Abrams on behalf of "the modern reader," who presumably is more at home with "bold speculation" than "religious orthodoxy." What is less fully articulated is the extent to which the poem's self-confutation threatens Abrams's entire project of understanding the properties of romantic lyric, especially in Coleridge's fully elaborated version, 1828 and after.

The questions raised by Abrams cannot be discussed meaningfully without a reading of the poem, in this case a reading which will highlight rather than evade the way in which issues of belief function in it. "The Eolian Harp" begins in a mood of mild erotic languor marked by a heightened, but essentially passive, sensory luxuriance:

> My pensive Sara! thy soft cheek reclined
> Thus on mine arm, most soothing sweet it is
> To sit beside our Cot, our Cot o'ergrown
> With white-flower'd Jasmin, and the broad-leav'd Myrtle,
> (Meet emblems they of Innocence and Love!)
> And watch the clouds, that late were rich with light,
> Slow saddening round, and mark the star of eve
> Serenely brilliant (such should Wisdom be)
> Shine opposite! How exquisite the scents
> Snatch'd from yon bean-field! and the world *so* hush'd!
> The stilly murmur of the distant Sea
> Tells us of silence.

Everything about the initial scene bespeaks passivity, from the postures of the lovers to the speaker's acceptance of traditional moral emblematism of nature. Meanings need not be sought, because this world is complete.

The second verse paragraph turns by association from the one sound which has confirmed the silence of the scene, the "murmur of the distant sea," to the eolian harp, "that simplest Lute, / Placed length-ways in the clasping casement," which will register plastically the changes in the breeze, setting in motion the poem's meditative excursion:

>   hark!
>   How by the desultory breeze caress'd,
> Like some coy maiden half yielding to her lover,
> It pours such sweet upbraiding as must needs
> Tempt to repeat the wrong! And now, its strings
> Boldlier swept, the long sequacious notes
> Over delicious surges sink and rise,
> Such a soft floating witchery of sound
> As twilight Elfins make, when they at eve
> Voyage on gentle gales from Fairy-Land,
> Where Melodies round honey-dropping flowers,
> Footless and wild, like birds of Paradise,
> Nor pause, nor perch, hovering on untam'd wing!

The poem moves into story-making here, as its speaker goes beyond the fixed analogies of the opening verse paragraph to develop a chain of associative comparisons. The breeze is to the harp as the masculine lover is to the maid, implicitly as Coleridge is to Sara. He is the force, she the response. In this mode of erotic dalliance, the maid's upbraidings encourage the lover, leading at last to full erotic engagement: "the long sequacious notes / Over delicious surges sink and rise." As the poem reaches this emotional pitch, its analogies shift, and the harp no longer reflects the human content of the scene, which is abruptly displaced, perhaps transcended. The notes of the harp, "a soft floating witchery of sound," now suggest a world beyond the moment, a world of elves, fairies, and mythological creatures. That complete and self-sustaining environment of the opening stanza has come to be merely proleptic to an alternative reality. Leaving casuality aside, we might observe that the movement to this alternative realm has coincided with the depersonalization of the poem's opening situation; as the speaker's active powers are exercised, "pensive Sara" becomes anything but thoughtful, objectified into an amalgam of generic coy maid and passive harp.

The poem moves immediately from its playful invocation of quaint superstitions, which are self-limiting, into a powerful metaphysical claim, which is not:

> O! the one life within us and abroad,
> Which meets all motion and becomes its soul,
> A light in sound, a sound-like power in light,
> Rhythm in all thought, and joyance every where—
> Methinks, it should have been impossible
> Not to love all things in a world so fill'd;
> Where the breeze warbles, and the mute still air
> Is Music slumbering on her instrument.

The first four lines of this passage are a late interpolation, first appearing in the errata of *Sibylline Leaves* (1817), and included in the text proper in 1828 and after. For Abrams and most other interpreters, these four lines are very near the core of the poem's difficulties.

The central purpose of Abrams's 1972 essay is to unpack these four lines of "The Eolian Harp," demonstrating the astonishing degree to which they interweave continuing threads of Coleridge's mature thought on nature and supernature. For Abrams they obviously constitute a signature passage. Adapting Coleridge on Wordsworth, we might say that if we were to encounter them running wild in the deserts of Arabia, we should immediately shout aloud, "COLERIDGE!" Here is the way Abrams frames his concluding citation of the lines:

> The poet breaks through sensation into vision, in which the phenomenal aspects of the landscape, its colors, music, and odors, are intuited as products and indices of the first manifestations of the creative Word, gravitation and light, in whose multiform unions all nature and life consist; and he goes on to celebrate the world's song of life and joy, which sounds through the wind-harp, in which the silent air is merely music unheard, and of which the subject is the one Life that, in marrying all opposites, also weds the single consciousness to the world without. (190)

For Abrams, the passage just given is at the heart of Coleridge's achievement as a poet and thinker. He begins and ends his essay with reflections upon it, claiming at one point that "every reader feels [it] to be the imaginative climax of the poem." Indeed, his essay implicitly rewrites the poem to make this utterance climactic and terminal as well as central. But within the poem itself, of course, the passage remains embarrassingly medial.

The third verse paragraph begins with yet another displacement. This time the movement of the speaker's consciousness is not upward toward a higher range of experience, but away in space and time:

> And thus, my Love, as on the midway slope
> Of yonder hill I stretch my limbs at noon,
> Whilst through my half-clos'd eye-lids I behold
> The sunbeams dance, like diamonds, on the main,
> And tranquil muse upon tranquillity;
> Full many a thought uncall'd and undetain'd,
> And many idle flitting phantasies,
> Traverse my indolent and passive brain,
> As wild and various as the random gales
> That swell and flutter on this subject Lute!

While Sara had before been the lute, played upon by the lover-harpist, Coleridge has now replaced her in the role of that "subject" instrument. Not incidentally, Sara has disappeared from the scene as it is imagined, or remembered, or both. It is no longer sunset but midday. Sara's cheek is no longer on Coleridge's arm, and it is his limbs which are stretched upon the "slope / Of yonder hill." From playing her, his "indolent and passive brain" has come to be played upon by random thoughts. From being an object of attention, Sara has receded to become an object of address, abandoned but un-seduced—a singularly mortifying predicament for the heroine of what looked as though it was going to be a seduction poem.

Or maybe it remains a seduction poem, while its temptations shift from sexuality to metaphysical speculation. I give here both the climactic verse paragraph of its speculative movement and the beginning of the palinode, so that the critical problem the work poses is clear:

And what if all of animated nature
Be but organic Harps diversely fram'd,
That tremble into thought, as o'er them sweeps
Plastic and vast, one intellectual breeze,
At once the Soul of each, and God of all?

But thy more serious eye a mild reproof
Darts, O belovéd Woman! nor such thoughts
Dim and unhallow'd dost thou not reject,
And biddest me walk humbly humbly with my God.
Meek Daughter in the family of Christ!
Well hast thou said and holily disprais'd
These shapings of the unregenerate mind;
Bubbles that glitter as they rise and break
On vain Philosophy's aye-babbling spring.

Abrams sees clearly enough from Coleridge's vantage point the dangers in this speculative train that necessitate its rejection. Even expressed hypothetically, the passage

> opens a possibility that filled Coleridge with metaphysical terror: the world-view he called "Pantheism." That is, the passage threatens to absorb a transcendent and personal Creator of the world, without remainder, into an Indwelling Soul of Nature, . . . which informs all the material universe and constitutes all forms of consciousness. . . . Coleridge's "intellectual breeze" even suggests a regressive form of the religion of Nature in which the unifying presence is a sacred wind or divine breath. (162)

Thomas McFarland, so often our best commentator on Coleridge's religious thought, describes the repudiated lines as "an example of pure Neoplatonic Spinozism." For McFarland, Spinoza represents one of the oscillatory poles of Coleridge's thought—Kant was the other—in which the struggle between pantheism and Christianity is continually restaged. Because McFarland adduces Coleridge's poetic text within the context of a book which is about belief, designed to illuminate the writer's entire theological project, he is comfortable with the turn the poem has taken, as the voice of the intellect and of Spinoza "is immediately counter-balanced by the voice of the heart and of Christianity."[6] The poem is a specific manifestation, then, of a conflict that runs throughout Coleridge's intellectual career.

Abrams's concern goes beyond historical elucidation of the passage. It is not enough for him or for his modern reader that the conflict expressed was an abiding one for Coleridge. The question is whether the poem makes its conflict real for us, or whether it is finally a disruptive intrusion, "timid and ineptly managed," that mars a poem. Abrams seems to have two concerns. The first is whether Coleridge's retraction does not in fact come from outside the poem, interjecting an issue that has little to do with the conduct of the poem itself. In this case Coleridge would be acting as his own non-poetic reader, rejecting a line of poetic thought because of personal doctrinal adhesions.[7] The second is whether the palinode must be taken as canceling not just the "organic Harps" and "intellectual breeze," which have come immediately before, but also "the one Life within us and abroad." As I read him, Abrams would in a pinch sacrifice the bauble of the lute, but his essay contests all assaults on "the one Life."

Our first recourse in addressing these questions can remain within the legal limits of modernist/romantic aesthetics by staying within the confines of the poem, attending to its rhetorical strategies. The role of Sara requires particular attention, because she is credited with providing the doctrinal check on its speculations. Interestingly enough, she is not allowed to voice her concerns, which Coleridge purports to read in the "mild reproof" of her "more serious eye." Coleridge's handling of the situation allows him to have it both ways: to attribute the motivation for his turn to orthodoxy to another person (who has, after all, been sitting there all along), but still to control the terms of the rebuff. Indeed, we know from McFarland (166–167) that Coleridge was conducting this debate with himself in his correspondence, using almost identical language, in the mid-1790s, close to the time he wrote the first version of the poem to include the palinode. Why, then, is Sara there?

In describing the form of the greater romantic lyric, Abrams noted that its "determinate speaker . . . carries on, in a fluent vernacular which rises easily to a more formal speech, a sustained colloquy, often with himself or with the outer scene, but more frequently with a silent human auditor, present or absent" (76–77). Abrams's priorities are revealed even in the structure of his sentence: he is finally interested in the colloquy with the self and/or scene, not any possible colloquy with the human other of the poem, even while admitting that a determinate addressee is normative. Nor, we might add, are these auditors invariably silent. Witness Wordsworth's "Resolution and Independence," which is not mentioned in the essay on the greater lyric, though a prime candidate for the form in every other respect, and think of "Expostulation and Reply" and "The Tables Turned," which if not "greater" lyrics, are frequently marginalized as "doctrinal" poems.

What I am suggesting is an incipient dialogical tendency in romantic lyric which subtly undermines claims for the self-sufficiency of either the individual poetic imagination or the monological lyric, greater as well as smaller. This dialogical quality governs the thematic development of "The Eolian Harp" and generates its theological conflict. Sara is more than a fictive convenience providing a beginning, turn, and end. She is that pole of the poem which represents human personality, the affectional life, and the present moment. Put simply, she is the embodiment of difference in the poem—sexual difference, human difference, temporal difference, ideological difference—against which its massive drive for unity strains.

The first verse paragraph is filled with minute, personalized, individualized particularities: "My . . . Sara"; "thy . . . cheek"; "mine arm"; "our Cot, our Cot o'ergrown"; "white-flower'd Jasmin"; "broad-leav'd Myrtle"; "yon bean-field." [8] The central meditation of the poem erases all difference, even perceptual difference ("A light in sound, a sound-like power in light"), in pursuit of a higher unity, "the one Life." Loving "all things" is poised against loving those individual things which began the poem, including Sara herself. If "all of animated nature / Be but organic Harps diversely fram'd," there is finally *no* difference, and the merely carnal, the merely affectionate, the merely sensual, and the merely personal are irrelevant. The drive of Coleridge's speculation is toward an ever more expansive sense of divine immanence, "one intellectual breeze, / At once the Soul of each, and God of all." The power of the poem lies in its discovery that immanence is alienating, that that which is everywhere can in fact be nowhere. The divinity it seeks is so depersonalizing and dehumanizing that the great marriage that Abrams celebrates, of "the single consciousness to the world without," is at war with the marriage of one man and one woman.

If we can read past the doctrinal truisms of the response imagined in Sara's "more serious eye," that glance through which she reasserts her personal presence, we will find it superbly balanced against Coleridge's speculations. To bid her husband to "walk humbly with . . . [his] God" is to reassert divine personality and specifically human characteristics; *walking* itself resonates against the recumbent *lying* posture of the speculative movement, acknowledging a world of effort which "the one Life" elides. Addressing Sara as "Meek Daughter in the family of Christ" reasserts the familiality of devotion, the humanity of worship. The poem's use of formulaic language in this section, language which is communally accessible and easily sharable, stands in sharp contrast to the brilliant singularity of the language of its earlier speculations. The poem has discovered paradoxically that hunger for immanence begets absence and alienation, and that acceptance of transcendence is the key to presence:

> For never guiltless may I speak of him,
> The Incomprehensible! save when with awe
> I praise him, and with Faith that inly *feels*.

The "Incomprehensible"—here divinity in all its austere transcendence—is twice renamed in the surrounding lines by the personal pronoun "him." This nominal sequence, "him . . . The Incomprehensible . . . him," expresses graphically the poem's closing insistence on the inseparability of transcendence and personality. Its recovery of personality is then extended to the speaker, "me, / A sinful and most miserable man, / Wilder'd and dark," and it restores those other individual blessings, presented as gifts and possessions, which had been threatened by speculation: "Peace, and this Cot, and thee, heart-honour'd Maid!"

My reading of the poem has attempted to work from within to determine the way in which it grounds its confrontation of beliefs. Its historical validity may be measured by the degree to which it confirms McFarland's observations about the strains within Coleridge's thought as he participated in the contemporary controversy over pantheism, the *Pantheismusstreit,* the ambivalences of which set

"Pantheism against Theism. Atheism against Christianity. Personality against the outer world. The head against the heart" (166). I would further argue, though, that one does not have to share or even honor the body of belief attributed to Sara in order to apprehend the dialogic of the poem. If the conflict between transcendence and immanence allows one entry, so do its conflicting modes of perception, of depiction of nature, and of love. Who among us has not at some time surmised that what Sara's eyes are really saying is "Shut up and kiss me," called to mind Don Juan's uncomfortably analogous fits of adolescent nature-worship, and entertained the possibility of a parody from Sara's perspective akin to Anthony Hecht's "The Dover Bitch," that magically funny riposte to Matthew Arnold's somber meditations?

My point is that conflicting beliefs are wholly functional elements of "The Eolian Harp," and that discussions which evade, minimize, or otherwise trivialize them cannot do the poem or Coleridge justice. Modern criticism's avoidance of belief, which often claims its warrant from Coleridge's own strictly circumscribed "willing suspension of disbelief for the moment, which constitutes poetic faith,"[9] distorts and enervates the romantic achievement. The dialogic of a poem like "The Eolian Harp" calls for an equally dialogical criticism, which is willing both to enter fully into a work's theological and metaphysical positions and to provide its best reasoned responses to Coleridge's open invitation, "What if?" What if this assertion were true? What would follow from it? What are its consequences for human life? In its final form of 1828, "The Eolian Harp" completes its own profound critique of "the one Life," which it had begun more than thirty years before. By coming to judgment on the conflicting beliefs it has embodied, it should encourage a criticism which will grant them equal seriousness, which might well include the seriousness of opposition which does not masquerade as aesthetics.

A purely aesthetic criticism of poems like "The Eolian Harp" is insufficient, however dense and compelling the historical detail with which it buttresses one side of its poetic argument. Its procedures reveal more about our need to bring romanticism within the compass of modernism than about the poetry itself. Of course such criticism is not entirely averse to dramatic conflict, upon which it purports to thrive. But it seems able to accept this conflict only when it can be made part of a positive, progressive, expansionist dialectic, incorporating all elements into some higher unity. It balks at embracing a poetic dialogic which is equally capable of rejecting beliefs which, however attractive, compelling, or characteristic of the age, are found somehow inadequate. "The Eolian Harp" may be the cleanest case we have of such conflict, and for this reason it may finally be one of the less interesting. I argue elsewhere that other central lyrics, such as Wordsworth's Intimations Ode and "Resolution and Independence," require equally rigorous examinations of their most quintessentially "romantic" sections, which seldom receive sustained critical attention.[10] Our inability to attend to unbridgeable conflicts of belief in romantic lyric is one of the clearest measures of the difference between the romantics and us. At the same time, it marks the distance between us, as academic readers, and the rest of us—them, as we are wont to think of that substantial portion of the world's population for which belief, creed, and doctrine remain central determinants for action. This is a distance we might find it worth narrowing.

Notes

1. M. H. Abrams, ed., *Literature and Belief: English Institute Essays, 1957* (New York: Columbia University Press, 1958).

2. Gerald Graff, *Poetic Statement and Critical Dogma* (Evanston, Illinois: Northwestern University Press, 1970). Graff has recently refined his critique of anti-propositional literary theory, although he now prefers the term "anti-assertional" as more technically accurate; see "Literature as Assertions," in *American Critics at Work: Examinations of Contemporary Literary Theories,* ed. Victor A. Kramer (Troy, New York: Whitstone Publishing Co., 1984), 81–110.

3. Cleanth Brooks, "Implications of an Organic Theory of Poetry," in *Literature and Belief,* 63.

4. See especially Jerome J. McGann, *The Romantic Ideology: A Critical Investigation* (Chicago: University of Chicago Press, 1983), and Clifford H. Siskin, *The Historicity of Romantic Discourse* (New York: Oxford University Press, 1988).

5. Abrams, *The Correspondent Breeze: Essays on English Romanticism* (New York: Norton, 1984), 159. Subsequent references to this and other essays by Abrams are to this collection and are given parenthetically. My analysis

follows the text of "The Eolian Harp" of 1828 and after, as found in *The Complete Poetical Works of Samuel Taylor Coleridge,* 2 vols. (Oxford: Clarendon Press, 1912), 1:100–102. My discussion concentrates on Abrams because of his towering presence in romantic studies. For discussions of "The Eolian Harp" with similar concerns see William H. Scheuerle, "A Reexamination of Coleridge's 'The Eolian Harp,'" *Studies in English Literature* 15 (1975): 591–599; and Douglas B. Wilson, *Two Modes of Apprehending Nature: A Gloss on the Coleridgean Symbol, PMLA* 87 (1972): 42–52.

6. Thomas McFarland, *Coleridge and the Pantheist Tradition* (Oxford: Clarendon Press, 1969), 166.

7. I borrow here the terminology of I. A. Richards, *Practical Criticism: A Study of Literary Judgment* (London: Routledge and Kegan Paul, 1929), 16.

8. For a provocative discussion of the role of particularity in another of Coleridge's conversation poems, "Fears in Solitude," see Karl Kroeber, *British Romantic Art* (Berkeley: University of California Press, 1986), 85–93.

9. Coleridge, *Biographia Literaria,* ed. James Engell and Walter Jackson Bate (Princeton: Princeton University Press, 1983), 2:6.

10. Gene W. Ruoff, *Wordsworth and Coleridge: The Making of the Major Lyrics, 1802–1804* (New Brunswick, New Jersey: Rutgers University Press, 1989). See 147–154 for a reading of the rhetorical function of the old man-stone-seabeast passage of "Resolution and Independence"; see 229–260 for a reconsideration of the function of the myth of pre-existence in the Ode, which is at issue in Abrams's "Belief and the Suspension of Disbelief," 24–28.

Wordsworth's Prescriptions:
Romanticism and Professional Power

❧

Clifford Siskin

A columnist for the *San Francisco Chronicle* recently bemoaned the loss of targets for his somewhat questionable brand of humor:

> Time was, you could go around pretty much trashing anybody you felt like trashing. Back then it was called "ethnic humor" or (even further back) "folktales." But then it was adjudged unseemly to select out one race or nationality and hold it up for ridicule.
>
> Now, politically, I was entirely in agreement with this thesis. But I also wrote humor for a living, and humor writers need objects of ridicule the way Richard Gephardt needs eyebrows.

After proceeding through a list of now forbidden quarry, he concluded:

> No go.
>
> And yet somebody had to keep changing those darned light-bulbs. . . . Stanford MBAs? Closer, but not broad enough. Then the revelation hit me like a ton of torts:
>
> Professions . . . are the only acceptable objects of ridicule. Anchorpersons, rich performers, doctors, accountants, lawyers and, yes, newspaper columnists are the current targets of opportunity.[1]

The word "current" should not mislead us into thinking this is only a recent phenomenon, for the professions have been targeted for centuries. Nor should the title of this essay, which links Words-worth to the professional, lead us to conclude that such ridicule was not one of that poet's favorite sports. In 1799, for example, he went down the list from lawyers through doctors to academics:

> A Lawyer art thou?—draw not nigh!
> Go, carry to some other place
> The hardness of thy coward eye,
> The falsehood of thy sallow face.
>
> . . . .
>
> Physician art thou? One, all eyes,
> Philosopher! a fingering slave,
> One that would peep and botanize
> Upon his mother's grave?
>
> . . . .
>
> —A Moralist perchance appears;
> Led, Heaven knows how! to this poor sod:
> And He has neither eyes nor ears;
> Himself his world, and his own God;
>
> One to whose smooth-rubb'd soul can cling
> Nor form nor feeling great nor small,
> A reasoning, self-sufficing thing,
> An intellectual All in All![2]

Clearly, Wordsworth did not perceive his interests to be aligned with those professions as occupational groups, although it should be noted that the effect of placing attacks such as these in a poem titled "A Poet's Epitaph" is not to deny "profession" as a category but to reinforce it through claims of hierarchical superiority: to be a Poet is to be a member of the *best* profession. The Romantic con-nection my title points to, however, is not with the concept of a "profession," for that clearly predates Romanticism, but to "pro-fession*al*" as an adjective denoting a kind of behavior that alters the social function of all of the professions. That term in that sense enters the language for the *first* time at the end of the eighteenth and beginning of the nineteenth centuries. Professionalism as we still know it today, then, has its origins in Romanticism, and I want to explore the way the literary and critical discourse of the latter has helped and continues to help to make the former a central form of modern power. I will begin, at the risk of seeming "A reasoning, self-sufficing *thing*" (emphasis mine), rather abstractly, asserting some of the reasons that at this point in time compel us both to study these two "isms" and to study them together. I will then return to Wordsworth to explore the generic construction of new behaviors linking work and the self in *The Prelude*.

When the anthologies tell us that Romanticism lasted a mere thirty-four years, from 1798 to 1832, they are, of course, merely conforming their historical narrative to a formula articulated repeatedly and powerfully in Romantic texts. "Oh, Sir!" wrote Wordsworth, "the good die first, / And they whose hearts are dry as summer dust / Burn to the socket" (*Excursion*, 1:500–502). Since only the good die young, and since Wordsworth was good but lived long, criticism since Arnold has killed him off early with the supposedly ahistorical aesthetic judgment that limits his "real" productivity to a Great Decade. Only recently have some Romanticists begun to question the truism of "sweet because short" by taking seriously the later Wordsworth.[3]

This is not the place to rehearse those arguments, but since the topic "The Romantics and Us" requires us to take periodization seriously, I will suggest that English literary history has in no date been more misleading than in that early end of 1832. Far from being the culmination of English Romanticism, as the anthologies insist, the 1830s marked the moment at which the constructs and strategies of Romantic texts became "normal" within and for the very culture that had produced them.[4] If I may be allowed a little license, a comparison between professions may be useful here. Just as the Romantic poets claimed to raise the standards of their profession by keeping themselves and their readers, in Wordsworth's words from the Preface to *Lyrical Ballads*, "in the company of flesh and blood,"[5] so the new medical men and women of the late eighteenth and early nineteenth centuries aspired professionally by anatomizing flesh-and-blood bodies snatched from the gallows, graveyards, and sometimes even streets. The Anatomy Act of 1833, which killed the corpse trade by permitting the use of unclaimed workhouse bodies,[6] may have made the doctors' close readings of their subjects—Wordsworth called it "look[ing] steadily"—less romantic in the superficial sense of adventurous, but it actually insured the flow of bodies, legitimized and made normal the new procedures, and valorized the knowledge those procedures produced.

Among the literary constructs normalized at the same time were Imagination, Creativity, and Love of Nature. Among the strategies was the telling of strictly literary and artistic tales about those constructs. To the extent that we accept those tellings as fully descriptive of Romanticism, our inquiries into "The Romantics and Us" will produce very specific kinds of knowledge: claims of direct or indirect influence, maps of shared themes and images, histories of ideas, catalogues of echoes. These have been, and are, of considerable value, but they also help to perform a specific historical and political function: they continue to divert our attention from the ongoing power of Romantic discourse—the ways that the literary and artistic have served within it to configure more than literary and artistic behavior.

The "more" at issue is in evidence all around us *if* we stop conforming our understanding of what is Romantic to the tales that Romanticism tells about itself. To do so is to recognize how Romantic art has prescribed—written before—both the "real" world it supposedly reflects and the very means by which we understand that world. From that perspective, Romanticism can be read and seen not only in the manuscripts and paintings exhibited as "William Wordsworth and the Age of English Romanticism," but also in the *professional* behaviors and formations that made that exhibition— and the accompanying conference that occasioned this essay—possible.[7] They range from a topic fashioned to produce knowledge about the present ("Us") by linking it developmentally to the past ("The Romantics"), to the late eighteenth-century form for sharing that knowledge (the "conference"),[8] to the enabling institutional framework (the public museum, the departmental university, the bureaucratic state).[9] The ongoing power of Romanticism, in other words, has to do with how, historically, Romanticism has empowered professionalism, both by generating the discourse of professional behavior and by turning our attention from it.

To claim that Romanticism is "about" professionalism is not to insist that the turns linking Romanticism to the secularization of Western thought, as taken by M. H. Abrams,[10] and to the mapping of consciousness, as executed in the early work of Harold Bloom and Geoffrey Hartman,[11] were wrong, but to point out that this new connection became visible only at a specific historical moment. On the one hand, Romanticists have only recently become concerned with the potential for a particular kind of repetition in their work: the resemblance I have already touched upon between the interpretation and that which is being interpreted. Even though disagreement persists as to the import of those resemblances, no issue is more central to today's Romanticists than clarifying their historical relationship to their subject matter. However their concern is voiced, scholars are finding Romanticism to be no longer just a passive object of knowledge, but something implicated in the act of producing such knowledge.[12]

Professionalism, on the other hand, has also over the past few years become increasingly problematic, something both threatened and threatening. The threat it faces is most dramatically evident in the scenario that sociologists call proletarianization.[13] Figures from 1985 show that almost one half (47%) of the physicians under thirty-six years old were not independent practitioners but employees of the large companies constituting the new health care market; that figure compares to less than 20% for those over fifty-five.[14] Independence among either age group, however, has only invited proletarianization in another form, as evidenced in Michigan where physicians carrying picket signs rallied in the streets of the state capital to protest rising insurance costs. The double bind is obvious: every such effort to preserve their independent financial status as professionals erodes both their public image and self-image as elite professionals.

Despite their difficulties, the doctors will probably not get much sympathy from professionals facing even more immediate and drastic threats: professors in the humanities, for example, who after a decade of job lists only a few millimeters thick now find that increased breadth means decreased depth—many of the new jobs do not hold the traditional promise of tenure. Neither will they draw much sympathy from a public that understands professionalization not as concept under siege, but as a force that has gone too far. Just consider, keeping in mind the newspaper columnist's glee in making the professions objects of ridicule, how many images we have for professional excess: yuppies who are too ambitious, specialists who are too narrow-minded, experts who are too elitist, theorists who are too esoteric. We yearn instead for what professionalism has supposedly disguised: an individual whose deep human feelings have somehow survived the chill. "The problem," as one literary professional has recently put it, "is that you can't talk about your private life in the course of doing your professional work." [15]

My work on Romanticism and professionalism thus occurs at a temporal and disciplinary intersection. At this historical moment in the late twentieth century, two phenomena of the late eighteenth century are in conceptual crisis. The personal, professional, and social stakes are high both for Romanticists trying to redefine the difference between what they study and how they study it, and for experts in professionalism, including sociologists, historians, and cultural critics, who are trying to work out a description of a category that purports, in turn, to describe the kind of work they do. Both efforts have already generated sufficient activity to produce the first signs of institutional change. Redefinitions of Romanticism have encouraged increased specialization in the job market, where a few listings now specify not just "Romanticist" but "New Historicist Romanticist" or "Gender Romanticist." That decidedly professional turn may be a subject for study by new faculty at Johns Hopkins where, I understand, the History Department will tailor future searches not to periods or other traditional distinctions, but to a few select concerns, such as The History of the Body and, significantly, The History of Professionalism.

As of yet, these two tasks, writing the history of professionalism and rewriting Romanticism, have not been linked. The overtly historical efforts regarding the former have frequently leapfrogged the late eighteenth and early nineteenth centuries, attending on the one side to early and mid-eighteenth-century changes in technique and status, primarily of medical men, [16] and, on the other side, to the mid- and late nineteenth-century statistical rise in the number of professionals. [17] The figures recorded by the census do, at first glance, seem to leave Romanticism out of the picture: at the end of the first three decades of the nineteenth century, for example, only 400 respondents classified themselves as professional authors whereas over 13,000 did so by the century's close. [18] This numerical difference could be read as a confirmation of the conventional period difference—a few enthusiastic Romantic amateurs versus the many sober Victorian professionals—but doing so does not explain the change. How did an England in which Samuel Johnson defined "profession" as, simply, "known employment,"[19] become an England that less than a century later made professional employment into an object of professional knowledge—recording, classifying, and reclassifying, from the census of 1841 onward, the occupation of every individual in the nation?

For a start, the word "profession*al*," as an adjective describing a kind of behavior, had to enter the language. As I pointed out earlier, it made its first appearances at the end of the eighteenth and beginning of the nineteenth centuries, a moment that was also marked lexically by the debut of terms of difference such as "amateur." Victorian professionalism, in other words, was written, word by word, before it became "real" and widespread. For most of the eighteenth century, professional behavior had simply been the behavior of gentlemen, for only gentlemen had held the status to enter the professions;[20] this new vocabulary, however, was part of a discourse of professionalism that rearranged the relationships among—and the functions of—character, identity, status, work, money, education, property, and propriety.

The rearranging as well as the naturalizing of the results was, I maintain, the work of Romantic literature. This essay thus differs in a fundamental way from most of the current literary scholarship on professionalism: rather than asking how professionalization altered literary activity, either then or now, I inquire historically into how literary activity constructed the professional. To do so is not to idealize the power of language, literacy, and the institution of literature, but to historicize it, identifying, in this case, what Romanticism did and what it might still be doing.

The complaint I quoted earlier, for example, suggesting an essential opposition between professionalism and the subject of private life misses a major historical point: for the past two centuries professionals have talked about little else. Their apparent detachment from their own private lives while working on others' has been but a blind to the productive power of such talk: far from preceding and being increasingly suffocated by professionalism, private life was and is a product of the same (Romantic) discourse. Without individual privacy of body, soul, and property, professionals would have nothing in which to intrude. Their power, as Robert Dingwall has observed, lies in the license

> to carry out some of the most dangerous tasks of our society—to intervene in our bodies, to intercede for our prospects of future salvation, to regulate the conflict of rights and obligations between social interests. Yet in order to do this, [professionals] must acquire guilty knowledge—the priest is an expert on sin, the doctor on disease, the lawyer on crime—and the ability to look at these matters in comparative and, hence, relative terms. This is the mystery of the professions.[21]

Romanticism deepened that mystery by producing the deep self. The boy who Wordsworth wrote up as "prepared, / By his intense conceptions, to receive / Deeply the lesson deep of love" (*Excursion*, 1:192–194) is primarily characterized by the capacity, actually the imperative, to change over time, to develop. But Romantic development, as I have shown in my earlier work on the construction of that type of self, is always idealized so that it can *always* be pathologically interrupted.[22] Those interruptions, after all, are the opportunities for professional intervention and surveillance; the authority to convert knowledge of the deep self into prescriptive expertise is what makes professional behavior a central form of modern power.

So central is that power to our society that the exercise of it is a staple of our popular culture. In a recent episode of *Miami Vice,* for example, "Sonny" Crockett is shot, and, as he lies near death, his professional friends from the force have flashbacks focusing on their personal debts to him. The scenario repeated again and again involves the first time each of them blew away a suspect. Sonny rids all of them of their debilitating remorse with the line he himself learned from his lieutenant: "It's your job, man." Two hundred years ago, a job was "petty, piddling work," or a "low, mean, lucrative, busy affair"[23] and it certainly did not make absolute sense of personal identity, morality, or fate. For that to happen, the concept of work had to be rewritten from that which a true gentleman does not have to do, to the primary activity informing adult identity; the tales that tell of it and the features associated with it were altered to produce a myth of vocation.[24] This was not just a work ethic, for it made work more than necessary: it made work desirable—and necessary for personal happiness.

Crockett's formulation—you are, finally, your work—should seem familiar to everyone acquainted with English Romanticism, for Romantic texts have long been understood to repeat, in a particularly demanding way, "I am a Poet!" Members of the lower social orders, of course, had been identified with their work as "millers" or "smiths," but this kind of link between the first-person pronoun and an occupation was different: it came to function as a claim to social mobility and privileged status. The exercise of such privilege—rationalized now by knowledge rather than blood—entailed a recodification of human behaviors. As one of the traditional "gentle" professions, for example, medicine had not needed an additional or special code of ethics, since gentlemen already had the obligation to behave like gentlemen. Thus, through the eighteenth century, Hippocrates was attended to not for his oath but for his techniques of passive observation and humoral pathology.[25] The public relations reduction of the classical past from a source of knowledge actively imitated and engaged into a self-justifying moral agenda for the professional present occurred later, becoming an ongoing and—as humanists such as Allan Bloom have recently demonstrated—profitable project of modern professionals and professional groups.

Works such as Thomas Percival's *Medical Ethics* (1803) first employed that professionalism by the particular way they rewrote gentlemanly commitments into occupational codes. "Perhaps the most striking feature of Percival's book," observes Ivan Waddington, "is that, whilst relatively little space is given to a consideration of ethical problems in doctor-patient relationships, a great deal of space is devoted to establishing a set of rules for regulating relationships between practitioners. Moreover, the advice which Percival gives to practitioners in this context is much more concrete and more detailed."[26] Doctors professionalized themselves, in other words, by learning how to relate to each other as professionals, writing up and codifying the appropriate behaviors.

Wordsworth's *Prelude*—a poem by a poet, addressed to a poet, about how "we" should behave as poets—shares a historical moment and function with Percival's tract. It is a codification that assumed a now familiar form: it has become, quite simply, the most famous resumé in English literary history. Repeatedly describing it in terms that link personal happiness with a particular kind of work, Wordsworth offered his poem to Coleridge as a "review" of what "had qualified him for such employment"—the "such" referring to the writing of a long poem (*The Recluse*) that he considered "the *task* of my life."[27] This tale of "I a Poet" was told to prove that the "I" really was a "Poet" by conducting a "history of the Author's mind to the point when he was emboldened to hope that his faculties were sufficiently matured for entering upon the arduous labour which he had proposed to himself" (*Prose*, 3:5). Although Wordsworth correctly understood this self-descriptive conduct to be at that time "a thing unprecedented in Literary history" (*EY*, 586–587), we are now so used to poets talking about themselves at great length that I want to de-naturalize that expressiveness by showing it to be something *made* out of far less familiar parts.

The most unfamiliar part to modern audiences is, not surprisingly, the georgic-descriptive. I say "not surprisingly" because that is the element of the poem that has to do with the value of work, precisely the aspect of *The Prelude* which our generally Romantic readings almost always ignore.[28] We are far more familiar, for example, with its lyric elements, such as the first-person pronouns and the numerous apostrophes, which confirm the standard emphases on the creative spontaneity of the poet's personal voice.

The English georgic has its origins in the middle element of the threefold Virgilian oeuvre which the Middle Ages developed into the *rota Vergilii* or wheel of Virgil. Pastoral, georgic, and epic served as the basis for a scheme that divided not only poetry but life, society, and human personality into three interrelated parts. They are written, according to Anthony Low,

> in three styles: low, middle, and high. They correspond to three social ranks or occupations: shepherd, farmer, and soldier. They may take place in three locales: pasture, field, and castle; and they may be symbolized by three kinds of tree: the beech, the fruit-tree, and the laurel. . . . above all, the three kinds of poetry correspond to three basic human activities, into which almost everything we do in life may be divided: pastoral celebrates play and leisure, georgic celebrates work, and epic celebrates fighting.[29]

The basic form of work that Virgil celebrates in the *Georgics* is husbandry, but he explicitly connects agricultural labor to all other forms of work so that the major emphasis is on the value of working hard. Because it opposes action to pastoral's ease, and construction to epic's destruction, it is understood to be the proper mode for nation-building and the affirmation of personal and civic virtue.

Among English poets, however, its propriety has varied considerably depending on how the connection with laboring on the land was interpreted. When the emphasis was on the base nature of that laboring, as during the Tudor and Stuart reigns, it was displaced by an idealized pastoral.[30] Beginning with Milton's emphasis on the patriotic labor of rebuilding England—Low notes that Royalist poets would have considered Milton's phrase "noble task" oxymoronic —the georgic grew in importance, assuming a place "under the overarching epic framework of *Paradise Lost*" (310) with its broad movement from edenic pastoral to redemptive work-in-the-world. Spurred by Dryden's translation in 1697, the georgic rose even further in the eighteenth century as a didactically descriptive form interrelating art and politics, the detailing of rural life, and the promotion of the landowners' virtues.[31]

Its fate in Romanticism has been largely ignored in favor of analyses focusing on the pastoral, describing the Romantics' love of nature, and the lyric, celebrating the poet's expressiveness.[32] But the georgic does not disappear at the end of the eighteenth century; it enters into new combinations with other forms with some surprising results. Most immediately important for our purposes is the mix of the lyric with the georgic: the "I," in other words, that works—that identifies itself in terms of its developing capacity to work. This combination informs the entire *Prelude:*

> When, as becomes a man who would prepare
> For such an arduous work, I through myself
> Make rigorous inquisition, the report
> Is often cheering
>
> (1.146–149)[33]

To detail personal identity in this manner turns maturation into a preoccupation with occupation. The nature of that occupation, however, remains at issue. It may be "arduous," but it is certainly not arduous in the way that Virgilian husbandry is arduous: Wordsworth returns to the land but not to till it.[34] His text, then, is innovative both in linking the development of the "I" to work *and* in the way it redefines that "I" by redefining and valorizing a particular kind of work. The latter task required yet another manipulation of literary kind, this one set up by the Miltonic echo that opens *The Prelude*. At the end of *Paradise Lost*, Adam and Eve leave their home, walking from Paradise "hand in hand with wandering steps and slow" to meet their georgic fate of work in "the world [that] was all before them" (12.646–649). The situation and the language are mimicked as *The Prelude* begins, with the poet faced by a world that appears new but is actually the home from which he has strayed. Is he returning to the ease of a pastoral eden or getting down to work?

His description of himself in prefatory prose as "a Poet living in retirement" (*Prose*, 3:5) begs the question by playing upon an ambiguity: one can retire to an occupation or retire from it. In the initial verse paragraph the emphasis does seem to fall on the pastoral, Milton's image of human activity—"wandering steps"—echoed here in the natural image of a "wandering cloud" (1.17). A few lines later, however, the pastoral and the georgic appear together as the poet thanks the breeze without and the "correspondent breeze" within for "breaking up a long-continued frost" and bringing "with them vernal promises, the hope / Of active days urged on by flying hours,— / Days of sweet leisure, taxed with patient thought" (1.40–43).

When Milton juxtaposed the pastoral and the georgic he did it to show, as Anthony Low has put it, "delight in leisure because he has worked for it, because he is content to seek it not as a permanent state but as a well-earned respite from labor" (314).[35] In Wordsworth, however, the rationale is not so clear-cut:

> It was a splendid evening, and my soul
> Once more made trial of her strength, nor lacked
> Æolian visitations; but the harp
> Was soon defrauded, and the banded host
> Of harmony dispersed in straggling sounds,
> And lastly utter silence! 'Be it so;
> Why think of any thing but present good?'
> So, like a home-bound labourer I pursued
> My way beneath the mellowing sun
>
> (1.94–102)

Set within the pastoral, this reference to work is capped by an image of a "home-bound labourer" who should, in the Miltonic formula, be getting a "well-earned respite." But the justification for imaging this poet as a labourer is unclear, for he has produced nothing and the extent of his effort does not appear to be at issue.

Pastoral is also a given, and not a separate reward, when the prospect of "humbler industry" is raised again in the next verse paragraph. The failure to produce is not just accepted, "'Be it so,'" but explicitly naturalized:

> The Poet, gentle creature as he is,
> Hath, like the Lover, his unruly times;
> His fits when he is neither sick nor well,
> Though no distress be near him but his own
> Unmanageable thoughts: his mind, best pleased
> While she as duteous as the mother dove
> Sits brooding, lives not always to that end,
> But like the innocent bird, hath goadings on
> That drive her as in trouble through the groves;
> With me is now such passion, to be blamed
> No otherwise than as it lasts too long.
>
> (1.135–145)

When, two hundred lines later, it does appear to have gone on too long, making the poet feel "Like a false steward who hath much received / And renders nothing back" (1.268–269), he defends himself by beginning the review of his life—his resumé—with the same question about the years of professional preparation that has since been asked in moments of self-doubt by graduate students struggling with their dissertations, lawyers befuddled by the bar exam, and doctors exhausted by their internships: "Was it for this" (1.269)?

The ensuing tale of "I a Poet" that erases that doubt continues to mix, not juxtapose, the pastoral and georgic, for it is that mixture that prescribes two of the most important characteristics of the professional ideal. First, it presents professional work as desirable work—an edenic georgic. Since the pastoral is not offered as a separate source of happiness, the georgic activity with which it is intertwined is taken to be a means to that end. Second, the mixture naturalizes what many sociologists consider to be the distinguishing characteristic of modern professionalism: the claim to autonomy. When the domain of work is assumed to be a personal Eden, the professional assumes ethical sway over his or her own actions: the Wordsworthian phrase "'Be it so'" signals the self-authorizing power of professionalism. Understood generically, in other words, Wordsworth's retirement can be seen as not just the peculiar act of a poet, but as a representative moment of professional privilege.

Having begun with a description of that moment, *The Prelude* proceeds through a now familiar sequence in which parental influence, formal education, and life experiences all contribute to a concluding epiphany which is a statement of professional purpose: "what we have loved, / Others will love, and we will teach them how" (14.448–449). "Love" and "teaching" became key elements in the new catalogue of professional behaviors as the possibilities of selfhood were configured along a professional/amateur axis. The drawing of that axis was crucial to resolving the negative ambiguities attached to the professions in the eighteenth century. As the province of second sons, the status of the professions had been tainted by an unseemly need for income. Once the motivation became love, however, money became a permissible consequence of work—work that was now linked, as we have seen, not to unfortunate circumstances but to happiness. Thus as home and work became separate, gender-encoded realms at the end of the eighteenth century, love assumed a strategic role in both: "falling in love" eclipsed parental bloodlines as the mythical key to both domestic bliss, with one's true love, and to worldly success, doing the work one loves.

That fall, however, is anything but a free fall; rules were imposed, for example, by the introduction of "amateur" into English. The amateur, of course, is one who loves, but, in regard to the professional norm, either too idealistically ("understanding, and loving or practicing . . . without any regard to pecuniary advantage" read one definition in 1803) or too enthusiastically (Edmund Burke warned in 1797 of "the greatest amateurs . . . of revolutions").[36] Propagating the norm became the imperative of education, which institutionalized into the various disciplines "what" was loved and "how" it was to be taught. Wordsworth's *Excursion,* like *The Prelude,* concludes with a plea for education—in this case, a georgic plea for a national education system that would supply everyone with the "intellectual implements and tools" required for the work of civilization (9.293–335). At this historical moment, those tools of professional behavior have themselves become the subject of professional work—work that can help us better understand what professional and therefore powerful teachers the Romantics were, and continue to be.

Notes

1. Jon Carroll, "Closing the Ridicule Gap," *San Francisco Chronicle,* 22 Feb. 1988, Sec. F, p. 12, col. 5.

2. These lines are from the version published in the 1800 edition of *Lyrical Ballads.* Wordsworth's later revisions are detailed in *The Poetical Works of William Wordsworth,* ed. Ernest de Selincourt and Helen Darbishire, 5 vols. (Oxford: Oxford University Press, 1940–1949), 4:65–67. All quotations from poems by Wordsworth other than *The Prelude* are taken from this edition.

3. The reasons differ, but critical interest in the later Wordsworth is evident in recent efforts by such critics as David Simpson, Peter Manning, and William Galperin. See, for example, Simpson's conclusion in *Wordsworth's Historical Imagination* (New York: Methuen, 1987): "And yet . . . in the preceding remarks on the later poems, I am uncomfortably aware of the degree to which I am repeating once again the standard position taken by almost all readers and critics: that there is a decline, a falling away in urgency and inspiration. A more truthful and sceptical verdict would be that we are not yet in a position to make such judgements. What I would say is that the terms in which I have tried to make sense of much of the poetry before 1814 do not appear to be so fruitful for the later work. But there may well be other terms, which we have not yet discovered" (215). Also, see Manning, "Wordsworth at St. Bees: Scandals, Sisterhoods, and Wordsworth's Later Poetry" *ELH* 52:1 (Spring 1985), 33–58, and Galperin, "Anti-Romanticism, Victorianism, and the Case of Wordsworth," *Victorian Poetry* 24:4 (1986), 357–371.

4. See my argument in *The Historicity of Romantic Discourse* (Oxford: Oxford University Press, 1988), 9–10.

5. *The Prose Works of William Wordsworth,* ed. W. J. B. Owen and Jane Worthington Smyser, 3 vols. (Oxford: Clarendon Press, 1974), 1:131. This source is cited hereafter in the text as *Prose.*

6. W. J. Reader, *Professional Men: The Rise of the Professional Classes in Nineteenth-Century England* (London: Weidenfeld and Nicolson, 1966), 37–39. Additional information on the corpse trade can be found in Peter Linebaugh, "The Tyburn Riot Against the Surgeons," in *Albion's Fatal Tree: Crime and*

Society in Eighteenth-Century England, ed. Douglas Hay, Peter Linebaugh, John G. Rule, E. P. Thompson, and Cal Winslow (New York: Pantheon Books, 1975), 65–117.

7. The exhibition appeared at the Chicago Historical Society from April 6 to June 5, 1988. The conference on "The Romantics and Us" took place April 22–24, 1988.

8. "Conferences" were not exclusively serious matters until the middle of the eighteenth century. The word had formerly applied not only to arranged meetings, such as the Hampton Court and Savoy Conferences, but also to the act of conferring in the more general sense of conversation or talk. The restriction to formal discourse, cited in Johnson's *Dictionary* ("the act of conversing on serious subjects, formal discourse"), coincides roughly with Wesley's calling of the First Methodist conferences in 1744. See the *OED* for earlier usages.

9. For an analysis of the power of "that relatively new institution, the public museum," see Francis Haskell, "The Artist and the Museum," *New York Review of Books,* 3 Dec. 1987, 38–42. In her history of the nineteenth-century construction of history into an academic discipline, Philippa Levine reveals how the institutional interaction between the bureaucratic state and the schools helped to produce the recent phenomenon of the modern departmental university. See *The Amateur and the Professional: Antiquarians, Historians and Archaeologists in Victorian England, 1838–1886* (Cambridge: Cambridge University Press, 1986). The relationship between literature as an institution and the rise of the modern state is explored in Gerald Newman, *The Rise of English Nationalism: A Cultural History 1740–1830* (New York: St. Martin's Press, 1987), 49–156.

10. See M. H. Abrams, *The Mirror and the Lamp: Romantic Theory and the Critical Tradition* (New York: Oxford University Press, 1953) and *Natural Supernaturalism: Tradition and Revolution in Romantic Literature* (New York: Norton, 1971).

11. See Harold Bloom, *The Visionary Company: A Reading of English Romantic Poetry* (New York: Doubleday, 1961) and Geoffrey Hartman, *Wordsworth's Poetry, 1787–1814* (New Haven: Yale University Press, 1971).

12. See *The Historicity of Romantic Discourse,* 3–63, and the questions and answers sections of Morris Eaves and Michael Fischer, eds., *Romanticism and Contemporary Criticism* (Ithaca: Cornell University Press, 1986).

13. The many efforts to articulate this issue include: Gloria V. Engel and Richard H. Hall, "The Growing Industrialization of the Professions," in *The Professions and Their Prospects,* ed. Eliot Freidson (Beverly Hills: Sage Publications, 1971), 75–88; Eliot Freidson, "Professionalization and the Organisation of Middle-Class Labour in Post-Industrial Society," *Sociological Review* Monograph 20 (1973): 47–59; Martin Oppenheimer, "The Proletarianization of the Professional," *Sociological Review* Monograph 20 (1973): 213–227; Terence Johnson, "The Professions in the Class Structure," in *Industrial Society: Class, Cleavage and Control,* ed. Richard Scase (New York: St. Martin's Press, 1977), 93–110; Magali Larson, "Proletarianization and Educated Labor," *Theory and Society* 9 (1980): 131–175; Charles Derber, "Toward a New Theory of Profes-

sionals as Workers: Advanced Capitalism and Postindustrial Labor," in *Professionals as Workers: Mental Labor in Advanced Capitalism*, ed. Charles Derber (Boston: C. K. Hall, 1982), 193–208; and John McKinlay, "Toward the Proletarianization of Physicians," in Derber, 37–62.

14. See Robert Pear, "Doctors Fear They're Losing Status," *San Francisco Chronicle*, 31 Dec. 1987, Sec. A, p. 16, col. 1. This is reprinted from the *New York Times*, 26 Dec. 1987, Sec. A, p. 1, col. 1.

15. Jane Tompkins, "Me and My Shadow," *New Literary History*, 19:1 (Autumn 1987): 169.

16. See, for example, Geoffrey S. Holmes, *Augustan England: Professions, State and Society, 1680–1730* (London: George Allen & Unwin, 1982) and W. F. Bynum, "Physicians, Hospitals and Career Structures in Eighteenth-Century London," in *William Hunter and the Eighteenth-Century Medical World*, ed. W. F. Bynum and Roy Porter (Cambridge: Cambridge University Press, 1985), 105–128.

17. Those efforts that do attend to the late eighteenth and early nineteenth centuries do not address literary activity. See Ivan Waddington, *The Medical Profession in the Industrial Revolution* (Dublin: Gill and Macmillan, 1984) and Magali Larson, *The Rise of Professionalism: A Sociological Analysis* (Berkeley: University of California Press, 1977).

18. See the tables assembled in Reader, 207–211, and Philip Elliott's observations regarding the sociology of Victorian professionalism in *The Sociology of the Professions* (New York: Herder and Herder, 1972), 54–57.

19. See W. F. Bynum's discussion of Johnson's definition in Bynum, 111.

20. Both Reader, 1–24, and Elliott, 20–27, provide useful analyses of the gentlemanly nature of the professions in the eighteenth century.

21. Robert Dingwall, Introduction, in *The Sociology of the Professions: Lawyers, Doctors and Others*, ed. Robert Dingwall and Philip Lewis (London: Macmillan, 1983), 3. Dingwall is summarizing the views of Everett Hughes.

22. See chapters 8 and 9 of *The Historicity of Romantic Discourse*.

23. See Reader, 5, on the attitude of the eighteenth-century gentleman toward a "job."

24. The "term 'the myth of vocation,'" according to Ruth Danon, "derives from the studies of contemporary philosophers, sociologists, historians and laborers concerned with the problem of work in modern life. They make evident that we live in a work-centered culture and that this culture cannot be described simply in Weberian terms. The Protestant work ethic does not explain the expectation people have that they be made happy by their work." See *Work in the English Novel: the Myth of Vocation* (London: Croom Helm, 1985), 2.

25. See the references to Hippocrates in Bynum and Porter, 209, 212, 263, 327, Waddington, 153, and Guy Williams, *The Age of Agony: The Art of Healing, 1700–1800* (1975; repr. Chicago: Academy Chicago, 1986), 7. The use of the Hippocratic oath to exclude surgeons from a "closed shop" is discussed by Frederick F. Cartwright, *A Social History of Medicine* (London: Longman, 1977), 41–42.

26. Waddington, 156–157.

27. *The Letters of William and Dorothy Wordsworth: The Early Years, 1787–1805,* ed. Ernest de Selincourt and revised by Chester L. Shaver (Oxford: Oxford University Press, 1967), 594–95. Cited hereafter in the text as *EY.*

28. A useful exception is Kurt Heinzelman's *The Economics of the Imagination* (Amherst: University of Massachusetts Press, 1980).

29. Anthony Low, *The Georgic Revolution* (Princeton: Princeton University Press, 1985), 4. Cited hereafter in the text.

30. In addition to Low, 14, see Raymond Williams, *The Country and the City* (New York: Oxford University Press, 1973), 13–34; Stephen Orgel, *The Illusion of Power* (Berkeley: University of California Press, 1975), 37–58, and James Turner, *The Politics of Landscape: Rural Scenery and Society in English Poetry 1630–1660* (Cambridge: Harvard University Press, 1979), 116–185.

31. See *The Historicity of Romantic Discourse,* 87–88. For information on the uses of the georgic in the eighteenth century, see John Chalker, *The English Georgic: A Study in the Development of a Form* (Baltimore: Johns Hopkins University Press, 1969).

32. Among the most insightful discussions of Romantic pastoral are Herbert Lindenberger, in "The Idyllic Moment: On Pastoral and Romanticism," *College English* 34:3 (December 1972): 335–351, and Lore Metzger, in *One Foot in Eden: Modes of Pastoral in Romantic Poetry* (Chapel Hill: University of North Carolina Press, 1986). Lindenberger stresses "The precariousness, the tensions, the historical dislocations which give idyllic moments their intensity—and also their momentariness" (351) in order to raise theoretical questions regarding literary periodization. Metzger asserts that "pastoral most frequently functions in English Romantic poetry to articulate radical ends of social reform attenuated by an insistence on conservative means" (xiv).

The major exception to the turn from georgic in the criticism of Romanticism is Annabel Patterson's analysis of Wordsworth's "hard pastoral whose entire rationale is georgic" in *Pastoral and Ideology: Virgil to Valéry* (Berkeley: University of California Press, 1987), 263–84. This remarkable book supplements my argument in two important ways. First, it shows how "the arbiters of European culture since Virgil" have turned to the *Eclogues* "as a paradigm of the intellectual's dilemma" (10). That turn necessarily involves the georgic because "Virgilian pastoral would have indicated its liminal status on the borders of georgic even if the *Georgics* had never been written" (134). Thus my analysis of the Wordsworthian use of the pastoral/georgic distinction to portray "intellectual" behavior in *professional* terms can be placed within a history of earlier portrayals in different terms.

Second, Patterson, expanding on an earlier effort ("Wordsworth's Georgic: Genre and Structure in *The Excursion," The Wordsworth Circle* 9:2 (Spring 1978): 145–154), also sees a mix of pastoral and georgic in Wordsworth. Her concern, however, is with the "ethical dilemma posed by rural labor" and Wordsworth's "solution" to it: an endorsement, both of its "necessity" and its "dignity," that makes the "hardship . . . *natural*" and therefore capable of "ennobl[ing] the spectator" (281–282). This analysis of "the socioeconomic conflicts that underwrite the literary ones" (280) is thus very useful, but the issue requires further attention, for her inquiry into Wordsworth's descriptions of his own work is subordinated to judging his depictions of, and reactions to, the labor of others. Having ignored the "professional" aspect of Wordsworth's mix, Patterson sees *The Excursion* as "an (aberrant) phase" between the early and late *Preludes*. But the call for "education" which she cites as indicative of *The Excursion*'s aberration is also, as I show in the conclusion to this essay, the professional impetus behind all of the autobiographical efforts.

33. All quotations are from the 1850 version of *The Prelude* as presented in William Wordsworth, *The Prelude, 1799, 1805, and 1850*, ed. Jonathan Wordsworth, M. H. Abrams, and Stephen Gill (New York: Norton, 1979).

34. Patterson quotes approvingly (278) from Fredric Jameson's argument, in *The Political Unconscious: Narrative as a Socially Symbolic Act* (Ithaca: Cornell University Press, 1981) that "one cannot without intellectual dishonesty assimilate the 'production' of texts . . . to the production of goods by factory workers: writing and thinking are not alienated labor in that sense, and it is surely fatuous for intellectuals to seek to glamorize their tasks . . . by assimilating them to real work on the assembly line and to the experience of the resistance of matter in genuine manual labor" (45). She uses the argument to caution against the "attractions" of Wordsworth's "claim" of "the hard pastoral of the mind at serious work," citing Kurt Heinzelman's use of the phrase "'a labor theory of poetic value'" (*The Economics of the Imagination*, 221). To point out that "such appropriations of Marxist terminology" are problematic, however, is only the first step in coming to terms with the issue of Wordsworth, Romanticism, and the professionalization of work. Historicizing the terminology itself is the next step: the relationship, for example, between Romantic discourse and Jameson's key (and ultimately *self*-glamorizing) adjectives—"real" and "genuine." For some angles on the Romantic/Marxist connection see my review of David Aers, Jonathan Cook, and David Punter, *Romanticism and Ideology: Studies in English Writing, 1765–1830* (London: Routledge and Kegan Paul, 1981) in *Comparative Literature Studies*, 21:2 (Summer 1984): 228–232 and also *The Historicity of Romantic Discourse*, 142–143.

35. Other writers also brought the pastoral and georgic together in different ways, producing, as Patterson asserts in speaking of Sir Francis Bacon, a "relationship between the two genres [that] became, in effect, a sign-system for other sets of relationships and arguments" (134). Wordsworth's combination, for example, shows both continuity and discontinuity with Bacon's "Georgics of the mind." It does link intellectual labor with images from nature, but both the nature of that kind of labor—from the inductive method of Baconian science to Wordsworth's deep knowledge of the developing self—and the nature of nature—from a source of "sweeten[ing]" (Patterson, 137) images of order to a conceptual category that redefines "real" feelings, language, and behavior—underwent significant change. In addition, Wordsworth's mixture entails not the mutual modification described by Patterson (Bacon's "pastoralized georgic," 138), but the assertion of their simultaneity in the activity of the professional.

36. The first usage cited in the *OED* is from 1784.

Suggestions
for Further Reading

Abrams, M. H. *The Mirror and the Lamp: Romantic Theory and Critical Tradition*. New York: Oxford University Press, 1953.

————. *Natural Supernaturalism: Tradition and Revolution in Romantic Literature*. New York: Norton, 1971.

————, ed. *English Romantic Poets: Modern Essays in Criticism*. 2nd ed. London: Oxford University Press, 1975.

Altieri, Charles. *Enlarging the Temple: New Directions in American Poetry during the 1960's*. Lewisburg, Pennsylvania: Bucknell University Press, 1979.

————. *Self and Sensibility in Contemporary American Poetry*. New York: Cambridge University Press, 1984.

Arac, Jonathan. *Critical Genealogies: Historical Situations for Postmodern Literary Studies*. New York: Columbia University Press, 1987.

Baker, Carlos. *The Echoing Green: Romanticism, Modernism, and the Phenomena of Transference in Poetry*. Princeton: Princeton University Press, 1984.

Bate, Walter Jackson. *The Burden of the Past and the English Poet*. Cambridge: Harvard University Press, 1970.

Berry, Wendell. *Standing by Words*. San Francisco: North Point Press, 1983.

Bloom, Harold. *The Anxiety of Influence: A Theory of Poetry*. New York: Oxford University Press, 1973.

————. *The Visionary Company: A Reading of English Romantic Poetry*. Ithaca: Cornell University Press, 1961; rev. ed. 1971.

————, ed. *Romanticism and Consciousness: Essays in Criticism*. New York: Norton, 1970.

Bornstein, George. *Poetic Remaking: The Art of Browning, Yeats, and Pound*. University Park: Pennsylvania State University Press, 1988.

————. *Romantic and Modern: Revaluations of Literary Tradition*. Pittsburgh: University of Pittsburgh Press, 1977.

———. *Transformations of Romanticism in Yeats, Eliot, and Stevens.* Chicago: University of Chicago Press, 1976.

———. *Yeats and Shelley.* Chicago: University of Chicago Press, 1970.

Butler, Marilyn. *Romantics, Rebels, and Reactionaries.* London: Oxford University Press, 1981.

Clausen, Christopher. *The Place of Poetry: Two Centuries of an Art in Crisis.* Lexington: University of Kentucky Press, 1981.

Frye, Northrop. *A Study of English Romanticism.* New York: Random House, 1968.

Garvin, Harry R., ed. *Romanticism, Modernism, Postmodernism.* Lewisburg, Pennsylvania: Bucknell University Press, 1980.

Heffernan, James. *The Re-Creation of Landscape: A Study of Wordsworth, Coleridge, Constable, and Turner.* Hanover, New Hampshire: University Press of New England, 1984.

Holden, Jonathan. *The Rhetoric of the Contemporary Lyric.* Bloomington: Indiana University Press, 1980.

Honour, Hugh. *Romanticism.* New York: Harper and Row, 1979.

Hooker, Jeremy. *The Presence of the Past.* Bridgend, Midglamorgan: Poetry Wales Press, 1987.

Johnston, Kenneth R., and Gene W. Ruoff, eds. *The Age of William Wordsworth: Critical Essays on the Romantic Tradition.* New Brunswick: Rutgers University Press, 1987.

Keith, W. J. *The Rural Tradition: Rural Perspectives in Poetry from Wordsworth to the Present.* Toronto: University of Toronto Press, 1980.

Kermode, Frank. *The Romantic Image.* New York: Macmillan, 1957.

Kroeber, Karl. *British Romantic Art.* Berkeley: University of California Press, 1986.

———. *Romantic Fantasy and Science Fiction.* New Haven: Yale University Press, 1988.

———. *Romantic Landscape Vision: Constable and Wordsworth.* Madison: University of Wisconsin Press, 1975.

Langbaum, Robert. *The Poetry of Experience: The Dramatic Monologue in Modern Literary Tradition.* New York: Norton, 1963.

McFarland, Thomas. *Originality and Imagination.* Baltimore: Johns Hopkins University Press, 1985.

———. *Romanticism and the Forms of Ruin: Wordsworth, Coleridge, and the Madness of Fragmentation.* Princeton: Princeton University Press, 1981.

McGann, Jerome J. *The Romantic Ideology: A Critical Investigation.* Chicago: University of Chicago Press, 1983.

Mellor, Anne K. *English Romantic Irony.* Cambridge: Harvard University ᵗ⁹80.

Ostriker, Alicia. *Stealing the Language: The Emergence of Women's Poetry in America*. Boston: Beacon Press, 1986.

Paulson, Ronald. *Representations of Revolutions, 1789–1820*. New Haven: Yale University Press, 1983.

Paz, Octavio. *Children of the Mire: Modern Poetry from Romanticism to the Avant-garde*. Cambridge: Harvard University Press, 1974.

Pinsky, Robert. *The Situation of Poetry: Contemporary Poetry and Its Traditions*. Princeton: Princeton University Press, 1977.

Reiman, Donald H., Michael C. Jaye, and Betty T. Bennett, eds. *The Evidence of the Imagination: Studies of the Interactions between Life and Art in English Romantic Literature*. New York: New York University Press, 1978.

Simpson, Louis. *A Company of Poets*. Ann Arbor: University of Michigan Press, 1981.

———. *The Character of the Poet*. Ann Arbor: University of Michigan Press, 1986.

———. *Collected Prose*. New York: Paragon House, 1989.

Siskin, Clifford. *The Historicity of Romantic Discourse*. New York: Oxford University Press, 1988.

Swingle, L. J. *The Obstinate Questionings of English Romanticism*. Baton Rouge: Louisiana State University Press, 1987.

Wordsworth, Jonathan, Michael C. Jaye, and Robert Woof. *William Wordsworth and the Age of English Romanticism*. New Brunswick: Rutgers University Press, 1987.

Notes on Contributors

CHARLES ALTIERI, Professor of English and Comparative Literature at the University of Washington, works primarily in literary theory and modern poetry. The author of *Act and Quality: A Theory of Literary Meaning and Humanistic Understanding* (1981) and *Self and Sensibility in Contemporary American Poetry* (1984), Altieri has forthcoming a book entitled *Painterly Abstraction in Modernist American Poetry*.

GEORGE BORNSTEIN, Professor of English at the University of Michigan, is the author of *Yeats and Shelley* (1970), *Transformations of Romanticism in Yeats, Eliot, and Stevens* (1976), *The Postromantic Consciousness of Ezra Pound* (1977), and *Poetic Remaking: The Art of Browning, Yeats, and Pound* (1988), as well as editor of collections like *Romantic and Modern: Revaluations of Literary Tradition* (1977) and *Ezra Pound Among the Poets* (1985). He is currently preparing the second volume of his two-volume edition of *W. B. Yeats: The Early Poetry—Manuscript Materials* for the Cornell Yeats series.

JAMES K. CHANDLER, Professor of English at the University of Chicago, is the author of *Wordsworth's Second Nature: A Study of the Poetry and Politics* (1984). His recent essays have centered on relations among literature, history, and politics in the romantic period. He is currently completing a book to be called *England in 1819*.

JOHN HOLLANDER is A. Bartlett Giamatti Professor of English at Yale University. His most recent volumes of poetry are *Harp Lake* (1988), *In Time and Place* (1986), and *Powers of Thirteen* (1983). *Melodious Guile: Fictive Pattern in Poetic Language* also appeared in 1988; his previous critical studies include *The Figure of Echo* (1983), *Vision and Resonance* (1975), and *The Untuning of the Sky* (1961). He is a Chancellor of the American Academy of Poets and a member of the American Academy and Institute of Arts and Letters and the American Academy of Arts and Sciences. He is currently at work on an extended study of ekphrastic poetry.

KARL KROEBER, Mellon Professor in the Humanities at Columbia University, has written widely on romantic literature and culture from multidisciplinary perspectives. His books include *Romantic Narrative Art* (1960), *The Artifice of Reality* (1964), *Styles in Fictional Structure* (1971), *Romantic Landscape Vision: Constable and Wordsworth* (1975), *British Romantic Art* (1986), and *Romantic Fantasy and Science Fiction* (1988). He is now at work on a book on visual and verbal narrative.

JOHN MATTHIAS is Professor of English at the University of Notre Dame and has been Visiting Fellow in poetry at Clare Hall, Cambridge. He has published five volumes of poetry, most recently *Northern Summer* (1984) and *Places, Poems* (1989). He has co-translated *The Battle of Kosovo* (1987) with Vladeta Vuckovic, and he has edited *23 Modern British Poets* (1971), *Introducing David Jones* (1980), and *David Jones: Man and Poet* (1989).

ANNE K. MELLOR is Professor of English at the University of California at Los Angeles. She is the author of *Blake's Human Form Divine* (1974) and *English Romantic Irony* (1980). Former director of the Feminist Studies Program at Stanford and the Women's Studies Program at UCLA, she is focusing her current work on the construction of gender in English romantic literature. Her edited collection, *Romanticism and Feminism*, appeared in 1988, as did her feminist literary biography, *Mary Shelley: Her Life, Her Fiction, Her Monsters*. She is currently writing a polemical study of *The Two Romanticisms*, contrasting the male to the female romantic ideology, and a study of English Women of Letters, 1780–1830, tentatively entitled *The Bluestockings*.

ALICIA OSTRIKER is Professor of English at Rutgers University. She is the author of six volumes of poetry, most recently *The Imaginary Lover*, which won the 1986 William Carlos Williams Award from the Poetry Society of America. As a critic she is the author of *Vision and Verse in William Blake* (1965) and editor of Blake's *Complete Poems* (1977). Her writing on women poets includes the essays published in *Writing Like a Woman* (1983) and *Stealing the Language: The Emergence of Women's Poetry in America* (1986). Her current project is a set of meditations on the Bible.

ROBERT PINSKY, Professor of English at the University of California at Berkeley, is a poet, critic, and translator. His recent books include *The Situation of Poetry: Contemporary Poetry and Its Traditions* (1977), *An Explanation of America* (1980), and *The History of My Heart*, which won the 1984 William Carlos Williams Award of the Poetry Society of America.

GENE W. RUOFF, Professor of English and Director of the Institute for the Humanities at the University of Illinois at Chicago, is the author of *Wordsworth and Coleridge: The Making of the Major Lyrics, 1802–1804* (1989), and the co-editor *The Age of William Wordsworth: Critical Essays on the Romantic*

Tradition (1987). He is now working on an historical study of the construction, reconstruction, and deconstruction of Wordsworth's idea of the imagination.

CLIFFORD SISKIN is Associate Professor of English at the State University of New York at Stony Brook. In *The Historicity of Romantic Discourse* (1988) he detailed the ongoing power of English romanticism. His current project examines the literary construction of professional behavior.

LOUIS SIMPSON is Professor of English at the State University of New York at Stony Brook. He is the author of eleven books of poetry, five books of literary criticism, an autobiography, a novel, and *An Introduction to Poetry*. He has recently published his *Collected Poems* (1988) and *Selected Prose* (1989).

DIANE WAKOSKI, currently Writer-in-Residence at Michigan State University, is the author of sixteen collections of poems and many slim volumes of verse. Her selected poems, *Emerald Ice: Poems 1962–1987,* was the winner of the 1988 William Carlos Williams Award of the Poetry Society of America. She is currently working on an epic poem set in the American west called *The Archaeology of Movies and Books.*

We would like to thank the following individuals and publishers for permission to reprint material copyrighted or controlled by them:

The University of Pittsburgh Press for "Everywoman Her Own Theology," from The Imaginary Lover, by Alicia Ostriker, copyright © 1986 by Alicia Ostriker; and for "What You Want," from Green Age, by Alicia Ostriker, copyright © 1989 by Alicia Suskin Ostriker. *Reprinted by permission.*

Louis Simpson and Paragon House for "'The Man Freed from the Order of Time': Poetic Theory in Wordsworth and Proust," from Selected Prose (New York: Paragon House, 1989). *Reprinted by permission.*

A. P. Watt Ltd. on behalf of Michael B. Yeats and Macmillan London Ltd. for excerpts from W. B. Yeats's poetry from The Poems of W. B. Yeats: A New Edition, ed. Richard J. Finneran (New York: Macmillan, 1983), copyright © 1916, 1919, 1928, 1933 by Macmillan Publishing Company, copyright © renewed 1944, 1947, 1956, 1961 by Bertha Georgie Yeats. *Reprinted by permission.*

Alfred A. Knopf, Inc., for excerpts from Wallace Steven's poetry from Collected Poems (New York: Alfred A. Knopf, 1968) and from Opus Posthumous (New York: Alfred A. Knopf, 1969). *Reprinted by permission.*

Marc Simon and Liveright Publishing Corporation for "To Brooklyn Bridge," from The Poems of Hart Crane, edited by Marc Simon. Copyright © 1986 by Marc Simon. *Reprinted by permission.*

Elizabeth Bishop and Farrar, Straus and Giroux, Inc., for "Night City," from Geography II, copyright © 1972, 1976 by Elizabeth Bishop. *Reprinted by permission.*

Ann Lauterbach and Princeton University Press for "Still" (previously published in Paris Review) from Before Recollection, copyright © 1987 by Princeton University Press. *Reprinted by permission.*

W. W. Norton & Company, Inc., and The Estate of Richard Hugo for "In Your Young Dream," from Making Certain It Goes On, The Collected Poems of Richard Hugo, copyright © 1984 by The Estate of Richard Hugo. *Reprinted by permission.*

William Stafford and Harper & Row, Publishers, Inc., for "With Kit, Age 7, At the Beach," from Stories That Could Be True, copyright © by William Stafford. *Reprinted by permission.*

Robert Hass and Ecco Press for "Songs to Survive the Summer," from Praise, copyright © 1979 by Robert Hass.

Alfred A. Knopf, Inc., and Faber and Faber Ltd. for "Anecdote of the Jar" and "Sunday Morning," from The Collected Poems of Wallace Stevens, copyright © 1923 by Wallace Stevens, © renewed 1951 by Wallace Stevens. *Reprinted by permission.*